Notes & Apologies:

✶ Hello again, dear readers. Thank you to everyone who supported our temporary absence. The rumors of our demise were, in this case, not at all exaggerated, but thanks to your advocacy and care, we have risen again. We stand before you humbled and appreciative, and we very much hope you enjoy this homecoming issue.

✶ Subscriptions to *The Believer* include four issues, one of which might be themed and may come with a bonus item, such as an original compilation or art object. View our subscription deals online at *thebeliever.net/subscribe*.

✶ The incidental illustrations in this issue, which imagine a future world where human and machine are still learning to coexist, are by Tim Peacock.

✶ Do you need an editor for your manuscript? Do you want to send a secret numerological message to your lover? *The Believer* Classifieds section (page 134) is back and open to your every need. Send us ads, polite commentaries, philosophical meditations, requests for mulch. $2/word, and the words are printed in the magazine for all of time. Write to classifieds@thebeliever.net.

✶ On page 135 you will find a new regular feature, which tracks best sellers from around the world. Future issues will highlight best sellers from many other fine countries, such as Estonia.

✶ We have a habit of spotting typos and circling errors in old books, so we decided to create a simulation of this experience. On page 133, our copy editor, Caitlin Van Dusen, has introduced ten errors into a passage of Kenneth Grahame's *The Wind in the Willows*, the 1908 children's classic about moles, water rats, and other woodland creatures. Feel free to mark up the page with your red pen. Readers can find the answers on page 144. We'll have a passage from a different classic in our next issue. It will be harder but also more fun.

✶ Sprinkled throughout the issue is a microinterview with Ling Ma, conducted by Rhoda Feng. Ma is the author of the novel *Severance* and a new short story collection, *Bliss Montage*. The title of her new book is inspired by a term coined by Wesleyan film professor Jeanine Basinger, which refers to the brief period in an old Hollywood film when a female main character is permitted to live a carefree existence. Coincidentally, Basinger is also cited in our interview with Miguel Arteta, conducted by Aubrey Plaza (page 37). Arteta names Basinger as one of his key early mentors.

✶ This issue of *The Believer* is dedicated to Brian Dice.

DEAR THE BELIEVER

849 VALENCIA STREET, SAN FRANCISCO, CA 94110

letters@thebeliever.net

Dear Believer,
I thought Amber Husain ("I Can't Wait to Get Started," March/April 2022) did an excellent job of defending the "lowliest intern" who pesters the artist with fake overexcitement—not at all because she hopes to be Maxwell Perkins, but because she hopes to accrue enough vacation days (five would be all right) so that she might have some adventures of her own. I am glad, however, that Helen DeWitt has made do with blogging, and therefore bypassed the gatekeeping editors who sabotaged her genius. To both Husain and DeWitt, this reader says without irony, "Wonderful marvelous wonderful cool."
Sincerely,
Janie Wells
Tucson, AZ

Dear Believer,
Please stop publishing reviews of tools that are not tools. A screenshot is not a "tool." I found Kim Beil's commentary on the screenshot interesting, but it is not a tool.
Alan Hammerstein
New York, NY

Dear Believer,
As a longtime fan of the show *My Cat from Hell*, I was very glad to see that you published an interview with Jackson Galaxy (March/April 2022). The internet likes to mock cat people like me, portray us as crazy, which,

broadly speaking, we are. But, as Galaxy shows, we have also tapped into some pretty key insights from our experiences with felines. I particularly liked the way Galaxy described doing a body scan before entering a new home and engaging with a new pet dynamic. "It's not possible to be in a relationship with another if you aren't in one with yourself," he says. That's exactly how I feel. I may be crazy, but at least I'm in a relationship with myself about it.
Carey Herbert
San Diego, CA

Dear Believer,
Are you still doing your Believer Book Awards? My favorite book of the year was *Trust* by Hernan Diaz. I just wanted to let you know.
Ed Yeung
Oakland, CA

Dear Believer,
What a painfully sweet paean to Mr. Joe Raposo ("Songs in the Key of Childhood," March/April 2022). I became a little angry on his behalf when, turning to Wikipedia, I found his personal section to be so reductive. Apparently, *f* is for *famous friends*, and *d* is still for *death*. Many thanks to Chris Feliciano Arnold for the thoughtful elaboration.
Sincerely,
Emma Frey
Brooklyn, NY

Dear Believer,
The other day I was at a bookstore when a man tapped me on the shoulder, pointed to an extremely long, ambitious novel, and said, "It's about time they took this off the shelf. No one has ever read it."
Now, I don't like conflict, so I agreed with him, and because I mirror the gestures of strangers to make them like me, I then pulled out another long, intellectually ambitious book: Helen DeWitt's *The Last Samurai*. The man, who later I came to recognize was a figment of Twitter come to life, said to me, "Do you think they ought to take *The Last Samurai* off the shelf too?" I'd like your editors to know that if I hadn't read Amber Husain's fine essay on DeWitt in issue 139 ("I Can't Wait to Get Started," March/April 2022), I might simply have said yes.
Instead, I pushed back. "They ought to get bigger shelves here. Helen DeWitt had a hard enough time publishing this novel. Her imaginative reality is sui generis and benefits from room to play. I just read a fine essay about this, in issue 139 of *The Believer*," et cetera, et cetera, after which he relented, probably because I spoke for a good five minutes.
"I just wanted to talk to you," he replied, paid $7.50 for a sparkling matcha, and went on his way.
Yours,
Man
Houston, TX

RESURRECTOR

A ROTATING GUEST COLUMN IN WHICH WRITERS REEXAMINE CRITICALLY UNACCLAIMED WORKS OF ART

by Hanif Abdurraqib

When *Angels in the Outfield* came out, in 1994, I hadn't yet buried anyone I loved. I hadn't been to a funeral, and I hadn't yet been in a hospital room, been an audience to the sounds that stitch together, forming an orchestra, a soundtrack to an eventual exit.

Even with this in mind, I found myself obsessed with the afterlife. Not in a way that troubled anyone. I rarely spoke the obsession out loud. Even at ten years old, in the early summer days of 1994, I maybe had just enough self-awareness to know that the adults around me weren't all that into my curiosity about what awaited us after death, and they likely didn't have the answers, anyway.

Angels in the Outfield worked for me. I loved sports, though I didn't care much about baseball. I also really didn't care about any narrative that might suggest that God cared about sports, even though the film turns on a young foster kid, Roger, praying to God for the lowly California Angels to win the pennant, all because Roger's no-good dad said he'd come back into his life if the Angels won the pennant (which presents its own, separate set of absurdities, but absurdity is often the engine of plot, particularly in a sports film about deities that's aimed at kids).

What did fascinate me, endlessly, was the fact that Roger could see the dead, when no one else could. Even his best friend, JP, cannot see them, but desperately wants to. I don't know if I considered this then, but I wonder now if there is a thin line between the framing of the dead and their reappearances. What, for example, separates an angel from a ghost, besides the intentions that history or stories or hope or fear might affix to them? Roger saw dead people doing miraculous things, which brought him closer to God, I suppose, or at least closer to a father.

Watching the movie now, as I did two nights ago, I see how it can easily present itself as religious propaganda, and would likely be dismissed as such if it were released today. So much of its story relies on conversion, getting people to believe in the unseen, through the lens of one all-seeing, all-knowing, youthful messiah. But I still gravitate toward it, if for no other reason than that the movie, more than any other piece of media, defined my initial relationship with ghosts, with an afterlife. When I buried people for the next two and a half decades of my life, it was easy to convince myself that I would, maybe, see them again. Even if my seeing wasn't *literally* seeing. The flower my mother loved fights its way up through gravel after a hard Midwest winter, and that is a type of seeing. The song my dearest friend used to sing along to on road trips comes on at a party I was making my way out of, and so I stay, and in staying I meet someone, and in meeting someone I fall in love, at least for a few moments. That is a type of seeing.

My house is haunted. It's an old house, in a historic neighborhood in Columbus, Ohio. A jazz singer owned it once. A sad and lonely woman. She died in the attic, I'm told. No one found her body for months. When I first moved in, I could hear her shuffling about up there at night. I'd check for squirrels or mice the next morning. I called in exterminators, just to conduct my due diligence. But I always knew it was her. It's a good time to be unafraid of ghosts. I figure she's just letting me know she hasn't gone anywhere, that maybe we'll make each other's lives a little less lonely for a while. ✶

Illustration by Kristian Hammerstad

STUFF I'VE BEEN READING

A QUARTERLY COLUMN, STEADY AS EVER

by Nick Hornby

BOOKS READ:

* *City of Lies: Love, Sex, Death, and the Search for Truth in Tehran*—Ramita Navai
* *Say Nothing: A True Story of Murder and Memory in Northern Ireland*—Patrick Radden Keefe
* *Trespasses*—Louise Kennedy
* *Limonov: The Outrageous Adventures of the Radical Soviet Poet Who Became a Bum in New York, a Sensation in France, and a Political Antihero in Russia*—Emmanuel Carrère

BOOKS BOUGHT:

* *The Hummingbird*—Sandro Veronesi
* *Always Crashing in the Same Car: On Art, Crisis, and Los Angeles, California*—Matthew Specktor
* *Tomorrow, and Tomorrow, and Tomorrow*—Gabrielle Zevin
* *Also a Poet: Frank O'Hara, My Father, and Me*—Ada Calhoun
* *Festival Days*—Jo Ann Beard

Well, here we are, back at Believer Towers, and before we get on to the subject of books, I'm going to have to lie down for a little while. It's been quite a journey. Regular readers of this magazine may know that the Polysyllabic Spree, the fragrant young men and women who founded this magazine, sold it to people in Las Vegas, some say for a price north of a billion dollars; the fragrance used to be patchouli and the smell of fresh-mown grass, but for a while back there in the Vegas days, it was reputedly Bvlgari and Henry Jacques. I say "reputedly" because nobody ever got near enough to the Spree to smell them. They were on a private Caribbean island, and the people who put them there—me and I suppose even you—were not invited. I understand that E. L. James and Lee Child were frequent guests.

Anyway, the new Vegas owners got bored of us discussing books about veganism and interviewing collagists, and passed us on to an internet hookup site. This odd coupling, between a left-field arts magazine and purveyors of sex toys and other titillations, shouldn't have worked, but it really did: those couple of weeks were the happiest and most lucrative of my professional life. The new proprietor and I had a mutually beneficial arrangement whereby… well. Maybe I should keep that story for another time. Suffice it to say that it's not often that one feels both understood and financially valued. The Spree went and ruined it, of course, by insisting that the sex-toy site was an inappropriate home for their precious magazine, so after all that, I'm back to where I was nearly twenty years ago, penniless and surrounded by chanting bohemians who are now well into middle age. (It looks to me as though they have burned through the reported billion dollars, if the quality of the catering and choice of herbal teas are anything to go by.) I am a little bewildered and resentful, but perhaps you will forgive me. Like professional athletes, *Believer* writers just go where they're told to go. No agency, no choice. We just make the best of it and turn in our copy.

I don't think the sex-toy man would have encouraged me to read the books listed above, however. I promised him "clickbait," but neither modern

Illustration by Kristian Hammerstad

Tehran nor the history of the Troubles in Northern Ireland would necessarily drive traffic toward the wares he had on offer. (It would probably be more accurate to say "the wares *we* had on offer," although that reveals more about our business arrangement than I wanted to disclose.) There is quite a lot of illicit sex in Ramita Navai's *City of Lies*, but if there is an unhappier book about the subject, then I'm not sure I want to know about it.

Navai's book consists of eight brilliantly observed and researched case histories, each dealing with a contemporary Tehrani at a point of crisis. And their crises are really not like ours: they invariably involve the police, repression, violence, a terrifyingly authoritarian interpretation of Islam, and, occasionally, death. Leyla's parents divorced when she was sixteen and immediately remarried, and the aftermath of all that produced a rebellious streak. She fell in love with another young rebel, and they married much too young. They didn't want to marry, but they had already started having sex, and they could live the life they wanted only if they were man and wife. The marriage went wrong quickly—Leyla found her husband having sex with his cousin in their marital bed—and she ran out of money. She could no longer afford her apartment, and moved in with a friend, who supplemented her salary through prostitution. Before long Leyla was turning tricks, too, and though she was arrested and given a whipping, eventually she became the mistress of a cleric and was well looked after.

It is in the chapter about Leyla that we learn of *sigheh*—"a temporary marriage approved by both God and the state, between a man (who can already be married) and a woman (who cannot), and [that] can be as short as a few minutes or as long as ninety-nine years." This is of course a rather neat trick for a married man, especially a cleric. It enables him to get what he wants without troubling his conscience. The worldly judge Leyla slept with was more cynical about the protection sigheh offers, but he took it anyway. Leyla ended up making a porn video for a client, and it became an underground sensation. She was extremely careful not to show her face, but the cyberpolice got hold of it and tracked her down via the visible serial number on her electricity meter. They hanged her.

"You can invent anything you like," Tolstoy said, "but you can't invent psychology." In a way, Navai's gripping, heartbreaking book shows a state and its citizens trying to prove him wrong. The book is called *City of Lies* because the author believes it's impossible to live in Iran without lying. Gay men cannot be gay men, not without living in fear of discovery and punishment. One character, Morteza, tries to "compensate" for his sexuality by belonging to a wild, violent, self-flagellating group of religious extremists and by beating up a gay man. Finally he finds peace by living as a woman. Kids can't listen to Lady Gaga, but they do anyway. Nobody can drink or take drugs; nearly everyone drinks and takes drugs. Hypocrisy is survival. People constantly have to make their interior lives disappear. *City of Lies* is an extraordinary piece of work about an extraordinary society.

If you have ever been in a London Underground station and looked for a rubbish bin in which to throw a banana skin or a disappointing betting

---

**MICROINTERVIEW
WITH LING MA, PART I**

THE BELIEVER: You've talked about how novels like Kazuo Ishiguro's *The Remains of the Day*, Garth Greenwell's *What Belongs to You*, and the works of Kafka influenced the writing of your novel, *Severance*. Were there short stories that inspired the writing of your new story collection, *Bliss Montage*?

LING MA: The novella *Mrs. Caliban* by Rachel Ingalls, which has a surreal premise but is emotionally very anchored, was an influence. It's about a frog-man and a housewife having an affair. It's so absurd, and yet I cried so hard reading that book. It felt so heavy. I like rewatching Miranda July's film *The Future* because I always forget how that movie unfolds. It makes these leaps that I would never have seen coming. It allows the emotion to unfurl the story, which is something I kept thinking about while working on the stories in *Bliss Montage*. I'd usually work on one story, get stuck at a certain point, work on another, push it as far as I could get, and basically rotate through the stories. ✶

slip, you won't find one. Rubbish bins were removed sometime in the 1990s, when the IRA were in the middle of their attempt to take their war to the British mainland. It was easy to leave a bomb in a rubbish bin. Londoners' troubles were not *the* Troubles, of course, but we were not unaffected by them, and they certainly helped shape who we are. To look at a list of bombs planted by the IRA in London between 1973 and 2001 is to remember that the threat was almost constant. There were fifty incidents in 1992 alone—most, though not all, caused no casualties, but they created an atmosphere in which there was danger under every bus seat, in every parked car and pub and department store. I was once on a Tube train when tourists who'd just arrived from Heathrow found a small case on the seat next to them; they picked it up, examined it, and then opened it, and every single other person in the carriage imagined the blinding flash, the thunderclap, and the pain that was bound to follow. The case turned out to contain a flute. In 1996 I was at home when a bomb exploded several miles away and my house shook.

So to read *Say Nothing*, Patrick Radden Keefe's definitive and addictive history of the sectarian conflict and the shameful part that the British Army played in it, is to be taken back to a past that we lived through but have maybe tried to forget. The large cast of characters contains many familiar names: Jean McConville, single mother of ten children, who was removed from her home and made to disappear; Gerry Adams, the consummate Republican politician, who

was arrested for the disappearance and released without charge; Bobby Sands, of course, but also the nine others who died on hunger strike, one after the other, in the summer of 1981, while Margaret Thatcher did nothing; Dolours Price, who took part in the first mainland car-bombing campaign, drove former IRA colleagues across the Irish border for execution, accused Gerry Adams of ordering the murder of McConville, and was emotionally and physically ruined by her war; Bernadette Devlin McAliskey, for a while Britain's youngest member of Parliament, who was shot nine times by the loyalist Ulster Defence Association in front of her young family, and lived.

These names were part of my life from my teenage years onward, and one of the many valuable services *Say Nothing* provides is context, some of it surprising to me. I didn't know that

when the Troubles began, the IRA was "practically defunct," with only a hundred or so members in Belfast. They were almost unarmed, as well, apart from a few antique guns left over from World War II—they had sold the rest to the Free Wales Army in 1968. (Wales, for those of you who don't follow the politics of the British Isles, is no longer a hotbed of armed revolution, and even voted for Brexit.) But the Loyalists viciously beat participants in a peaceful Catholic march in 1969, while the Royal Ulster Constabulary mostly watched, and then three thousand soldiers raided the Falls district of Belfast, where Catholics lived, and then, and then, and then. The IRA robbed banks and shot informants, and the British Army tortured suspected IRA members, and before too long Belfast had become as hellish, as dangerous and violent, as Tehran.

Say Nothing, like *City of Lies*, personalizes its terrible story—Patrick Radden Keefe never loses sight of his characters for very long, and they are threaded into the narrative. Northern Ireland is a small place, after all, and everyone knew everyone else. Dolours Price was one of the three IRA members who shot Jean McConville, the mother of ten. She deliberately missed her shot, but she was there, and knew all the time what had happened to her. The disturbing thing about both *City of Lies* and *Say Nothing* is that they make you think about what these places at those times would do to you. If you are a liberal, would you be a liberal in Tehran? What kind? The kind who must behave like a conservative, through fear? The kind who reports on neighbors who have had a drink or own a satellite dish? Or the kind who has a drink and owns a satellite dish and faces imprisonment? If you had grown up in Divis Flats, would you own a weapon? Would you avoid any trouble? Or would you remain defenseless in the face of army brutality and Protestant hatred? Because those would be the only choices you had. You couldn't be *you*, the you that is reading this in a California coffee shop or a New York independent bookshop, that's for sure. (Go to the cashier and pay for the magazine, by the way, cheap New Yorker.)

I read a second book set during the Troubles recently, *Trespasses*, a very fine first novel by Louise Kennedy. Her people are trying to be themselves, to live between the fault lines, but for Cushla, a young Catholic woman, that means falling in love with an older married man, a Protestant lawyer with Republican sympathies. If this makes the novel sound schematic in some way, it's really not: these people are complicated, damaged both by their choices and by the environment. And this being Belfast in the 1970s, there is no unlikely romantic outcome. It's a beautiful book, serious, deeply felt, wry. I have to say it was a real pleasure, also, to read a first novel by someone who has lived a life before attempting to write. Kennedy, now in her mid-fifties, was a chef for thirty years before writing her debut story collection; she lived through the Troubles herself.

I haven't left myself much space to write about Emmanuel Carrère's *Limonov*, and there's a lot to say about both the author and this book. Carrère is something of a phenomenon

in France. He has directed films and written scripts, fiction and nonfiction. On a recent visit to his native country, I found that everyone knows who he is and has firmly held views about which of his books is the best. There is a lot of love for *The Adversary: A True Story of Monstrous Deception*, a short, brilliant nonfiction account of an apparently ordinary man who murdered his own family, while others prefer *The Kingdom*, a longer novel about the early history of Christianity. That probably gives you a sense of his extraordinary range. He has recently been in trouble for writing about his ex-wife, after promising her that he wouldn't, although, as you can imagine, that's a complicated story. *Limonov* is a novel or a biography, depending on where and when you bought a copy, but either way it is a thrilling book, and this is a perfect

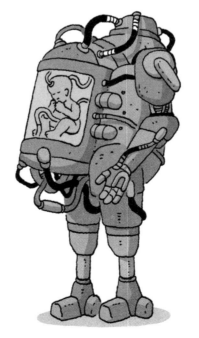

time to read it: the hero of the story, Eduard Limonov, was born in Dzerzhinsk in 1943, and his story is the story of the Soviet Union, and Russia, and quite a lot of other places, as it turns out. Eduard is a no-hope teenage hoodlum who is beaten unconscious by the police after starting a brawl; he could have gotten five years, but his father was in the military and someone recognized his name. He works in a foundry, he writes poetry, he's sent to a mental institution, he moves to Moscow, he makes jeans, he emigrates to the United States, he writes polemics for a Russian-language newspaper, he becomes a butler, he sleeps with women, he sleeps with men, he writes a novel. His work is published in Paris. He becomes a literary sensation. *This shit actually happened.* We are now halfway through the book. He fights for the Serbs in the Bosnian War and ends up back in Moscow at the dawn of the cowboy oligarch era, founding the quasi-fascistic National Bolshevik Party. This is really not a dull book. I can see I'm going to end up reading a novel about early Christianity.

I am not a great reader of science fiction, mostly because I don't understand a lot of it. But these last few weeks I have been visiting worlds almost beyond comprehension—at least, beyond comprehension for those of us who live in Western Europe or the United States. The way things are headed, though, we'll understand better soon enough. Who am I? Someone hiding in the corner, with my books and my music and my streaming subscriptions. Someone will probably take it all away soon enough, but until then, it will do. ✶

UNDERWAY

WE ASK WRITERS AND ARTISTS:
WHAT'S ON YOUR DESK? WHAT ARE YOU WORKING ON?

LAUREN GROFF

PROFESSION: *Writer*
DESK LOCATION: *Gainesville, FL*

My desk is a giant slab of waxed cherry that I had a local artist make into a desk when I received my first substantial check for writing. It is a thing so beautiful that I feel like I'm failing it if I don't visit every day, which is good motivation when I've taken too much melatonin to get to sleep and the project of rising and writing feels like a grind. I just can't disappoint the desk. The grain is as soft as an inner arm, but I'm not able to feel it at the moment, because it is covered in projects, all in the same enormous brown Muji sketchbooks with ties that are no longer available in the United States, and I will be devastated when I run out of them. There are short story projects here that I have been unable to complete to my happiness for decades, a poetry project, a quarry toward the strangest project I have ever attempted, a book in five Muji notebooks that I've written all the way through and restarted from scratch three times, a book that is so endlessly capacious I may never finish it, a notebook full of other people's quotes, a notebook that's a running list of images and phrases, a notebook, a notebook, a notebook. I start the day when I'm still asleep, coffee in hand, and go where the joy goes. What we do is serious play; sometimes the joy is all we have.

LESLIE JAMISON

PROFESSION: *Writer*
DESK LOCATION: *Brooklyn, NY*

The desk in my current bedroom is the only desk I've had in the past decade. Years of cramped-apartment living in Brooklyn have acclimated me to working at kitchen tables, on couches, in bed. But now, here it is—improbable as a spaceship, or an alchemist's stone—facing a towering catalpa tree, covered with stacks of books: a pile of vintage 1980s *Choose Your Own Adventure* books (for a magazine essay); a 1975 hardcover called *The Inner World of Daydreaming* ("Suppose your doorbell rings and you open it to find yourself confronted with a gorilla"). On the back cover, a black-and-white photo of a daydream scientist named Jerome L. Singer. Who knew it was a discipline?

Every once in a while, I prune the stacks. When they get too high, they interfere with the view: the dangling green catalpa pods as big as string beans for a giant, and the frantic, inscrutable soap operas of the squirrels who scuttle along the branches; or my neighbor's garage—once a horse stable, now a storage shed—with a Mr. Potato Head visible in the window. So many times my gaze has landed on that Mr. Potato Head—in moments of distraction, procrastination, frustration, occasional inspiration, frequent daydreaming (it's a discipline). So much of being *at* my desk consists of letting my gaze wander beyond my desk, and then letting my mind return to its materials, to find them somehow rearranged—even just slightly, fingers crossed—like the shards of glass in a kaleidoscope.

Like a bowerbird, like a woman whose Twitter bio reads "professional bowerbird," I've started gathering objects around the edges of my desk. These are artifacts from that other civilization—all the living that happens when I'm not sitting down. I keep a postcard from the Getty Villa in Los Angeles, the city of my youth: it's a reconstructed Roman villa—at once garish and breathtaking, antiquity rebuilt by oil money—that I loved as a kid and now like to visit with my daughter, who is currently obsessed with Greek mythology. She likes to make her own mythology. She likes to jump over the sleek, shallow fountain near the gift shop, saying, "I'm crossing the River Styx! I'm crossing the River Styx!" Life to death and back again, just like that. I keep that postcard to remind me of the sunlight of my hometown—its relentless illumination, its particular coastal beauty—and also to keep my daughter close, not just the fact of her existence, which is never far from mind, but her insatiable hunger to take the things of this world (its myths, its fountains) and re-create them. Like a bowerbird. An amateur.

Next to that postcard from the Getty, I keep a single tarot card, propped against my mug of pens. The Chariot. A wistful warrior with curly hair and a crown of stars, riding a chariot pulled by two sphinxes: one is black striped with white; the other, white striped with black. I salvaged this particular tarot card from the home of my aunt, who lived a troubled life and left behind a small cabin filled with what many people would just call "junk." I won't write about her life here, or her death, except to say that there will always be more I don't understand about her than I do.

Which is maybe true of everyone. But feels particularly true with her. While helping clear out her cabin after her death, I found this single tarot card resting on the dusty plastic covering of a stack of unopened cans of cat food. It's associated with overcoming conflict. That's what the internet says. I'm more interested in what it says next: The sphinxes represent opposing forces that the charioteer must learn to control—they often try to pull him in opposing directions. If you can navigate their disagreements, their combined power is tremendous.

AMY KURZWEIL
PROFESSION: *Cartoonist*
DESK LOCATION: *The Open Road*

I've been working on my second graphic memoir for six million years. *Artificial: A Love Story* is about me; my father, an inventor; and his father, a Viennese musician who escaped the Nazis in 1938 and died of heart disease in 1970. The book explores my father's attempt to resurrect his father's identity through AI and salvaged documents. It's also about what it takes and what it means to love someone.

I'm now inking the book's 316 pages. I'm on page 128. Lately, I've been moving around too much for my own good. Luckily, I have a traveling desk:

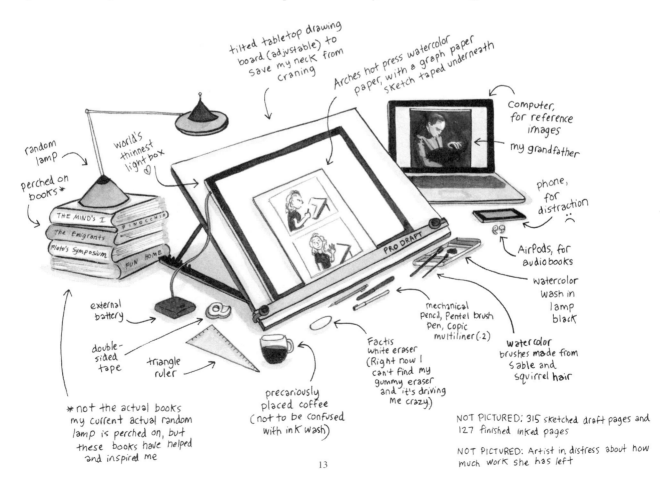

tilted tabletop drawing board (adjustable) to save my neck from craning

Arches hot press watercolor paper, with a graph paper sketch taped underneath

Computer, for reference images — my grandfather

phone, for distraction :(

AirPods, for audiobooks

watercolor wash in lamp black

watercolor brushes made from sable and squirrel hair

mechanical pencil, Pentel brush pen, Copic multiliner (.2)

Factis white eraser (Right now I can't find my gummy eraser and it's driving me crazy)

precariously placed coffee (not to be confused with ink wash)

triangle ruler

double-sided tape

external battery

THE MIND'S I / PINOCCHIO / The Emigrants / Plato's Symposium / FUN HOME

perched on books *

random lamp

world's thinnest light box ♡

* not the actual books my current actual random lamp is perched on, but these books have helped and inspired me

NOT PICTURED: 315 sketched draft pages and 127 finished inked pages

NOT PICTURED: Artist in distress about how much work she has left

13

TWO AMERICAN SONNETS
STARRING OCTAVIA BUTLER

by Terrance Hayes

I.

In Julie Dash's *Octavia Butler* the director washes Octavia's
Monumental feet & toenails in buckets of government water
When there are no seas or rivers handy. It takes too long
Awaiting God's drizzle though there are open barrels outside
The camera's frame in the scene where Butler lies outdoors
Letting her entire mouth fill with tap-water, then spitting the water
Into the air as rain blessed & better after the taste of her speech.
If you don't see suffering's potential as art, will it remain suffering?
When Butler tells Dash she's dreamed of storms all week,
Dash asks to film the dreams. The camera watches Butler sleep
A full moon humming something in the same baritone she uses
When she speaks. Of course, Octavia Butler stars in *Octavia Butler*.
She buys blouses with patterns of leaves & flowers in the off hours
And listens to the young hotel desk clerk worry about precipitous weather.

II.

In Gordon Parks' lost *Octavia Butler* photos Parks parks Butler
In Central Park & shoots her against the stars beginning to burn
Between the leaves & city some twilight evening in 1963.
She's a teen, but tall & nearly as quiet as the trees & policemen
Hovering over the scene. Parks shoots her near the tallest tree
Leaning into its shade, then clutching a hatchet, then transformed
Into a small black bird perched in its branches. No police dogs
Are on the attack. Rain makes the tree bark appear
To be sweating. The surface of everything cries over the black
Holes between capitalism & spirituality; the manholes between
Building & property. When asked about the banter shared
During their time together, Butler & Parks recalled different things.
If you see suffering's potential as art, is it art or suffering?
If you see life's potential as art, is it artful or artificial living?

ASK CARRIE

A NEW COLUMN FROM CARRIE BROWNSTEIN,
WHO IS BETTER AT DISPENSING ADVICE
THAN TAKING IT

Send questions to advice@thebeliever.net

Dear Carrie,

I'm a musician based in Brooklyn, and I reluctantly find myself trying to understand TikTok. I've always struggled to navigate social media, and these days it seems there's no possible way of getting my music to the people if my band and I are not perpetually creating content. I even tried to go the Halsey and Charli XCX route and made some TikToks about how hard it is to make TikToks, but I'm not famous enough, so no one really cared. Is it naive to think I can just create and produce my own work and listeners will somehow find me? Should I just forget about this whole social media marketing thing if it doesn't feel natural to me?

 Thanks,
 Bushwick Uninfluencer
 Brooklyn, NY

Dear Bushwick Uninfluencer,

First, I hope you take comfort in the fact that you are not the only person—young or old—struggling to understand TikTok, or to be confounded and exhausted by social media as a marketing tool. Next, try to rid yourself of the burden to create online content; I feel certain that's not the reason we were put on this earth. In fact, I find the idea of "content" to be incredibly cynical, reductive, and unimaginative. The rebranding of every aspect of our lives as content feels like one of the biggest (and darkest) victories for late-stage capitalism. I admit, some people are quite good at being

content creators, and that's probably because they actually enjoy it (or are masters at making the viewer believe they enjoy it). This isn't to say you shouldn't want to make money with your music or have fans or even get famous! Go for it! But the idea that content is tantamount to art is degrading. There is no faster way to forfeit uniqueness or grow weary than to reframe your passions as void-filling pabulum, particularly if you're doing so against your will. My advice is to stay true to yourself, focus on the music and songwriting, and become an artist who can perform live and command the stage. I can't guarantee it won't break your heart or be difficult. But would you rather have a moment or a career? I think the latter comes from being authentic and developing a strong point of view, and if neither is possible while creating content, avoid it. Trust that people will find your music.

Dear Carrie,

Why is the weather always wrong?
 Heike D.
 Madison, WI

Dear Heike,

Is it the weather or is it you? Or me? Or all of us? In other words, bad weather is the easiest and most obvious thing to blame for our ongoing dissatisfaction with life. Maybe we should be thankful for the pouring rain that ruined our visit to the llama farm. And feel gratitude for the scorching heat and blazing sun that made everyone look pained, armpit-soaked, and squinty-eyed in the annual family photo. If we couldn't blame our woes on the weather, then, frankly, we'd have to blame ourselves or one another. The weather's consistent failure to meet our expectations has likely prevented countless arguments and divorces. And don't get me started on how the weather does a lot of heavy lifting when it comes to small talk. Last, images and anecdotes about the weather's wrongness are a staple of social media, so let's not rob people of that joy.

Dear Carrie,

I'm wondering if you have any advice on how to manage a male partner who is constantly pointing out that I'm overweight. Could I lose a few pounds? Yes. But I would not by any means consider myself overweight. This has become a chronic topic of

Illustration by Kristian Hammerstad

conversation that always results in tears (for me) and frustration (for him). And now it has crept into comments about my food choices, etc. I don't agree that it should be a "free" topic, and my stance has been that this type of communication is not helpful, but he disagrees. Am I totally off base to think that this is somewhat taboo? I have multiple friends, male and female, who have never had this topic broached in any way by their partner. And I don't think the resentment or insecurity it elevates in me are helpful. I should add that I routinely keep up on my doctor visits and my overall health is in good shape. What would you do?

Lucy
St. Louis, MO

Dear Lucy,

The first thing I want to say is that it's not OK for anyone to body-shame you. Perhaps I'm not the first person to say that to you, and I may not be the last—because sometimes we all need to hear things multiple times before we believe them, and that's all right!—but here is the bottom line: your partner's behavior is not merely "taboo"; it is harmful.

It sounds like you've tried to set a boundary: you've told your partner that his comments about your weight and food choices

---

MICROINTERVIEW
WITH LING MA, PART II

THE BELIEVER: Many of the characters in your stories are in their late twenties or early thirties. As you say, they kind of exist on the periphery of their own experiences. What about that age appeals to you as a fiction writer?

LING MA: For me, that was the age when I had to make a lot of decisions about myself. In your late twenties, you either actualize what you want or you let the world define you. That sounds like it's from a graduation speech or something. Anyway, I think those are the years you become an adult and decide what kind of life you want to lead. In my late twenties, I was working and living in Chicago. I would take really long walks at night around the neighborhood, and those walks gave me a lot of ideas of things to write about. It was also the age when I was the most alone. ✸

---

are unhelpful and leave you feeling insecure, and that you want him to stop. Yet he's choosing to ignore that boundary. I find it ironic that your partner is supposedly concerned about your health while blatantly ignoring the deleterious effects his comments are having on your emotional and mental well-being.

Since I mentioned health, a quick detour to reiterate something you hinted at in your letter. You are correct that body size is not indicative of health. For more info, I reached out to my friend Caity Robinson (MPH, RDN, CD), and this is what she said: "There always has been and always will be inherent diversity of body shapes and sizes. 'Health' is a culmination of factors, many of which go beyond a person's individual behaviors."

Basically, your partner's comments are not about your health but rather about his highly subjective and narrow standards of beauty. Which brings me to my next point: you deserve to be with someone who (1) loves you for who you are, (2) doesn't shame you, and (3) makes you feel safe, heard, respected, and beautiful.

So if I were you, and if all the other aspects of your relationship with this man make it worth working on, I would clearly and unequivocally state my boundary one last time. Ask him to stop the comments and criticism. Tell him that your body is not up for debate, nor is your weight a "free" topic of conversation. I would also let him know how hurtful his behavior has been. Furthermore, I might see if he's open to some self-examination and reflection of his own.

Does he or someone in his family have a history of disordered eating that makes food a sensitive topic for him? Is he insecure about his own body and projecting that onto you? Is there something else he's upset about? In other words, perhaps there's a way this can become a productive dialogue about what you need and want out of this partnership.

But, Lucy, please always remember the bottom line—that is, it's not OK for anyone to body-shame you! And remember what you deserve! Because I really want you to feel loved! And not to feel like you need to change anything about yourself for the sake of someone else! You don't! Sorry, I can't stop using exclamation points! But I really mean it.

Finally, if your partner isn't willing to change and do some work on himself, then here's what I'd do, in all honesty: I'd lose the only weight that's holding you back, and that's the weight of this man and this relationship.

OK, before I go: if you need further inspiration and ballast, Caity kindly gave me recommendations to pass on:

MICROINTERVIEW WITH LING MA, PART III

THE BELIEVER: Peking duck is featured in *Severance*, and one story in *Bliss Montage* is titled "Peking Duck." In that story, the dish is described as "an image of near iconography" for the narrator. What is your relationship with the dish?

LING MA: The only time I remember eating it was in London, on a work trip. At first, I felt a little self-conscious about calling that story "Peking Duck," because it's an Oriental-seeming title, you know? It starts off like every other Chinese immigrant story. But I realized the title needs to be "Peking Duck." There's just such an Oriental vibe about that dish that I was interested in unpacking as a symbol in that story. Growing up in the US, I often heard that dish mentioned in recountings of US history, like with Nixon going to China and eating Peking duck. For some reason, it's associated with US presidents. It's almost like that dish is used for East-West diplomacy in some odd way. ✱

Dear Carrie,
I live in a small town. A rumor started that I am in the CIA. It was funny at first, but now it's not. People genuinely seem to believe that I'm a spy, and everything I say, no matter how innocuous it might be, is further proof to them that I am one. I have always been transparent and honest in all my relationships, even if it cost me. I feel insulted and misunderstood. What should I do?
  Name Withheld
  Location Withheld

Dear Name Withheld,
It makes me nervous even to answer this question, because I don't want to end up on a watch list. Not to say that you *are* in the CIA. But if you are—and this isn't an accusation—could you please give me a sign? Can you call me on my cell phone, right now, without me giving you my number? Could you start my car remotely? Are you currently sitting next to me on my sofa, disguised as my dog? I'm waiting… Hm, it's been a full ten minutes, and none of those things came to fruition. I will soldier on. BTW, I mean "soldier on" figuratively; I don't have any military training; please don't perceive me as a threat. Anyhow, I will now proceed to give advice to an average citizen who's presented me with a completely run-of-the-mill question. Wink, wink. Dammit. This is harder than I thought. OK, Name Withheld, I suppose if you're hell-bent on changing the narrative, you could use your training (I'm not saying you have any special training, of course) to place secret messages inside people's smart speakers. *Alexa, is my friend a spy?* Alexa: *No. Stop being paranoid. Your friend is not a spy. They're obviously just a very private person with a dubious income source who travels frequently for work and has never invited you into their home. Now playing Eminem's "The Real Slim Shady" for the next twenty-four hours.* Alternatively, what if, instead of feeling misunderstood, you embraced the whole CIA thing?! What if you hosted a CIA Day in your small town or rode atop a CIA-themed float at the next parade? You could make T-shirts for everyone that say, I'M NOT A SPY BUT MY FRIEND IS! Because I imagine that part of the fun for your fellow townspeople is the mystery, and once that's gone, they'll likely move on to new speculations. Like, I'm curious about who's leading this charge that you're a spy. Seems like a diversionary tactic to me… ✱

SACRIFICE ZONE

A SEMI-REGULAR GUEST COLUMN ABOUT REGULARLY IGNORED PLACES

by Claire Vaye Watkins

LOCATION:	LATITUDE, LONGITUDE:
Yellow Pine, Nevada	*N 36°03'59.1", W 115°46'30.6"*

There is no place in Nevada's Pahrump Valley called Yellow Pine, yet I arrive. Yellow Pine is a place invented for sacrifice. It is a new name given by NextEra Energy—a gigantic energy company from Florida worth about $175 billion—to a trapezoid of land stolen by the United States. Here, NextEra wants to build an industrial solar array on public land. Yellow Pine is located in Nevada and, preceding that place's invention, in Newe Sogobia, unceded territory of the Western Shoshone Nation as well as the Nuwu (Southern Paiute), namely the Pahrump band of the Nuwu, themselves unrecognized by the federal government. The land is in a valley between Las Vegas and Pahrump. I grew up here.

For years now I've come to Yellow Pine to witness the avoidable carnage occasioned by NextEra's array-in-progress, one of a vast patchwork of industrial for-profit solar arrays in the works across 124,000 acres of the Mojave Desert and the Great Basin, a region its devotees call America's Outback. Yellow Pine is home to about 90,000 old-growth yuccas and, until recently, 139 adult desert tortoises. It's an undulating creosote sea that I credit for making the air I breathed throughout my girlhood. Shannon Salter, a friend who's been living in a camper near Yellow Pine to document the desert's destruction, calls Yellow Pine "5,000 acres of pure spirit." It's obviously true: from Yellow Pine one looks up to Mount Charleston, the highest peak in the Spring Mountains and a key site in the Salt Songs, the ceremonial creation myth song cycle of the Nuwu.

The adult tortoises of Yellow Pine have been relocated across the highway to a dried-up spring, making them "refugees," as a tortoise biologist I met there put it. Tortoises are not intrepid travelers. They spend their whole lives in one small, intimately memorized patch of desert, maybe a mile square. I heard about a tortoise who'd been transplanted from another site—"mitigated," in the banal-evil lexicon of the Bureau of Land Management—dug up from her burrow and moved out of the path of industrial order only to return in search, probably, of water. The place she scratched a certain groove in the dirt so water would gather. Or perhaps in search of her mate. Instead of home or love, the tortoise met a "tortoise exclusion fence," a tight black grid, about two feet high. The tortoise followed the exclusion fence for five square miles, until she died. The juvenile and baby tortoises of Yellow Pine were too hard for contractors to find and relocate, so they were effectively left to die.

Illustration by Jackie Ferrentino

It seems to me the tortoise is being mitigated into extinction. About thirty of the adult tortoises relocated from Yellow Pine were promptly eaten by badgers. Even in this grimness there is wonder: I lived my whole girlhood in this valley, and I did not even know we had badgers.

Wonder has its limits. I take little solace in the poetic names of proposed industrial solar arrays that, if built, would kill a massive swath of public land from Arizona to Death Valley: Yellow Pine, Copper Rays, Sawtooth, Bonnie Clare, Chill Sun, Titus Canyon. Busted Buttes 1 and 2. Gemini, Virgo, Jackpot.

According to the Bureau of Land Management's environmental impact statement on Yellow Pine, the industrial array will result in between zero and ten jobs and the "permanent loss or degradation of native vegetation on up to 2,000 acres." The vegetation in question is older than we have cared to determine—yucca colonies grow for hundreds of years; creosote bushes spread rhizomatically for thousands. The plants and fungi and lichen crusts here feed every category of life, from bacteria to mammals. At Yellow Pine, a suffering, yet intact and alive, ecosystem will be pulverized by "graders, excavators, bulldozers, backhoes, cutting machines, end loaders, delivery trucks." These machines will crush the living microbiotic crust unfurled across the land like clumps of crusty velvet and scrape off the ancient and delicate interlocking stones geologists call "desert pavement," an intricate formation of rocks, sending up a tremendous explosion of potentially toxic "fugitive dust." The short black tortoise exclusion fence has now been replaced by tall chain link. Once, before any fences went up, I knelt beside a geologist on a cobble of desert pavement and listened as he told how these stones were once trod upon by giant ground sloths.

Newcomers call a place like this "nothing" or "empty," in an effort (I choose to believe) to grasp its vastness, a worshipful cry at the staggering expanse of land that is an obvious balm to city sprawl, to the long-plowed former prairies of the Midwest, the ill and raided forests of the East, the poisoned, burned, cow-chewed, bombed, and plundered ranges of the American West. Yellow Pine is public land, as fraught as that notion is on stolen land, and it is

our commons, part of one of the last swaths of intact wilderness on a fabulously abused continent.

The alternatives to greed-drunk, avoidable carnage are also obvious to us watchers at Yellow Pine: free, abundant, distributed community solar in the built environment. Publicly owned panels covering parking lots, military bases, dead alfalfa fields, and golf courses that never should have been built in the first place. My activist buddies demand solar in the cities, where environmentalist politics are more palatable, rather than the "all of the above" policies that would kill this land and drive the people who live nearby into deeper alliance with climate deniers and violent fascists. We hope to reject the false choice between transitioning off fossil fuels and conserving biodiversity, which threatens to shred what remains of the American environmentalist movement. The wilderness deserves life, and we need wilderness, not only to live but to live well. I would love to see California insist on truly public utilities that put solar panels on every rooftop in the state. I dream of Nevada modeling a real, sustainable energy revolution with a holistic land ethic, rejecting wasteful supply chains, for-profit extraction, and overconsumption. I fear that instead, the southwestern states will, at the Biden administration's urging, turn the Mojave Desert into the "Texas oilfields of the twenty-first century," as another tortoise biologist put it.

It's been a long and bloody couple of centuries in the American West. It's looking to be a perilous decade, especially in cities like LA, Phoenix, Reno, and Las Vegas, where, by the end of this century, it will be too hot for asphalt. Sacrifice zones are a convenient concept, but seen from against the fence around Yellow Pine, they are plainly a figment of the imagination. Embracing optional mass death to profit the same few who got us into this mess is self-harm on a geological scale. It is a deep, grievous injury to the collective soul, and such injury can never be contained. The loss my friends and I gather to mourn at Yellow Pine cannot be cordoned off. The grim folly we watch here will be a part of all of us forever. Perhaps no region of this country knows the lie of the sacrifice zone more deeply, more intimately than the thirsty, ever-irradiated desert Southwest. ✷

COLORADO SPRINGS

A NEW POEM

by Danez Smith

she crying for all us – her brother, son, me, everyone someone's boy – before
the wedding, henny wrecked, lovewhelmed, meaning well   *so much* –
she says – *Black boys go thru these days: gay, transgender, gangbanging* – i know
what she means, i try to   not be criminalized   i know she doesn't see us as crimes,
maybe sins, but sense to her, since i know my own mother – i know she means
the bodies we didn't think our sons would lay down, the men we never imagined
would seek our sons in the night   our boys   dressed in those colors
monochrome & prismstrained, flagging what we hoped wouldn't find them. i know
when i pressed my purple stone to my mother's breast, what flooded her wasn't disgust
but sickness, knowing what violences might rush her once blue babe now cut to pink
meat, red as honesty, those blood ill premonitions: love – their own bodies – other boys
all mothers know anything can hunt a son – a fear so animal language cannot tame
nor reason. later, before the wedding, in the woods at the mountain's feet, love
points out a mushroom *that looks like a coin*. it do. earthy currency, a metal soft
& chewable, fragile platinum. even if i was Mother Earth I couldn't expect this
wild change, fleshy & star bright steel bloom. I wouldn't know it grew like this
too, dirt rising into armor. she didn't know we grow up fine, my mother loves
her purpled child deeper & truer even though what she feared would scar me
left its mark. i know she meant well, i know love shots beyond language or sense.
mothers, if we make it, we make it through it all.
love, find our sons.
body, hold our babies well. free them from all cages even if it's what we named them.
violence, don't lust after our boys & call it kin. if you must find our babies in the midst
of their lives, please leave only a wound we can dress
& may we not be the scars they stitch lonely in the mothergone dark.

THE HOPPER-CONSANI CONNECTION

HOW A VISUAL MASH-UP OF FOUR TANGENTIALLY RELATED
CELEBRITIES BECAME AMERICA'S PREFERRED DINER ART

by Ryan H. Walsh

I f you're sitting in an American diner that happens to have any predilection for nostalgia—and it's extremely rare that any diner does not—there's a good chance you're going to see a certain painting somewhere inside the establishment. It's a series of paintings, actually, but they will have one thing in common, whether the setting is a casino, a gas station, a movie theater, or a pool hall: they will *always* portray four specific people: Elvis Presley, Marilyn Monroe, James Dean, and Humphrey Bogart.

In one painting, titled *Classic Interlude*, Monroe and Presley sit happily together at the cinema as James Dean slouches in the row in front of them, too cool to care that he's not on a date with Marilyn, tossing a kernel of popcorn up into the air. But his gaze back toward the pair betrays his *whatever*-veneer. There's no mistaking it: he wishes he was Elvis, cozied up next to the beautiful woman with the million-dollar smile. Meanwhile, here comes Humphrey Bogart, ambling down the theater aisle, a flashlight pointed toward the trio's seats. Perhaps Dean, always the rebel, didn't pay for a ticket.

Another tableau depicts the outside of a drive-in restaurant. Presley sits on the back bumper of a car, banging out a song on an acoustic guitar. Monroe appears to be swept away by the tune; Dean eyes Presley half with contempt, half with envy. Meanwhile, Bogie stares off into the middle distance with the intensity of a man who has lived more life than he has left in front of him, much of it marked by regret. It's always some semblance of this dynamic with the four: a love triangle, plus an older man who oversees, chaperones, or is trapped in his own inner world in proximity to their young(ish) romance.

These four American celebrities never appeared in a movie together. None of them were good friends. There are stray stories of their lives briefly intersecting, but nothing consequential. All three of the men met Monroe and, of course, all three were rumored to have had a fling with her. Two of them died in the 1950s; Monroe in the '60s; Presley in '77, at the age of forty-two. Most of them reached the height of their fame in the 1950s, though Bogart's star certainly shone brightest in the '40s, when he made such movies as *The Maltese Falcon*, *Casablanca*, and *The Big Sleep*.

In other words, this isn't the most obvious foursome to occupy a painted, nostalgic eternity together. But now, ironically, thanks to these ubiquitous paintings, Monroe, Dean, Presley, and Bogart seem forever inseparable. So who decided on this grouping, and why? The answer is comically, unnecessarily complex. It begins with an impressionist painter from New York who created one of the great odes to American loneliness in the early 1940s.

Edward Hopper was born in Nyack, New York, in 1882, the son of a dry-goods merchant and a woman whose love of art led to her son's initial interest in painting. Elizabeth encouraged Edward's pursuit of the craft, even hand-selecting the boardinghouse where he resided during his first trip to Paris, in 1906, to study the masters. After Hopper spent six years at New York School of Art,[1] his work—etchings, watercolors, and then oil paintings—began to develop its own style.

He was an impressionist, initially in the style of Degas and Manet, who ignored modern movements, even audaciously claiming never to have heard the name Picasso *mentioned* during his visits to Europe. By the time Hopper's point of view was fully formed, he had figured out how to capture the mood of noir cinema in his city scenes, with or without people inhabiting them. But instead of the stark black-and-white tones of the silver screen, he made his scenes work with saturated colors.[2] In Hopper's hands, the most mundane tableau is imbued with a deep mystery, and a sense that something unusually intense is about to happen, or just has.

For nearly two decades after his schooling, Hopper made a living creating commercial illustrations—a job he passionately disliked—while his serious work was largely ignored by the art market. But right around the time he reconnected with his old classmate and future wife, Josephine Nivison,[3] at an artists' colony in Gloucester, Massachusetts, his career took a turn for the better—much better. In 1933, he enjoyed his first major retrospective at the Museum of Modern Art. By the close of the decade, he was among the most successful living American artists, right on the cusp of creating his finest masterpiece.

Hopper was fifty-nine when he began working on *Nighthawks*, just as the country formally entered World War II. His lauded position in the art world had been well-earned, due not only to his unwavering work ethic but also to his refusal to conform to trends that might lead to higher asking prices for his work. He later remarked that he based his most famous painting's setting on an all-night lunch counter he'd observed on Greenwich Avenue in Manhattan, two miles from his apartment.[4]

---

1. It was known as the Chase School at the time. There, one of Hopper's teachers, Robert Henri, would publish a 1923 book titled *The Art Spirit*, which would go on to become a kind of bible for film director and painter David Lynch. Hopper's influence on Lynch's work, on both the screen and canvas, is often vividly clear and at times seemingly presented in overt visual homages.

2. Hopper loved the cinema; if he wasn't painting, he was reading or at the movies, and soon cinema would love him back.

3. This was not a coincidence. Jo, a painter herself, became both Hopper's manager and his only model, and she excelled in both roles. Their relationship was complex, to say the least, and often deeply fraught, Jo serving simultaneously as his muse and foil. "Someday I'm going to write the real story of Edward Hopper. No one else can do it," she wrote in a journal. "You'll never get the whole story. It's pure Dostoevsky. Oh, the shattering bitterness!" There is a plainly valid interpretation of the fact that her rising career was derailed, or willfully sacrificed, in service of Hopper's.

4. An enormous amount of amateur detective work has gone into ascertaining the precise location of Hopper's inspiration. Bob Egan of PopSpotsNYC.com places it at 70 Greenwich Avenue, but he also notes that this inspiration goes well beyond a building. Hopper biographer Gail Levin writes that he loved a 1927 Hemingway story titled "The Killers" so much that he wrote to the editor of the magazine that published it—*Scribner's*—to express his admiration.

Nighthawks. © 1942 by Edward Hopper. Oil on canvas. 33 1/8 x 60 in. Courtesy of the Art Institute of Chicago.

Routinely cited as one of the most recognizable American paintings of all time, *Nighthawks* presents an illuminated diner at the intersection of two desolate, darkened streets, with a man and woman sitting stoically inside. The unmistakable emotional distance between them could be decades in the making, or they could have met earlier that night. A blond male employee in a crisp white hat tends to something unseen just below the counter, while another well-dressed customer with his back to us hunches over his late-night cup of joe. There is one unifying mood that looms over the entire scene: loneliness. Gordon Theisen's book-length meditation on the painting, *Staying Up Much Too Late: Edward Hopper's Nighthawks and the Dark Side of the American Psyche*, called it a "twentieth-century masterpiece… a deeply cold and alien work, despite its immediately recognizable subject matter," one that "exerts a seductive pull."

While Hopper was dubbed "the visual bard of American solitude" by *The New Yorker* in 2020, and received countless variants of this sentiment over the years, he never intentionally set out to capture Americans' unique, shared feelings of separateness. But in his artistic quest to express his own inner loneliness,[5] he accidentally bottled

---

The story opens with a scene not unlike the one depicted in *Nighthawks*. Furthermore, the story was accompanied by a line drawing by C. LeRoy Baldridge depicting two men wearing fedoras, interacting with a male diner employee; examining it, one feels as if they're potentially looking at an early Hopper sketch exploring the concept of these type of men inhabiting a locale like the one also seen in *Nighthawks*.

5. Of his introverted, stoic nature, Jo Hopper once remarked of her husband, "Sometimes talking with Eddie is just like dropping a stone in a well except that it doesn't thump when it hits bottom." The artist disliked explaining where the lonely feelings expressed in his paintings originated, only offering some version of "the whole answer is there on the canvas." Hopper's biographer Gail Levin highlighted how his unusual tallness naturally

Boulevard of Broken Dreams. ©1985 by Gottfried Helnwein. Watercolor on cardboard. Reprinted courtesy of the artist.

a zeitgeist. "I don't think I ever tried to paint the American scene," Hopper once explained; "I am trying to paint myself." Just as everyone in a dream is some representation of the dreamer, according to Jungian theory, every figure in *Nighthawks* is Hopper.

In 1942, the Art Institute of Chicago purchased the painting for three thousand dollars, and it has resided there ever since. *Nighthawks*'s influence was immediate and long-lasting. In 1946, director Robert Siodmak clearly re-created the painting in the opening scene of his film *The Killers*, an adaptation of the Ernest Hemingway 1921 short story, which in turn had been one of the inspirations for *Nighthawks*— a perfect loop of influence. Later, Alfred Hitchcock

---

separated him from everyone else, and Jo even went so far as to suggest that his lonely portraits of lighthouses were meant to represent that isolation. The models for the *Nighthawks* couple who seem so distant yet so intertwined? Jo and Edward Hopper.

unabashedly re-created Hopper's *House by the Railroad* (1925) as the ominous setting for his 1960 masterpiece, *Psycho*. Knowing the director's appreciation of Hopper's eye, it's hard to watch 1954's *Rear Window* without feeling as if each glimpse into each apartment owes a heavy nod to the voyeuristic point of view we encounter in paintings like *Nighthawks* and 1928's *Night Windows*. From there, the painter's influence on film grew exponentially, to a point where it's hard to differentiate between direct influence and the influence of influence. Countless cinematographers and directors—Abraham Polonsky, George Barnes, Gordon Willis, Wim Wenders, and David Lynch, to name a few—have referenced Hopper explicitly and tacitly in their work. On it went, with artists from musician Tom Waits to writer Joyce Carol Oates drawing on *Nighthawks* for their output.

Then, in 1985, something very strange happened in the *Nighthawks* chronicle: an intense Austrian Irish artist named Gottfried Helnwein, fresh off creating the horror-shock cover of the 1982 Scorpions album *Blackout*, painted *Boulevard of Broken Dreams*.[6] *Boulevard* is an extremely faithful re-creation of Hopper's *Nighthawks* setting, except that Helnwein replaced the four anonymous figures with Elvis Presley (as the diner employee), Marilyn Monroe (one-half of the seated couple, here gleeful), Humphrey Bogart (the only figure who maintains the same mood as the original figure he's standing in for), and James Dean (as the loner, here staring wistfully at Elvis's dumb joy in doing menial service work).

If the visual mash-up was meant as a biting commentary on Hopper, or on American celebrity, or both, it misses the mark, but in doing so, ironically, it became massively popular.[7] In 1994, in a piece about the persistent influence of Hopper's work, *The New York Times* noted how the parody painting

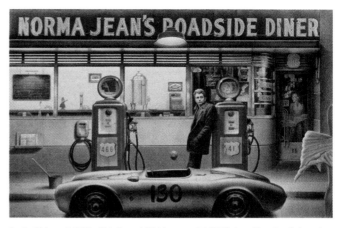

had become a "best-selling poster… a favorite from Brooklyn pizza parlors to California shopping malls." Journalist Tim Foster described it as "the absolute *epitome* of kitsch— a work so godawful that it's hard to actually think of it as anything other than 'product.'" Foster is, as far as I can tell, the only reporter ever to get a quote from Helnwein on the work. (Multiple interview requests went unanswered for this piece.) The writer of an otherwise praise-laden profile of the artist in 2011 notes:

> I did the mental equivalent of a spit-take when I realized that Helnwein had painted *Boulevard of Broken Dreams*, the all-too-familiar parody of Edward Hopper's *Nighthawks*… The artist fumbled uncomfortably when I asked him about the painting. "That was meant as a joke… it got a life of its own and it got so big—that was not my intention."

Perhaps it was Helnwein's attempt to pull an Andy Warhol: after all, the New York pop artist had already famously painted two of the Fakehawks gang, Presley and Monroe.[8] This theory is supported by the fact that Helnwein met Warhol the year before he created *Boulevard*, in an encounter that sounds akin to a religious experience:

---

6. The original source of the painting's title is the 1933 Al Dubin and Harry Warren song "Boulevard of Broken Dreams," which itself has a serpentine history of influence. Originally released by Dubuque, Iowa's, Brunswick Records, it appeared the following year in the 1934 film *Moulin Rouge*, which has no relation to subsequent films of the same name. (The song was later used as the A side of Tony Bennett's major-label debut 45 with Columbia Records in 1950.) After Helnwein's repurposing, it became the title of a biography of James Dean in 1994; Green Day's Billie Joe Armstrong explained that he "nicked" the title of the band's 2004 song from Helnwein's individual portrait of Dean by the same title, which the artist created in conjunction with the painting of the foursome. One of the most popular uploads of the song—116,695 views, 883 likes, 78 comments—is set to a montage of Hopper paintings, though no commenter has pointed out that the song is related to *Nighthawks* and Hopper only by way of parody. It's as if Helnwein's *Boulevard*'s influence has equaled that of the original, which is a tremendous, unlikely accomplishment in itself.

You can keep boring down into this vein. Jochen Markhorst's book entirely about Bob Dylan's 1965 song "Desolation Row" makes a convincing case that the chain of influence for pairing loneliness or despair with specific locales in pop music titles went something like this: "Boulevard of Broken Dreams" (1933) to Hank Williams's "Lost Highway" (1945) to "Heartbreak Hotel" (1956) to "Highway of Regret" (1959) and then to Dylan's "Desolation Row." This is worth noting only because Dylan's own painting style has so often been compared to the aesthetics of Edward Hopper, and recently, the singer's 2020 painting *Night Time in St. Louis* was identified as a clear homage to *Nighthawks*, with the *Telegraph* remarking that "it's as though Dylan has taken the realism of Edward Hopper for a big night out on Desolation Row and left it reeking of nicotine, gasoline and regret." Furthermore, Helnwein's *Boulevard of Broken Dreams* is not unlike the concept of Dylan's "Desolation Row" expressed visually, complete with famous figures standing in for the lonely lives and actions of regular folks (he had to "give them all another name," you see).

7. You could make the case that Helnwein is playing with Hopper's symbiotic relationship with American cinema—both drawing inspiration from it and directly influencing it—by having some of its biggest names literally invade one of his paintings, but this really does not seem to have been his intent, nor is it a popular interpretation of the work.

---

8. Warhol had infamously painted Presley and Monroe in the early 1960s, but in 1985, a few years after the arrival of Helnwein's painting, Warhol produced a portrait of James Dean too. Only Bogart, forever the odd man out, never received the Warhol treatment.

Andy invited me to the Factory in New York [in] 1983 and after he told me how he loved my work, he asked me to follow him into an empty room where we sat down opposite to each other and he just froze and he didn't say anything and he didn't move. We sat there in silence for some time and I didn't know what to do—at first it was strange and it felt kind of awkward, but then slowly everything started to transcend and the tension dissipated and nothing seemed important anymore. Andy looked like a wax-dummy in the posture of a pharaoh that had been dead since thousands of years—the room around us became darker and darker and the white of Andy's face and hair got a glow so intense that it started to burn my eyes. I realized that we were floating now somewhere in outer space and nothing mattered anymore and I raised my Nikon and shot.

Lou Reed later told Helnwein, "Your picture of Andy is the only one I have seen that shows his true self."

The instinct to alter a famous painting and call it a new piece of art is not without precedent. For his 1919 "ready-made," *L.H.O.O.Q. or La Joconde,* Marcel Duchamp painted a moustache on da Vinci's *Mona Lisa* and added his signature. In 1964, Walt Disney animator Ward Kimball published *Art Afterpieces,* in which he added contemporary details to famous paintings for laughs, like placing a gigantic cheeseburger in the lap of *Portrait of a Young Woman in White* (c. 1798). Nevertheless, Helnwein's popular painting seems to function as a kind of ground zero for contemporary visual mash-ups. It presages so much of what we now see on social media daily, accomplished by anyone with basic Photoshop skills—think of the image of Bernie Sanders wearing mittens placed in every setting imaginable, post–Biden inauguration.

With this in mind, it might be surprising to learn that Gottfried Helnwein is *not* the artist who continually recombined these four celebrities into the nostalgic scenarios on the walls of so many American diners. That's

someone else. They've never met, it turns out—but they do share a publisher.

Helnwein had no interest in taking an artistic cue from *Boulevard*'s success, combining pop culture with high art in easily sellable ways. You can tell this by glancing at his subsequent output, which has grown only darker and more disturbing over the years. R. Crumb, of all people, once called him "one sick motherfucker," and later collaborators would include Marilyn Manson and the band Rammstein. But *Boulevard* was a bona fide poster best seller, so not creating more work like it was akin to setting a pile of money on fire.

"The way I got into doing these posters," Chris Consani tells me over the phone from Manhattan Beach, California, "is that Helnwein didn't want to do it anymore, because he wanted to be a serious fine artist. And what an *amazing* artist that guy is."

Consani was born in Washington, DC,[9] the son of a Secret Service agent and a painter. "The house could be burning down and she'd still be painting because she was so intense," he explained of his mother's artistic devotion. Watching her, fascinated, Consani soon developed his own interest in painting. He attended the University of Southern California and the ArtCenter College of Design in Pasadena, going on to create memorable commercial work, like the poster art for *National Lampoon's Christmas Vacation* and Michael Jackson's *Moonwalker.* Well into his professional art career, Consani met Dennis Gaskin, the publisher of Helnwein's *Boulevard* image, and offered to pick up where he left off.

"You know those *Highlights* kids' magazines in the dentist's office?" Consani asks. "They had these black-and-white pictures with hidden images in them. I always thought that anyone who was a hard-core black-and-white

9. The fact that the few online biographies of Consani claim he's Canadian is a great example of his indifference to his internet presence. Consani was already doing well, he figured, and he thought, "Why upset the apple cart? *I* know I was born in DC."

movie buff, like me, might be able to spot a lot of hidden trivia in my paintings. So there's little references to all of their movies and lives in the paintings." The visual-puzzle concept was paired with the idea that the tragic spirt of Helnwein's *Boulevard* could be ditched for a more playful mood, where all four figures are interacting with one another in some way. Consani pitched this concept to Gaskin, who agreed to try it out, and thus his *Hidden Truths* series was born.

From the start, Consani tried to make the paintings different from Helnwein's original. He initially substituted Clark Gable for Humphrey Bogart, but fate intervened when they couldn't get permission for Gable's image. (Gaskin was one of the rare producers of these kind of posters, Consani explains, who actually paid royalties to the estates of the dead celebrities.) In this way, the Fakehawks Four were preserved as a unit, and Consani set out to develop a fresh dynamic. "I wanted an emotional interplay between Dean, Elvis, and Marilyn, and almost to insinuate that [the two men are] vying for her [at the same time]," Consani says. He agrees with my assessment that Bogart is the perpetual odd man out, but stops short of cosigning my interpretation that he's trapped in some kind of cursed existence as a permanent witness to others' lives yet never living his own.

Consani isn't the only artist who paints scenes with the Fakehawks Four, but he is the most prolific and best-selling. ("I've seen a lot of the other ones that have been done," he says, "and I didn't like them, because it doesn't look like they're relating to each other."[10]) Even as he critiques his competitors, Consani remains humble about his success. Reviewing his paintings with me, he can only see things he wishes he could change. We look at *Royal Flush*, in which the Fakehawks are seated at a blackjack table. Bogart deals, Dean has just won big, Presley is shocked at the loss, and Monroe eyes Dean as if he may now finally be worth her time. Consani is right about its flaws: this one *does* look like a janky collage onto which he has forced facial expressions from old photos to fit a story. The other paintings have a more effortless, realistic feeling to them.

I admit I sometimes find it oddly comforting to look at these four icons living on together in a painted midcentury eternity—where James Dean is tending bar for the other three and Humphrey Bogart can't be bothered to look up from his newspaper—even as another part of me winces at how deeply cheesy they are. But the paintings are also a stubborn reminder of a fading monoculture in which there was nothing unusual about selecting a group of four white people meant to represent the best of what Hollywood had to offer. Even with their high-art origin story, these paintings are examples of nostalgic, accessible pop cultural imagery; none of them would ever appear in a serious exhibition in America.

Still, there's an argument to be made that these posters are viewed and enjoyed by far more people than most pieces that sit in museums. While a brilliant canvas can challenge the viewer to determine the intent and meaning behind it, Consani's *Hidden Truths* paintings tell you exactly what they're about the moment you see them. If you *then* want to be challenged, don't worry: he has stocked these images with Easter eggs meant to reward attentive observers. It's the perfect kind of thing to toy with while sitting in a diner, trying to decode all of the posters' secrets with a friend, or alone—like an activity placemat for adults.

Consani completed thirteen *Hidden Truths* posters before calling it quits. He and Gaskin felt they had saturated the market with the concept, though he notes that sales and licensing of the images continue, even if their popularity is nowhere close to its height in the '90s and aughts. Consani and his friends encounter the images out in the world all the time. I do too. As I stare at one painting framed and hanging in the '50s Diner in Dedham, Massachusetts, I wonder if their unchallenging, comforting tone betrays Hopper's original *Nighthawks* in a meaningful way, and whether or not that matters. Then I have a realization: If someone were to paint this diner scene right now, with myself and three other people, all sitting alone at the counter just after dawn with coffee and the paper, they would surely include the detail of a Consani painting hanging on the wall. In other words, a modern-day *Nighthawks* might contain a *Hidden Truths* painting within the painting. There is something absolutely uncanny about Consani's images looping their way back toward their original, twice-removed inspiration, and how they now reside almost exclusively in the original setting of Hopper's masterpiece: a diner. ✶

---

10. Google "Evening at Rick's by George Bungarda" for a good example of a clumsy attempt at the Consani concept. Bungarda also has a 1993 work titled *Legends Theatre*, in which Jimi Hendrix, Buddy Holly, Elvis Presley, and Jim Morrison are all performing together onstage (that's a *lot* of singers), while Bob Marley, Janis Joplin, and even Beethoven(!) are reduced to audience members.

GOODBYE, IRONMAN TATE.
GOODBYE, VICIOUS ABUNDANCE.

A FAREWELL NOTE TO GREG TATE

by Rachel Kaadzi Ghansah

What is a writer? He writes for readers, but what does "for" mean? It means intended for them, a writer, he writes to his readers just as he writes "for" readers. He also writes for non-readers, that is, not intended for them, but "in place of them." So "for" means two things: intended for them and in their place. Artaud famously wrote, "I write for the illiterate… I write for idiots." Faulkner also wrote for idiots. That doesn't mean so that idiots might read, or the illiterate might read. It means "in the place of" the illiterate. I write "in the place of" barbarians, I write "in the place of" animals. And what does that mean? Why does one dare say something like that? I write in the place of idiots… the illiterate… animals?

Because that is what one does, literally, when one writes, when one writes, one is not pursuing some little personal matter. Dumb asses! It's an abomination of literary mediocrity in every era, but particularly quite recently, that makes people think that to create a novel, for example, any little private matter suffices, any little personal affair, one's grandmother who died of cancer, or a love affair, and there you go, one can write a novel! What a disgrace to think such things! Writing is not a private affair. It's an act of throwing oneself into a universal affair, be it a novel or a piece of philosophy… writing

necessarily means pushing language and syntax... up to a certain limit, the limit that separates language from silence, or the limit that separates language from music, or the limit that would be the wailing, the painful wailing, the painful wailing....
     —Gilles Deleuze, in *L'abécédaire de Gilles Deleuze*

Don't look at the sun! Feel it! Death is imminent. My fire is unquenchable.
                    —Charlie Parker, in a letter to Nico Konigsberg

That Gregory Stephen Tate was born in Dayton, the birthplace of American aviation, in Ohio, the free state of so much lore and legend, makes too much sense. What many others ran toward and dreamed of, Greg Tate was born into, on October 14, 1957.

All of us are in a constant state of becoming, cataloging, and putting into place the references that will define us, but few of us will have the sheer talent of assembly that Greg Tate had. He turned himself into an archive, an infinity room of everything Black, magnificent, and mythic.

Tate once wrote that "what Black American culture—musical and otherwise—lacks for now isn't talent or ambition, but the unmistakable presence of some kind of spiritual genius: the sense that something other than or even more than human is speaking through whatever fragile mortal vessel is burdened with repping for the divine, the magical, the supernatural, the ancestral."

If that was true a decade or so ago, when he wrote it, it might be even more so now. When Tate died, I was sent a small army of links to his writing by his dear friend dream hampton, and I read them all with the unbroken attention of a student, with the furrowed-brow focus that one must summon whenever one sits in the presence of a master. Some I had read before, some were new to me, but now, when I recall those days of wonder of returning to his sentences, there are too many perfect ones lodged in my brain to select those I thought were his most seminal.

These days, I understand all his essays to be a kind of uncollected liturgical book on love. In his commentary on the minor war between Amiri Baraka and Spike Lee over the legacy of Malcolm X, Tate sagely decided that:

> What makes the oratory of Malcolm endure as a source of enlightenment isn't just his clarity about how white supremacy works, but also his desire to see us love our African selves more than we love the world of the oppressor. We still listen to Malcolm because we hear the voice of a lover, sometimes asking what Bob Marley asked—*could we be loved*—other times asking us why do we love white America, or at least its status symbols, more than we love ourselves.

All Tate's writing has a density that I associate with memory but also with the repping for and of the divine. Tate was making art for the most high. He was also a lavish and unabashed lover of Black people. And he refused to let us forget all that he knew about us, not out of arrogance, but out of care. His writing offers us grace. And meaningful instruction on how to treat one another with intelligence and tenderness. What is dazzling, if not staggering, is how each sentence of his goes forth from the embassy of his intellect, weighted down with all he has to say and heavy with everyone and everything he cites, and somewhere between where it left his desk, carrying his aims as a craftsman, he also then gave those words the ability to alight, run to the sun, and never touch down until they had kissed the sky.

Greg Tate was the eldest son of Florence Tate and Charles E. Tate. In *Sometimes Farmgirls Become Revolutionaries,* Florence's biographer, Jake-Ann Jones, coyly describes her as "a middle-class Dayton housewife and mother of three children." But, as Jones writes in her fascinating study of Florence Tate's evolution toward activism, she was also "the first African American female journalist at the *Dayton Daily News*." Charles and Florence were committed and engaged, if not enraged, members of the Congress of Racial Equality (CORE) and founders of the Dayton Alliance for Racial Equality (DARE). They were a cultivated and sophisticated couple; in 1968, they left the kids behind to attend Miriam Makeba's wedding to Stokely Carmichael, dressed to the bohemian nines. They were also two people with unrelenting drive, who were discontent with the laggard pace of overdue progress and who became increasingly radical. Tate's father worked as an economic development theoretician, while Tate's mother acquired a voluminous FBI file from being surveilled for her pan-Africanist efforts, which ranged from her support of the National Union for the Total Independence of Angola (UNITA) to her later work as a press secretary both for Mayor Marion Barry and for Jesse Jackson's 1984 presidential campaign. If Tate's parents were laboring hard to envision a new world, he found himself a child citizen well prepared for it in so many ways. From the Rust Belt's veldts and a small agro-industrial city in the middle of America, the boy sent away for news of life occurring elsewhere. Greg Tate was a quiet child, an observer of the universe around him. Recalling his adolescence, Tate once wrote:

> The one known as Samuel Ray "Chip" Delany first entered my frame of reference in Dayton, Ohio, circa 1968. He arrived through the mail via something called the Science Fiction Writers of America book club. SFWA would send you three books a month, and in my first batch was Delany's *Nova*. Before even opening the book, I was struck by the author photo, which presented a wooly-headed young Black dude said to have been born in Harlem on April Fools' Day, 1942. My 13-year-old self had been reading science fiction since second grade, but I'd never seen nor even imagined an Afro-American writing science-fiction novels at the height of the Black Power movement.

By the time the family moved to Washington, DC, in 1972, Greg Tate was old enough to understand the statelessness of the district itself as a metaphor that extends to Black people everywhere. Dispossession not only lends itself to the construction of our art; it also gives it that bottom, that ineffable ache. It provides ready-made proof of the odd paradox that the wounds of history are always the basis of our glory, that all harnesses can be altered into superpowers in the realm of wild imagination.

But sometimes it be your own people who don't understand you. A family friend tells me that, like so many of us, Tate struggled in school with bullies who tried but failed to flatten him into being the sort of boy they thought he should be. Their failure might have done him and us the inadvertent favor of sending him forever searching for a tribe he must have dreamed of discovering.

When Samuel R. Delany's *Dhalgren*, a masterpiece of science fiction, was published in 1975, Tate remembered: "Taking possession of the black leather La-Z-Boy in the family den, I would spend the next four days devouring the novel in 200-page gulps."

One decade later, Tate, now on staff at *The Village Voice*, published "Yo Hermeneutics! Hiphopping toward Poststructuralism," his audacious review of Henry Louis Gates Jr.'s anthology *Black Literature and Literary Theory*. In it, Tate, with his signature knowing, acknowledged that "perhaps the supreme irony of Black American existence is how broadly Black people debate the question of cultural identity among themselves while getting branded as a cultural monolith by those who would deny us the complexity and *complexion* of a community, let alone a nation." All of Tate's work felt rich with an understanding owed to growing up

---

MICROINTERVIEW WITH LING MA, PART IV

THE BELIEVER: How do you write? Do you draft things by hand first?

LING MA: I do write a lot of things by hand first. The ideal writing day, which doesn't happen as much anymore, is: In the morning you have your coffee, you write by hand, you try to inhabit the scene. What's important about writing by hand is you slow yourself down. Also, it's usually my first time trying to scratch out a scene. All I'm doing is observing the details, trying to envision the setting, certain dialogues. Then in the afternoon, you input all of that into the laptop, editing and adding more details as you go along. Essentially, what this process forces you to do is inhabit a scene multiple times, in order to give it new layers of detail. I feel like a story improves the more times that you can inhabit a scene. It's like going underwater—you have to keep going underwater multiple times before you can get everything you need. A lot of beginning writers get discouraged because they feel they're not imaginative enough. But I think that's just your first time inhabiting a scene. You have to submerge yourself multiple times to get all the details and snippets of dialogue. You can't just go once and then think that's all you can do. You've got to do it so many times. ✶

in DC, surrounded by a city brimming with people who looked, sounded, and experimented like he did, with all the many ways they could perform their personhood while being fully aware that defiance and endless elasticity are the bedrocks of Black American culture. For his "arkestra chamber" that he founded in 1999, Tate chose to call the thirty-person band, Burnt Sugar. Was he thinking of the agonizing, almost alchemic historical process that turned us from enslaved Africans into Black Americans—in which by necessity we became the molten, dark, and liquid presence running rebellious through the bleached bones of the white whale that consumed us? The majority of Black Americans here have learned the obvious with ease: that we can only pledge allegiance to ourselves and whatever we create artistically must try to articulate the strangeness of being the animating life force of a nation that despises you but needs you. It's no wonder that Bad Brains and Greg Tate both came of age in DC. There is something renegade and inherently riotous about being able to see the Capitol Building from the hills of Anacostia, with only other Black people around you for miles. In those sections of DC, everyone seems to reside under an invisible David Hammons flag, where a Black utopia, politically and sonically, is the destiny, the obligation, and the only intended audience. As Tate told Camille Goodison in a 2012 interview in *Callaloo* magazine, Chocolate City was where he first "got interested in music, collecting music… and reading music criticism too. It kinda all happened at the same time. I had a subscription to *Rolling Stone*. I was really into Miles Davis. He was like my god in the 1970s. Miles, George Clinton, Sun Ra, and locally we had a serious kind of band scene going on. All the guys in my high school were in a band. You were either in a band or you were just deep into music. That was definitely the major activity that all conversation and passion flowed around. More than sports, more than politics." It was the music. "The reason black music," explained Tate in his obituary for Miles Davis, "occupies a privileged and authoritative place in black

aesthetic discourse is because it seems to croon and cry out to us from a postliberated world of unrepressed black pleasure and self-determination. Black music, like black basketball, represents an actualization of those black ideologies that articulate themselves as antithetical to Eurocentrism. Music and 'ball both do this in ways that are counterhegemonic if not countersupremacist—rooting black achievement in ancient black cultural practices. In the face of the attempt to erase the African contribution to world knowledge, and the diminution of black intelligence that came with it, the very fact of black talents without precedent or peers in the white community demolishes racist precepts instantaneously."

To read Greg Tate is to wonder: Who taught Greg Tate high school English? They knew the operations of the language. He knew the operations of the language. You just know Greg Tate sat somewhere under the watchful eye of a Black teacher who cared, learning how to diagram sentences into perfection. His sentences are so clean and architectural—balancing the brutality and beauty of fact with Tadao Ando's, Louis Kahn's, and Álvaro Siza's smooth lines. They are the evidence of a teacher, peering over the rims of their glasses, who knew that the building can't just be pretty, it has to stand and be strong enough to endure any oncoming catastrophe, any form of doom. And so, prepared and extremely well trained in a way that some say no longer occurs, he entered the city's "Mecca," Howard University, to study journalism.

Greg Tate met many of his closest friends at Howard. He watched Betty Davis tantalize homecoming with her sweat and the gyrations of her hips. But, most importantly, at "the Mecca," he started to claim the title he would wear for the rest of his life, that mysterious cloak of authorship: he began to be and to call himself a writer. A gift-and-a-curse decision that anyone who writes knows is like James Brown's cape: something you try to throw to the floor, only for it to be put back on your shoulders as your responsibility, your craft, your gorgeous duty to the rest of us who need your screams to articulate our highs, our lows, our grim day-to-day, with words that make sense of it all.

"Let's be clear. Editing Greg," said Joe Levy—Tate's editor at *The Village Voice*—in his NPR eulogy, "…was a little bit like being the coach who looks up from his clipboard and says it'd be a good idea if Michael Jordan played that night. He's writing about film. He's writing about books. He's writing about culture. He's writing about scholarship. He's writing about philosophy. Any writing he did was a revelation." Beginning in 1981 and continuing for the next twenty or so years, Greg Tate dominated the pages of *The Village Voice*. New Yorkers everywhere got to read a writer not only working in his prime but as much at the top of the game as anyone ever has been. Many of these articles were compiled into his book *Flyboy in the Buttermilk.* Published in 1992, *Flyboy* has become an anchor text that shows what modern criticism can do. But there is something worthwhile and intimidating about looking back at Tate's essays piecemeal as cover stories instead of as a collection. The velocity with which he produced his mastery is astonishing. He wrote like he knew his writing propped up a misunderstood, decontextualized generation—and it did.

Tate once said his ideal readers were "postfunkateers well read in literature and cultural theory, conversant with black politics of the last four hundred years, visually literate, musically eclectic, and as at ease with themselves in Watts as they are in Paris. If I reach one person like that out there, the rest don't matter." Did he know we were all out there waiting to be hit by him and his vicious abundance like a heavy storm, and to stand there, stunned by the recognition and the thunder of his gift?

Tate homed himself in Harlem, and, having found his peers, other outlandish and intelligent Black people, he pulled them close and made a tribe: Julie Dash, dream hampton, LaTasha N. Nevada Diggs, Joicelyn Dingle, Joan Morgan, Stefanie Kelly, Imani Uzuri, Tamar-Kali, LaRhonda Davis, and Michaela Angela Davis, were his homegirl goddesses and Geechee women; Vernon Reid and Thulani Davis created all over the map; AJ and Mikel Banks seemed made of thangs past. He often quoted his found family in his work, many of them bold in their deep purple. In those essays, he flashed a message to the rest of us that there was life on another planet, where God was a Black woman, and her lyre

played P-Funk, and if we stayed strong, we, too, could get there and gather over sushi at his table at Sharaku.

Once, I got tagged in a Facebook conversation in which Tate told two of his friends, Ginny Suss and Paula Henderson, that Julio Cortázar's *Hopscotch* was one of his favorite novels. Of course it was. It is a time-jumping story, but most of all, it is a love story. Tate himself was a love story. That is why we must hold his family, his people—Chinara, Nile, Brian, and Geri—so close: because they were the absolute center of his enormous love. Although they shared him with us, their loss is colossal, because anyone who knew Tate knows that Nile and Chinara don't just share his blood. They not only carry his face, borrowing and replicating that same broad smile, but they were and are the focus of his devotion, the sum of his love. But anyway, in the conversation that day, Tate quoted three lines from *Hopscotch* that didn't make sense to me then, but they do now, so I'll share them here:

> I love you because you are not mine, because you are from the other side, from there where you invite me to jump and I cannot make the jump, because in the deepest moment of possession you are not in me, I cannot reach you, I cannot get beyond your body…
>
> As if you could pick in love, as if it were not a lightning bolt that splits your bones and leaves you staked out in the middle of the courtyard.… You don't pick the rain that soaks you to the skin when you come out of a concert…
>
> La Maga did not know that my kisses were like eyes which began to open up beyond her, and that I went along outside as if I saw a different concept of the world, the dizzy pilot of a black prow which cut the water of time and negated it.

Greg Tate's love "cut the water of time and negated it." And there must have been, always, throughout time, people—not many, but of much importance—who knew how to teach us to recall the songs we once sang but have forgotten, who recalled memories that our motion away from our pasts had disfigured. And for as much as we speak about our journey here over the water, the wood and wicker of the ships, the pitch and night-colored waves, there must have been someone who, knowing how to sustain people in moments of utter despair, a shattering of their spirits and selves, asked them to lift their eyes up toward the infinity of the stars that have and will always point us toward our true selves that are beyond possession, anyone's control, and always free.

What we are mourning is that Greg Tate kept our secrets. Some have said he was a griot, but I'm not sure about that, because, as Tate pointed out, a griot must live away from his people, be buried in the stump of a tree away from their reclamation, as a tax for his knowing. But Greg Tate was our bard, our storyteller, and our generous, ego-free high priest, who held in his hands the blueprints to our most profound shrines, who whispered to us that we always know how to get back home. Greg Tate reminded us that we don't need a place at their petrified tables; we can gather under a living tree and love, create, in our own making. And that is more enduring and powerful than anything we can be offered from the outside. The part of us that knew to see him and claim him also knows in our abiding love, respect, tutelage, and recognition of him that there will never be another Greg Tate. He was from above. He was a conductor of the beyond.

Greg Tate never let anyone shackle his devotions. He permitted no attenuation of his brilliance so that others who feared an unimpeded Black brain might remain comfortable in his presence. The apotheosis of cultural criticism, Tate was calm and esoteric, but he was not a coward. He was also our best critic, in that the critic discerns, and through them we understand, because we are returned to what Amílcar Cabral termed "the source." Sometimes they point the way to good taste. To decay. Or to a better understanding of our aesthetic and intellectual limitations. At the height of his fame, Chuck D of Public Enemy told *Spin* that the only piece of criticism he was "furious at over the past year is Greg Tate." Tate's crime? To point out in 1988, publicly, "[Public Enemy] are obviously making it up as they go along. Since PE show sound reasoning when they focus on racism as a tool of the US power structure, they should be intelligent enough to realize that dehumanizing gays, women, and Jews isn't going to set black people free." Tate recognized that

at our best, we must forget the easy seductions of misogyny, colorism, provincialism, and vacant capitalism.

At the center of his critical project was the legacy of his powerful Black mother as the emotional and intellectual root of his abiding concern for Black women as peers, artists, and thinkers. Greg Tate was surrounded by men who professed to be radicals, busy thinking up new worlds, but who, for the life of them, seemed adamant in their ignorant refusal to figure out how to treat Black women right in this world here and now. "We'll all still have to get up the next morning and deal with being Black men and women in America. Which at the end of the day is about what? Learning to love and struggle with one another, end of story," he wrote. I don't think I ever once heard Tate sound angry. But I almost always saw him know what was up. Black excellence? So inherent, one must almost be suspicious of the people and iffy moments that have gathered up under it. Black ambivalence? The clever, quiet space where what is understood needs no branding, cannot be bought or sold—the interior that hovers above translation or transaction? Yes. The decadent rigor of Tate's thinking let us witness someone who knew the ins and outs, the folds, the fantastic planets, and the heft of Black culture, and therefore the madness of America at large.

When Greg Tate died, his devoted friend Imani Uzuri put together a video call where his friends gathered to say goodbye. Some played the bass, some cried, and almost everyone told stories. One friend asked that we do what Greg Tate would have wanted most from all of us as artists: that "we leave nothing on the shelf." I think that is the best way to describe what he did as a writer.

Greg Tate understood that Blackness is essentially just a bibliography. Those who know not only know but also contain and further it. The importance of capacious citation is really just a matter of love. We hat-tip what we love and acknowledge whom we learned it from, not only out of obligation but because citation is devotion and puts us in constellation.

When things first got bad two years ago for me, as they did for us all, I fell into the practice of listening to—no, blasting, to be honest, to my neighbors—Pharoah

Sanders's *Pharoah* album. While every song on it is a plea and a prayer, "Love Will Find a Way" always makes me want to cry like every cell inside me is experiencing deep pleasure and absolute disbelief at what we can do here when we leave nothing on the shelf. It is the same with good, thick, dense writing like Tate's, full of memory and rich with an account of what can easily get lost. Isn't writing like this just an attempt to transmute onto the page what Pharoah screams on that track? *Sometimes I feel so good giving love to you. And hope you will feel the same as I do.*

I feel lonelier now that Tate is gone, not because we spoke often or because he was my closest friend. But because when

---

A PARTIAL PLAYLIST OF SONGS MENTIONED IN VIRGINIE DESPENTES'S *VERNON SUBUTEX* TRILOGY

* "I'd Rather Be an Old Man's Sweetheart (Than an Old Man's Fool)," Candi Staton
* "So weit wie noch nie," Jürgen Paape
* "Work Bitch," Britney Spears
* "Les paradis perdus," Christophe
* "Breaking Up Somebody's Home," Albert King
* "Construcción," Daniel Viglietti
* "Push the Sky Away," Nick Cave and the Bad Seeds
* "Temps mort," Booba
* "Fight or Die," Code of Honor
* "Diamonds," Rihanna
* "The Modern World," the Jam
* "All Nite (Don't Stop)," Janet Jackson
* "Rumble," Link Wray
* "Get Lucky," Daft Punk
* "I'd Rather Be with You," Bootsy Collins
* "Sexy M.F.," Prince
* "Personal Jesus," Johnny Cash
* "The Hanging Garden," the Cure
* "Bombay Tension," Tuxedomoon
* "Blackstar," David Bowie
* "Real Love," Mary J. Blige
* "Mr. Bojangles," Nina Simone

—list compiled by Ginger Greene

I knew that Greg Tate was in the world, I knew there was someone out there playing his kalimba, walking down Adam Clayton Powell in a turquoise silk scarf, or suggesting some *Guardian* article about a punk band in Libreville— someone who always knew what time it was, even if I don't always. I knew there was someone worth listening to, because they often had the correct answers.

I met Greg Tate when I was twenty, as the starstruck juvenile creep assistant of dream hampton. I was invited to join them for a spicy tuna roll lunch at his office (Sharaku), and I sat there stunned into silence by my good fortune and Tate's cool, but also terrified that the rice would get lodged between my braces and embarrass me. Instead, Tate let me sit with them like I was an actual human and asked me what I was reading. This is to say, I cannot think of a time in my life as a writer when Greg Tate was not present with a generosity that is rare.

Early into this hope of mine to be a writer, back in 2011, Greg Tate messaged me, as I'm sure he did many others, with the following tremendous but tender lie: "YO-… No condescension or patronizing or hubris intended but you're now officially the new Me. At the very least."

I am very hesitant to share this, for all of the logical reasons, but it tells so well of the sort of man that Greg Tate was. He wanted to, at all costs, esteem the ones who often only knew 400 blows, the kids who had almost been flattened by life. Do you have any idea what a gracious lie like that does for someone, particularly for a young Black woman writer, a juvenile creep, starting out? Helado Negro, who makes gorgeous music, has an album called *Private Energy*, where he sings about what it means to be enclosed by your people and held by those you cherish:

> *You grow older*
> *Knowing that you'll*
> *Always be this one thing*
> *And you'll always have*
> *This to be you*
> *And the people*
> *Who'll be here waiting*
> *For you*
> *Always will be one with*
> *You*
> *And you'll be one with*
> *Me*

When Tate sent me that note, I think he was aware that I would need jet fuel to try and write and live in this skin. However, with words like those, I needed no shield. I needed no mercy. What could I need from them? Those out there. Why not avoid ceremonies, why not turn "no" into your favorite reply, why not pull stories? He had alerted me silently to the moral and creative lassitude of certain magazines that had never published him when he was our absolute best. If he was our best, and I was certified by him, I was already given entrance into the private energy of what matters most and what is true. You can give others harbor, and that note did as intended: it helped me float past other lies and unforgivable injuries that I would hear, assaults that were intended to sink me as a Black writer. It was a raft against the precarity and erasure that I know Tate, as a one-of-a-kind Black genius, must have known well and seemingly didn't want others, especially a young Black woman, to be bruised and undone by.

In an exchange we once had, Greg Tate told me, "We boost America even in reporting our slow genocide. There's no critique or gesture that doesn't feed the beast up in this shit. Whut we fighting for at best is to become co owners of Indian country. U dig? With a corner office? We gotta get Pan-Africanist again so that our notion of winning is a Continent not fukn prison or prosecutorial reform. We need a more visionary end game than a fairer master-slave dynamic."

Although it forever haunts me as a generational question, I dislike having to ruminate on what having the kind of bold vision that Tate had cost him. To stay free is a sacrifice, to remain sovereign is a commitment, and to consider what his liberty, his womanism, and his vanguardism might have cost him is disquieting. To fully appreciate Tate, we cannot be naive from the safe perches of tenure, staff positions, or trust funds, and romanticize or minimize his professional independence. Now that he is gone at sixty-four, which is really no age at all, I have to read his classic essay about Basquiat as a doubling or as a self-portrait of Tate's own battle with the loathly lady of commercialization:

> This business of speaking for Black culture and your own Black ass from outside the culture's communal surrounds and the comforting consensus of what critic Lisa Kennedy once described as "the Black familiar" has taken many a brilliant Black mind down to the crossroads and left it quite beside itself, undecided between suicide, sticking it to the man, or selling its soul to the devil. The ones who keep up the good fight with a scintilla of sanity are the ones who know how to beat the devil out of a dollar while maintaining a Black agenda and to keep an ear out for the next dope house party set to go down in Brooklyn, Sugar Hill…

One could read this for the literal geographies of a generous man providing directions for how to be, but what I'm also speaking of here is extra-literary and deeply personal. Greg Tate showed every generation coming behind him not simply who to be but also how to do it. With Greg around, the orientation of things was righted and like the position of the sun tells you what you need to know about how to order your day, he was always cheering you toward the way without saying more than a few words.

So are you still very sad? Because I am. I feel withered by his absence. There are moments when the reminder of his passing catches me, and I feel spun around and stupid and unsure of what I should do next and for whom, and it feels as if something omnipresent in the order of things has vanished.

When that happens, what occasionally steadies my vertigo, my feeling of such premature, injurious loss, is that I know Greg Tate must have felt so good when he wrote, not because writing is ever easy, but because Tate was always leaving behind an illuminated record of genius, reverence, magic, and subculture, and therefore he was always giving such love to us.

And how lucky we were to witness that ever-expanding mind. It was like watching Max Roach solo on and on and faster and faster, at a vertiginous pace, but never letting the pocket sag with slowness or a stick fly loose from his fingers. It was orbital how much information he could summon and loop in on the spot—he was to Black history what the moon is to Saturn or Mars or the other planets. He was located in it. So close to it. You could call him with a question about Quincy Troupe, Betty Carter, or Amiri Baraka, and suddenly you'd know what Tony Williams said to Miles on March 23, 1963, in Boston. Rich Nichols, the Roots manager, always told me that in terms of writing that rivaled the sound, the boom bap, the rush, and the wail, you had to start with Greg Tate. Which was true, so it was hard to care what anyone else thought about the work or what it should be, because early on, Greg Tate said to so many of us all, *Do that shit*. And we all tried to trail that comet of him, knowing it was utterly impossible. ✶

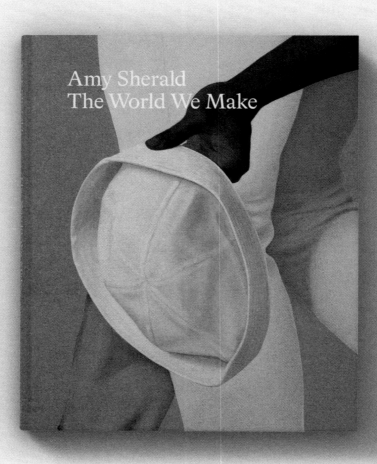

MIGUEL ARTETA

[FILMMAKER]

— INTERVIEWED BY —

AUBREY PLAZA

[ACTOR]

"AT OUR CORE, WE ARE DESPERATE TO BELIEVE IN SOMETHING."

Things Jonathan Demme taught Miguel Arteta about filmmaking:
You need to be discovering something as you're telling the story
Directing is about responding, not controlling
You can't force your vision

In an interview, Miguel Arteta once characterized his film The Good Girl (2002) as a prison escape story. The Retail Rodeo, the fictional big-box store that serves as the setting for the film, is the metaphorical prison, and its employees are the inmates. Some of them turn to religion to survive, some revolt, and one duo looks to break out. "It's a great metaphor," Arteta said, "because everyone feels trapped." This is how many of Arteta's films function: he finds an unexpected vehicle through which he can express a universal human experience. He gives agency and humanity to those whose work lives are seen, by many, to be less than heroic.

Born in San Juan, Puerto Rico, in 1965, Miguel Arteta moved to Costa Rica at a young age. After getting kicked out of school there, his parents sent him to the US, where he attended a boarding school, and later matriculated to Harvard. He left Harvard for Wesleyan University, where he studied film under Professor Jeanine Basinger, and also met future collaborator Mike White. Arteta's breakthrough came with Star Maps (1997), which tells the story of a Latino teen trying to make it in Hollywood by selling maps of famous people's homes. He found further success with classic of indie cinema Chuck & Buck (2000) and Cedar Rapids (2011). He directed Salma Hayek in one of her most poignant roles in the acclaimed Beatriz at

Illustrations by Kristian Hammerstad

Dinner (2017). Hayek plays the maid to a wealthy couple, who in an act of condescension, invite her to dinner with their wealthy friends. What ensues is both farcical and deeply spiritual, and, like much of Arteta's work, begins by examining American class issues but eventually transcends them.

He is interviewed here by Aubrey Plaza, whom he met in 2006, when he was staging a reading of Lucas Moodysson's movie Together *(Arteta was considering an English-language version). Plaza is well known for her role on* Parks and Recreation, *and has starred in many independent films, including* Ingrid Goes West *(2017),* Emily the Criminal *(2022), and* Black Bear *(2020), which she and Arteta discuss in this interview. Plaza began her career in improv, and this is often evidenced through her deadpan stage presence, which was on full display when she accepted her 2012 Young Hollywood Award by saying, "Fuck you, old people. Old people can go fuck themselves. I'm going to live forever."*

—*The Editors*

I. "I, MIGUEL"

THE BELIEVER: OK, first of all, and I know this is an interview, so it doesn't matter visually what's going on, but I noticed the shirt you're wearing.

MIGUEL ARTETA: I figured it was appropriate for this interview.

BLVR: Does it have something to do with Jonathan Richman?

MA: It does. For my fiftieth birthday, my wife, Justine, and a few friends made a T-shirt based on Jonathan Richman's album *I, Jonathan*. But they put my face on it instead, with a lot of things I love, like Justine and anteaters and things like that. And whales.

BLVR: OK, so just to be clear for our readers, you're wearing a T-shirt that has all these things.

MA: Yeah. It says I, MIGUEL. Figured it would be, uh, you know—being interviewed takes a certain amount of hubris. So I figured I'd wear this shirt.

BLVR: That's a perfect start, because I was gonna say that I never feel qualified to be an interviewer, and especially to

interview someone like you, who I see as like a mentor and a hero and all these things.

MA: No, I really respect the way you deal with your work and the way you love your work. You're having an incredible career, and I can almost see the rest of your career in my mind. So I'm interested to learn from you about how to be so focused and passionate.

BLVR: All right. Well, this isn't about me. I know what you're trying to do, and I'm not gonna let you do it. Let's start with your mentors—who do you consider your mentors?

MA: I was very lucky to meet Jeanine Basinger at Wesleyan University. Through her, I fell in love with the golden age of Hollywood. But my first love of movies was European movies, like Fellini and Buñuel and Kurosawa. I was very pretentiously in love with all those movies in high school. Seeing *Juliet of the Spirits* made me realize: Oh, this is just filming your dreams. And I was like, That's a fun job. I want that job.

BLVR: Was this in Costa Rica?

MA: Yeah, I was born in Puerto Rico, and then my father retired early and moved us to Costa Rica for high school. And I hated it there. I got myself thrown out of high school.

BLVR: Why were you kicked out?

MA: I had an American girlfriend, and it was a very conservative environment in the '70s in Costa Rica. And, um, we were making out a lot. And we kind of wanted to get kicked out. And we were making out on the lawn—

BLVR: [*Laughs*]

MA: —and all the other students got very riled up. There were meetings about us. And my parents got a letter from the headmaster saying, "For having horizontal affection on campus premises, we must dismiss Miguel."

BLVR: Oh my god.

MA: It was a great day 'cause I knew my parents would

then send me to boarding school in America. And when I landed in Miami at sixteen—they still had those steps down from the plane—I stopped the whole line so the first things that touched America were my lips. I kissed the ground.

BLVR: How did your relationship to movies develop in boarding school?

MA: I think having the language barrier was very important. When you don't have command of the language, going to the movie theater becomes a source of comfort 'cause you're understanding most of what's going on. In your daily life, you're not able to communicate quite as well. So I think that's why I started to go to the movies a lot at that time. And eventually I fell in love with the golden age of Hollywood, which has been my passion. Me and my wife still watch Turner Classic Movies. To me, it's the most inspiring kind of filmmaking because those people are not trying to show off. They're not going to point the finger at themselves and say, *Look. Look how clever I am. Look how much style I am adding.* They're actually trying to make you think deeply. And tell you how people are. And get you to be an active participant in the story. Their style is a little bit, you know, hidden inside the seams. And that has been my style and the style of the filmmakers I really love, like Jonathan Demme, who is a modern-day inspiration for me.

BLVR: What was the first movie you saw of his?

MA: I saw *Something Wild*, which is—

BLVR: I love that movie.

MA: Ray Liotta, Melanie Griffith, 1986. The joy of the filmmaking and the irreverence of it all were so contagious. It was a crystallizing moment where I was like: I have to be a filmmaker. You know, something I thought about when I knew you

were gonna interview me is luck. Luck plays such an important part in all our lives. I really think luck is the primary reason we end up having something interesting to say. Or end up in a position to be heard. Luck has played such an important role in my life. Like, I was born with parents who could afford to send me to college. Then *Something Wild* blew my mind, and I was like, This is what I wanna do. Jonathan Demme had not done *The Silence of the Lambs* yet; he was not a famous director at the time. And I happened to give a short movie of mine to my car mechanic. And then he called me back, after I moved to New York, and was like, "I've given your short movie to this director, Jonathan Demme."

BLVR: No shit.

MA: Um, and my car mechanic was somebody who was, you know, unstable—

BLVR: Emotionally, or?

MA: Yeah, very unstable. A little bit out-there. He would fix my car for free if I talked to him about Central America. And a year after I moved to New York, I got a call from him [*mimicking voice*], "I finally tracked your number! Jonathan Demme!" And I was like, "Whoa, you know who he is? I love him." And he says, "Listen, my ex-wife is married to his cousin, who is an incredible minister in Harlem [Robert W. Castle]. And Jonathan is making a documentary about that cousin. It's called *Cousin Bobby*." 'Cause, you know, this is a guy who fought with the Black Panthers. "Anyhow," he tells me, "I've given him the tape. They want you to go there this Sunday. Jonathan's gonna come and sit down and watch the movie with you."

BLVR: From your—your car mechanic? Your emotionally unstable car mechanic? OK, so I just have to say this. Something that I wanna say about you—that I have always felt from the day I met you, and that everybody who knows you feels—

is how open and kind you are. And you can describe it as "luck." I think luck is one way to describe it. But I think it's more than luck, because I think things like that happen because of how you are as a person. Like, if you weren't somebody that was willing or open to talking to your car mechanic about whatever the fuck you were talking about… to me, that's everything. And that's something I don't think people realize—especially when they're younger—but you never know what will lead to what. And it's not even about trying to make those connections happen. It's really just about the nature of who you are. And, like, yes, you're lucky. But I think it's more like you're curious about another human being, and then you make a connection. Then something beautiful happens.

MA: I think you're right. The element of curiosity is important because art is about feeling like you are being seen. Why do we like a performance? It's because we can see ourselves in it, you know? So I think having a willingness to see people is important. I don't think you can succeed as an artist unless you have some element of that.

BLVR: So going back to Jonathan Demme: He gets your short film and then what happens?

MA: He watches it. He likes it. And he says, "Listen, I'm making this documentary called *Cousin Bobby*. We're shooting with this Super 16 camera—do you know how to change the reels? We need a loader." And I said, "Yes." And he could tell I was lying and started laughing and said, "We'll teach you how to do it. Stick with us." So I got to work with him on and off for a year—the year he was preparing *The Silence of the Lambs.* And we got to travel to where Cousin Bobby had a house, in northern Vermont. And we went and spent a few days there. Cousin Bobby was obsessed with Jonathan's movies. So I got to watch Jonathan's movies with the two of them and, you know, got a great education. Jonathan was very generous to many young filmmakers. He's stayed my mentor and taught me so much about the transference of energy that is filmmaking.

BLVR: What do you mean by that?

MA: He said that directing wasn't about controlling— it was about responding. If you try to be all controlling as a director, your movies will be boring. You need to be discovering something as you're telling the story, so the audience is invited to be part of the discovery. If you are like, *I know everything about this character, about this world*, you might end up making the kinds of movies that feel closed off.

BLVR: Right—like something's off about them. Movies have to evolve.

MICROINTERVIEW WITH LING MA, PART V

THE BELIEVER: You've written about working as a fact-checker at *Playboy*. I'm curious about the mechanics of that job. Can you say more about it and what kinds of pieces you worked on?

LING MA: It was all over the place. At the time, they still did these long investigative articles, many of which were about the Mob or drug smuggling. The longer investigative pieces took a couple of weeks to get through. Some of it was just reading interview transcripts, and some of it was calling up sources that the reporter had spoken with, and working with the legal department to make sure there wouldn't be any liability issues. Sometimes I called up the Playmate of the Month and asked, "Is *The Little Mermaid* your favorite movie?" They always liked *The Little Mermaid* for some reason. Maybe that was a generational thing. It was an interesting place to work. I also helped edit the forum section at the back of the book. We got some great pieces from Jaron Lanier and others. I was there for close to three years. I have some mixed feelings about that job, but I have to say I worked with some really talented editors and writers. Also, I had a boss who did not mind that I wrote fiction at work. I started *Severance* during my last days at the *Playboy* office. ✱

MA: Yes. He said, "You gotta respond to how you're feeling that morning, how the actors are feeling, what the location feels like on that day in particular." If you just force your vision on all these things, it's not gonna go right. I'm not sure if I'm recording his words exactly, but he said it's like there's a highway and you're the person that's telling the highway: *That's the destination way over there, we think.* But there's many different routes to get there. And you need to be very open, you know? Like sometimes you think you're gonna go one direction the whole time, but somebody makes you think better of it.

III. "HUBBIES"

BLVR: What are your memories of Puerto Rico? At what ages were you on the island?

MA: From the time I was born till I was thirteen. And my memories were, um, of being an awkward kid. My fondest memories were of going snorkeling with my dad. I liked being underwater and looking at the fish. I was, like, a hobby-oriented kid. I would make rockets and go fly them. You know those Estes Rockets? Model rockets? I was obsessed with those. And then I was obsessed with origami. I was very proficient in origami. And then I was obsessed with fish tanks. I made my own fish tanks. And we would go get saltwater fish while we were snorkeling and I was very obsessed with that. So, um, I think hub- hobbies saved my life.

BLVR: What is "hubbies"?

MA: It's a mispronunciation of the word *hobbies.*

BLVR: [*quietly*] *Hubbies*… Oh, *hobbies*! Sorry. Sorry. Hobbies.

MA: I still have a funny accent.

BLVR: Your hobbies in Puerto Rico. Got it.

MA: Yeah. You know, I rejected Latin America so, so strongly when I left. There was something about the machismo. And probably conflicts with my dad. And I think I have had this sick accent for forty-something years because of that active rejection—my subconscious is, like, fucking with me.

BLVR: I love your accent. It's the most fun when we play Balderdash. Um, so is it true that you ripped people off by reading their palms? And did that start at a young age?

MA: That happened in Boston. At the Cambridge School of Weston. When I was sixteen and seventeen, I had the mystique of being from another country. So I was able to use that to my advantage at parties and say, "Listen, if you give me a dollar, I will read your palm." And I could make up to sixty dollars in one night. I said that, you know, a shaman lady had trained me in Costa Rica. That definitely made me realize how suggestible people are.

BLVR: Yes, we are.

MA: I think that's the strongest drive. Even stronger than procreation or self-preservation. I think it's the thing that drives humans the most.

BLVR: What do you mean? Just wanting to believe in something?

MA: Yes. You know, it's like how if you go to a dinner where three people are drinking a lot, then most people will drink a lot more. There's a reason why we have countries and religions and tribalism—because at our core, we are desperate to believe in something.

BLVR: Yeah. Did you grow up religious at all? Or do you consider yourself spiritual?

MA: Um, I worship the sun. I like the sun. I think the sun is the source of everything. But the sun is just a lot of gravity. A lot of matter, throwing off energy. So I guess I believe in energy.

IV. BATHROOM CRITICS

BLVR: Have you always felt like a confident person? Especially in terms of trying to become a filmmaker? Or do you suffer from, um, deep insecurities and anxiety, and doubt yourself every step of the way?

MA: I am very insecure in life, and, you know, I joke all the time that I'm fragile like a little flower.

BLVR: Are you sensitive?

MA: I am very sensitive with people. I don't have the personality of a film director. But something magical happened when I started to make my pretentious little movies at sixteen. There was something that just immediately fit. And a lot of confidence became accessible to me. And I remember that first day, saying, *This is it*, like, *I have found my niche*. There is something about the element of taking a camera and trying to tell a story with it. I think it's the feeling of being a spectator—watching an actor get into the zone is like watching human beings fly, you know? And it is such an amazing thing to be a part of it. Like, to help propel someone else to just levitate and fly, and to have the front-row seat.

BLVR: I love that. I wonder if most directors have that feeling. I don't know if they do. Like, what do you really think of actors? 'Cause I've met a lot of directors in my life that—whether they say it out loud or not—it's almost like they don't actually respect the process of acting or something.

MA: I think a lot of directors are jealous of actors because they have this ability to go into a zone that is just so beautiful. It's a superpower. I'm constantly shocked by how disrespected and mistreated actors are. You know, when they become very famous, everybody's mostly blowing smoke up their butts. And so they don't have any idea who to trust. And that's a difficult position to be in.

BLVR: Do you think directors always secretly pick favorite actors when they shoot movies? And that they secretly have a favorite one? And do you do that?

MA: Yes. Yes.

BLVR: Do you fall in love with your actors when you work with them?

MA: I do. If the movie's gonna turn out well, you want to fall in love with more than one in the film, you know.

BLVR: With all of them.

MA: With as many as possible. There's usually, in stories, one point of view, and then there's the object of what that person's pursuing. Which tends to be another person. So you wanna try and fall in love with those two people in most movies. And I definitely do.

BLVR: Did you ever wanna be an actor?

MA: I wish I could do it. You know, I've taken classes from Sundance, and worked with this teacher named Joan Darling. She was one of the first female directors on TV. She's wonderful. I took her class just to see what it was like. And she thought I was great, wanted to cast me [*laughs*] in a feature that she was—

BLVR: I heard that you starred in a movie called *In Good Company*. Is that true?

MA: [*Laughs*] I get a residual check for *In Good Company*, for about seventeen cents, every couple years, yes.

BLVR: What was your role in *In Good Company*?

MA: I was the AV guy that tells Clark Gregg that it's OK to move the furniture.

BLVR: He was in that? I don't remember that. He played my dad one time.

MA: The truth is that when friends have asked me to be in films, they always end up cutting my lines down to, like, one little grunt or something.

BLVR: What about rituals? Do you have any superstitious things you do when you make a movie?

MA: My favorite part of making movies is something that doesn't happen that much anymore, which is sitting down in a dark movie theater and watching it with an audience. Especially if the audience doesn't even know I'm there. I used to go see the finished movies in the theater, on the opening weekend. I would look around like: Are they having fun? Did it work? Did this go well? And then I used to go into the bathroom right after and I would stay in that stall for, like, fifteen minutes, because that's where you get the best criticism. It's amazing how people open up in the bathroom. They would just be like, "Oh man, fuck, [the lead actor] was so bad. I can't believe this movie. The ending was so stupid."

V. THE GNARLY TRUTH

BLVR: What's the worst criticism you've ever gotten?

MA: I was very hurt about—I made a movie with Alia Shawkat, which we wrote together, called *Duck Butter*.

BLVR: I love this movie. I love *Duck Butter*.

MA: Thank you. The critic that had praised *Chuck & Buck* (which is a movie I did with Mike White, twenty years before), who had named it Movie of the Year in *Entertainment Weekly*, and really got my career going—that same critic went on to just say the meanest things about me and the movie [*Duck Butter*]. How "paper-thin" it was and how it didn't have any insight into human beings. It was hard.

BLVR: Oh, wow. Well, fuck that guy. That guy's wrong. I love *Duck Butter*. Of all your films, what would you say you're most proud of?

MA: I think *Duck Butter* and *Beatriz at Dinner* are, like,

sweetest in my heart. Making them was such a pleasure, and I adore them. But I do think that *Chuck & Buck* is probably the best movie I've made. I met Mike White when he was very young and he was starting to write. And I put him in my first movie with this other writer, Zak Penn. Mike and Zak were a writing team at that time. This was like in the early '90s, and I cast them as racist writers 'cause I knew they were both very funny. Mike rewrote every word of dialogue but didn't tell me about it. Zak came in and said, "Listen, Mike has rewritten our whole thing. I think it's much better. And I think you should do it this way." I took a minute to read it and I said, "Holy shit. I wish he had rewritten my whole fucking script."

Mike and I just had a nice connection. He had written both *Chuck & Buck* and *The Good Girl*. And I wanted to try to do them both. But *Chuck & Buck* had a difficult birth. We were trying to find traditional ways of financing it, and eventually we were like, "Let's just start making it." 'Cause that's the way you actually get funding, when people feel the train has left the station. And after deciding this and getting everybody riled up like that, I just had a moment of tremendous fear. Like: This is a movie about a gay man. And I am not gay. You know, maybe I'm not the right person to make this movie. So I tried to get other filmmakers to do the movie, like my friend Ira Sachs. Eventually, somebody else was gonna make it—a friend of Mike's. But the characters kept floating in my head—I was obsessed with

---

MICROINTERVIEW WITH LING MA, PART VI

THE BELIEVER: One trend I've been hearing a lot about lately is quiet quitting, which you may be familiar with. A software developer on TikTok described it like this: "You're not outright quitting your job but you're quitting the idea of going above and beyond." Candace, in *Severance*, almost represents the reverse phenomenon. She's "quiet working" and goes into the office regularly, even when everyone else has stopped doing so. Do you have any thoughts about this phenomenon?

LING MA: I just read about it like a week or two ago. It sounds a lot like compartmentalizing. As someone who

worked in offices, I would always attempt to compartmentalize and would constantly fail. There's a John Cheever quote that goes something like "He felt like he was a spy in the suburbs." Cheever's whole topic is suburban lives in Westchester County, and his task was to be like a spy or an observer so he could write about it all. But what he found was that the spy became the subject. I think about that quote all the time. Working at places like *Playboy*, you begin by observing but eventually get sucked in. It's very hard to compartmentalize and keep a distinction between yourself and the roles that you're paid for. ★

them. I had knee surgery around that time, and I remember having a delirious moment in Kentucky—at a film festival there—where I couldn't sleep all night, 'cause this character Buck was haunting me. And I called Mike and said, "Let's just make it in video and make it for no money. And let's not even worry. I need to make it."

BLVR: You were possessed by it.

MA: Yeah. So we went and made it. We cast my friend Chris Weitz, and then I was like, Well, his brother, Paul Weitz—you know, they're a filmmaking team—could play a role too. And I told Mike that, and he was like, "Well, if you're casting your friends, then you need to cast me as Buck." And so it felt like we weren't making a movie for the world. It was a movie that we were making with our friends, on a little three-chip camera. I really loved making it and watching Mike White perform.

BLVR: He's incredible in that movie.

MA: Yeah, he put his heart into it. When he had to cry in a scene, he would cry in every single take. Even if it was a wide shot. He couldn't help it. I think he felt that story so deeply.

BLVR: Before that you had done *Star Maps*, right?

MA: *Star Maps* was my first film. Matthew Greenfield helped me write the story. And we begged for money from strange people in Los Angeles. We made our first movie difficult. It was around the time that *Clerks* came out, and everybody was like, *That's the way to make a movie: two characters in one location.* And instead, we shot it on thirty-five-millimeter film at, like, forty locations, with eight main characters. It was an act of stupidity. But there was something fun about that. When you

make your first movie, you have a unique opportunity. 'Cause you don't know what you're doing, you know? It only happens once and it's a very delicious thing.

BLVR: And that movie went to Sundance, right?

MA: It went to Sundance, yes.

BLVR: That's like a dream come true—your first film getting into Sundance. Do you still believe in independent films? I just think of that era of movies—there was something so magical about someone making a movie like *Star Maps* and then taking it to Sundance. And having it, like, break through the noise.

MA: I think, you know—going back to luck—I hit Sundance at that time when there was an appetite to have independent movies in theaters. And they were starting to win awards and you could get paid for them. So that was very lucky. And I've been wondering where that has gone. Where has the mumblecore scene gone? It's difficult—there's not a market for these movies. But, you know, there's always somebody breaking through, which is incredible. You know the filmmaker that did a movie called *Waves* [Trey Edward Shults]?

BLVR: Mm-hmm.

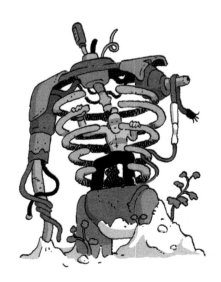

MA: There's just incredible people like him, figuring out how to do it. People are still doing it. I believe in personal storytelling. My dream is to make one more movie that is done very purely that way, just for the pleasure of involving the audience in a journey—where I'm going to learn something new that I need to learn. I'm very curious right now about the nature of humans and hope. How are humans having hope when the evidence suggests we should not have hope at all?

BLVR: Because the planet is dying?

MA: Yeah. The planet is dying. We are going backward in terms of, politically, how to deal with each other. Racism is coming back with a vengeance. Women's rights are being destroyed. Russia is trying to just invade places. The advances in science and artificial intelligence are probably—you know, the world's gonna have a computer that's a dictator soon. It's hard to think about somebody being born now. And yet people are finding hope still. So I'm very curious about how to do that. Where does that come from? And is it legitimate? Or is it—is it sad that we have to have hope? Or is it great?

BLVR: Yeah. For me, that's the point of making movies, in a lot of ways—it's hope. 'Cause it feels like movies that have hope, even if they're really dark—that's what makes me fall in love with them.

MA: You know, I was gonna ask you about the movie you made with Christopher Abbott.

BLVR: *Black Bear.*

MA: *Black Bear.* Where was the hope in that? What made you go there?

BLVR: Well, I think for me, that was an exercise in confronting the truth. And the black bear was a symbol of the truth, however gnarly it is. I think, I mean, it's debatable what the end is in that movie, because the movie's broken into two parts and it's kind of unclear: Did the first part follow the second part? Or the second part follow the first? And are both parts not real? It's kind of like the movie is a commentary on the creative exercise of writing. But for me, even though the end is so fucked up—even though she's basically been confronted with her worst nightmare, which is this paranoid fantasy that she's been having the whole time—she is eventually confronted with what's true. Her worst nightmare is true, and she sees the bear. In my head, I mean, it cuts away so fast, but in the way it worked out for me, in my brain, was that she just lets the bear eat her alive. And, um, I guess that's not really hopeful, is it? But the point is [*laughter*] that she found the truth.

MA: She surrenders.

BLVR: Yes, she surrenders to the truth of it. And, I don't know, is that hopeful?

MA: It is. Any act of surrendering is an act of hope. A leap of faith. I think your performance in that film was like Gena Rowlands in a Cassavetes movie. Raw. Just incredible. I think that performance is gonna be discovered and rediscovered many, many times. And, um, I'm in an introspective mood because I found out I have prostate cancer last week, which I think you know.

BLVR: I did know. I was not gonna bring that up in this interview. But you go for it. We haven't even talked about this.

MA: You know, it changes, a little bit, the way you look at things. I'm hopeful everything's gonna go well. The prognosis is pretty good. Not perfect, but pretty good. So hopefully when this interview comes out, I will be on the other side of it. And not as worried. But it does make you think a lot about what matters, and I feel very lucky 'cause this is a treatable form of cancer. By all accounts, we have found it early enough that I'm gonna be OK. But you can't help but think about your life. I guess that's why luck has been on my mind. You know, I was so rebellious against my parents when I was young. And then they lived long enough, and I lived long enough, to realize that they actually loved me. And gave me an incredibly privileged start in life. I've had so much love in my life, so many friends. And then I've had the luck of doing what I love to do, which is making movies. And I feel like—I've done ten films. And if that's it, it was pretty great.

BLVR: Well, I don't think that's gonna be it. Don't say things like that.

MA: Well, I feel blessed, and I hope I get to make ten more. But I definitely feel like transferring energy is really what's on my mind. Since this thing has come into my life, what I think about is wanting to help people—encouraging everybody to seek engagement and be kind. And, you know, those are the seeds of trust, and within them are the seeds of love. And I think that, at the end, that's the only thing that matters. I'm trying to look back, because I didn't have this perspective when I made my films. But as I look back, I feel like some of the good ones express that. ✶

SNOW IN JUNE

A NEW POEM

by Jane Wong

Months after ending
my engagement, I woke
with my ears plugged up,
stoppered like a bath, chain
dangling a rusty tongue.
Television static filmed
my cochlea like milk
I can't drink. I couldn't even
hear the massive truck wrestling
by outside, splintered logs stacked
atop each other like all
my lovers. I was pressed cider,
leaking mash. I gulped,
I yawned false at first, then
grew very, very tired. My jaw
unlocked nothing, hinged
disappointment each
time. I shook my ears side
to side, imagined warm wax
pouring out like the maple syrup
he used to drown waffles in, puffed
squares resembling the indecipherable
garden boxes he built me. When I left,
he demanded I pull my starts out.
Those are most certainly yours.
It was horrible to yank them up,
roots kicking like something caught
in my throat. Worms encircled
my wrist like a prom date I never
had. *You dodged a bullet*, everyone says,
and I hear *you lodged a bull* – horns
tearing up our walls, snout slapping
the bed with sentient fury. I lived there.
I lived in what I thought was love,
lumbered. *It's cottonwood season*,

our neighbor said to me, *snow in June!*
Isn't it something? She touched my arm
like a piece of mail she'd been expecting.
I couldn't tell if she knew I was leaving.
It was relentless. The cottonwood tails
hailing all over the house, feverish
fluff. Like some invisible beast
gutted a thousand rabbits all at once.

MISSED CALLS

THE EXQUISITE TENSION—AND IMMENSE CHALLENGES—OF A SECRET
TELEPHONE COURTSHIP IN 1990s KARACHI

by Rafia Zakaria

I sit alone in the dim, book-lined room waiting for the phone to ring. Outside, a hot Indiana summer drags its swampy feet. I stare at my smartphone's screen. The time, neat numbers superimposed on a picture of my daughter, stares back. My thoughts are steeped in the past, and so the device feels strangely alien and incongruous in my hands. Then it rings, and a man's voice reaches out into the stillness of the room. It is a voice I have not heard for nearly twenty-five years. It is a voice I have not heard since the day I was married.

"You didn't wait for me," he says.

"You never called," I respond.

There are no doubts in our minds but we test each other anyway. I ask him to recite my telephone number, not the one he has just called but the one from long ago, from Karachi. He laughs and recites it easily. I do the same with his old number, surprised that it is on the tip of my tongue.

This story is a love story, though its main character is not a person but a thing. The telephone, in this story, determines the possible and the impossible. Back in the 1990s, there were two telephones in my house in Karachi. The downstairs phone was a pale gray rotary model, which was placed on an end table in our formal sitting room. A phone call was still an occasion for the elders in our house, especially for my grandparents, who had known life without it. Each call cost money, and since every expenditure was closely monitored in our home, so, too, was the use of the telephone. When you did make a call, you would sit on the edge of the armchair, so as not to create an imprint or a sweat stain on the good furniture, and carefully dial each digit. Anyone walking by the glass door of the sitting room was entitled to ask who was on the other end of the line. Unlike now, one phone belonged to a whole household. Unlike now, it had to be shared.

The upstairs phone was in my father's study—a room even more off-limits than the sitting room downstairs. This phone was "new," bright orange with black buttons. It sat on the edge of a tall dresser that my father sometimes used as a standing desk. If you were upstairs and wanted to make a call, you had to stand—a deliberate arrangement meant to cut all calls short. My father did not like anyone lingering in his study, spending his money. Both these rooms, these telephones—I can say without exaggeration—would determine the course of my life.

While meeting boys face-to-face was forbidden to me, looking at them was not. That is how everything began—by looking. F and I first laid eyes on each other entirely by accident, on an otherwise unremarkable day. My father, my mother, and I had gone to the drugstore for cigarettes. My mother and I were in the white sedan we had at the time,

The author on her wedding day. All the gold embroidery on the dupatta worn on her head was done by hand,
and it weighed over five pounds, making head movements difficult. Photo courtesy of the author.

with her sitting primly in the front passenger seat and me in the back. Next to the drugstore was a copy shop. F, who had an exam the next day, was there making copies of his friend's class notes.

F was really striking. Athletic and broad-shouldered, he was dressed that day in a button-down shirt and khakis. His hair was gelled back, and his wide mouth curled into something between a grin and a smirk. He had a sharp aquiline nose, and his dark brown eyes were set in a way that gave him a perpetual look of mild intoxication. And he was supremely confident—in the way the youngest son of a very wealthy government official can be.

My attention would not have been drawn to him had my mother not noticed him herself and said something quite out of character: "What a handsome boy." I turned to look at the same moment that F finished paying for his copies, and in that instant our eyes met and our lives changed. We fell in love in the traditional way of a gender-segregated society. It is how most people in Pakistan fall in love, not knowing each other's names, not having uttered a word. My mother's voice seemed miles and miles away.

F made sure that we saw each other again. It wasn't too difficult: the drugstore we frequented, the photocopy store, the grocery store, the video rental store were all clustered together in a neighborhood market square not far from our house. My family visited the shops at the square every day—my father to rent whichever movie was to be his evening viewing, my mother for fresh bread and eggs from the store, and I because it was the only way I was allowed to leave the house other than to go to school. My twin brother had once regularly joined us on these excursions, but puberty had given him considerably more freedom just as it had taken mine. He played cricket with the neighborhood boys in the alley next to our house, rode his bike around the nearby streets, did whatever he wanted in that hour before dusk when the rest of us went to the shops.

A few days after our chance encounter, F and I saw each other again. And then yet again, so often that I began to look for him every day. He drove a new burgundy Toyota Corolla, which I soon came to recognize as he drove up and down the short streets around the market square to catch a glimpse of me. Then one evening, while my father was taking his time mulling his selections in the video store and my mother had slipped into the bakery, F stopped his car directly next to ours.

My heart thumped as his friend leaped out from the passenger seat and threw a small card through my open window and onto my lap. The front of the card was just an advertisement—I don't remember for what—but on the back F had written his name and his phone number. As quickly as I could, I stuck the card in a book I had with me, hoping that my euphoria was invisible to my watchful parents. In my head played a single refrain: I have his number and I know his name.

We would have scores of telephone conversations before we could be alone together.

During these months, he continued to try to see me any way he could. We faced a difficult dilemma: If we wanted to see each other, we could not talk to each other. To talk, I had to call, which required excusing my way out of the daily trip to the market so I could be alone with the telephone in my father's study. With my parents gone—and my grandparents not yet used to paying attention to what I was up to—F and I could sate our hunger to hear each other's voice. But if I wanted to see him, the call would have to be foregone. I would accompany my parents to the market, follow my mother into the grocery store. F would trail me as my mother shopped for sugar or spices or milk, and our eyes would meet silently across aisles laden with food. In those moments, we soaked up the heady intimacy of being close to each other even if we could not speak.

Some days we tried to evade the choice between seeing or speaking. Instead of waiting until evening to see me, F would skip class and show up outside my school's premises before dismissal. He would already be there, waiting and watching for the small glimpse he would get of me as I walked out the gate, before my mother arrived to take me home. When F and I spoke on those evenings, with me sweating at the edge of the armchair in the fanless sitting room, we felt victorious.

The first time we touched came a bit later, after we had professed our love for each other; he first and hurriedly at the end of a phone call, I embarrassedly at the beginning of the next. I was standing in a grocery store aisle helping my mother select ingredients for a special recipe she planned to try, my back to the aisle as I scanned the shelf in front of me. It was then that I felt fingers lightly graze my back. Startled, I turned around just fast enough for our eyes to meet for one second through the gaps between boxes of crackers. It was nothing and it was everything.

We became friends, best friends. I was so terribly lonely in those first few years of puberty, still stunned at how furiously quickly all sorts of things were forbidden. It was also a time of deep confusion as I tried to make sense of divergent messages from my parents. My mother would tell me every day to "study hard," but she would also say that she, my father, and my grandfather would never permit me to study with boys. All the colleges and universities that taught law or medicine or engineering, the subjects I was told I should study, were mixed-gender institutions, where I would have to study with boys. What was I to do, then, with all the hard studying?

The restrictions that had been imposed upon me arose, I knew, from my father's fears. The first was the trademark fear of all refugees: a distrust of the new "home," which never seemed to match up to the expectations that had been pinned to it. (Originally from Bombay, his family was among those who had migrated to Karachi from India following the 1947 partition.) The second kind of fear was all his own: a dogged risk aversion that saw female freedom (mine) as a threat to male honor (his). In his cynical calculation, being a father to a daughter was a no-win situation. In order to ensure that I would be married off to one of the transplanted Bombayites he thought suitable for me, he had to make nice and stay in their good graces. My father, a gruff and eccentric man who chafes at social expectations himself, hates being forced to be nice.

My family's feelings of rootlessness probably played a role in why I fell for F. Unlike us—descended from Indian Muslims who had been instrumental in conceptualizing Pakistan—his family was Punjabi and very much rooted in the country. His ancestors had been in the Punjab region for generations and were fast becoming the dominant elites in Pakistan. F was a son of the soil, as unquestioning of his own sense of belonging as I was ambivalent about mine. My family, once rich, was keeping up appearances in the grand house my grandfather had built, which we now struggled to maintain. F's family was among the prospering new, rich members of a tight Punjabi trading community. But in the eyes of a cultured and cosmopolitan family from Bombay, they were country bumpkins, no matter how much money they had or how deeply I loved him. My father never would have approved.

F could not remove these burdens, but in listening to me and loving me and showering me with attention, he made them a bit more bearable. Just hearing his voice on the line made me feel hopeful about the future. Somehow, I believed, we would convince our parents, and we would marry, be together forever. Foolish and idealistic, I underestimated my father's resolve that I would marry only within the tiny community to which we belonged. I misread the intent behind my parents encouraging me to cultivate intellectual depth; I wrongly thought the books I was given to read—*Anna Karenina* and *Madame Bovary* and *Moby-Dick*—signaled an openness to letting me determine my own fate. First love entrances, casts a spell that blots out the existence of everyone else, of pesky concerns and cares. Reckless and selfish as I was in those days, I refused to consider what might happen if my secret romance were exposed to my conservative family. At seventeen and thirteen, respectively, F and I had never known heartbreak. All things were possible. We knew nothing and so we loved fully and without fear.

The new rules were strict even by Pakistani standards. Most of my school friends were allowed to visit one another's homes after school. Many attended extra tutoring lessons, where they studied with boys. Some even arranged outings to restaurants or parks. All of these things were forbidden to me. School was the only place I went by myself, and it had its own set of exacting rules. After school, I could go nowhere at all, not even to my maternal grandmother's house, five minutes away. Sometimes, if I really nagged, my mother would relent and intercede with my father on my behalf so that I could, for instance, attend a friend's birthday party. Before asking him, she would confirm with the girl's mother that no boys, not even older brothers, would be present.

To amend what Simone de Beauvoir famously wrote in *The Second Sex*: a girl is not born but is made. In retrospect, it is not surprising that the restrictions made me rebellious. Practically speaking, these restrictions meant that meeting F would be possible only if I lied to my parents. This seemed unthinkable in the beginning, but as we came close to a year of knowing each other, the intensity of our feelings began to exert its own pull. Yearning all the time, I began to devise a plan to sneak out of school.

Ten minutes was all I could promise him. As soon as the dismissal bell rang, I would sneak off the grounds through a different gate from the usual one, where my mother picked me up. Then I could get into his car, and we would have ten minutes together before I had to sneak back across school grounds to meet my mother.

The author with all her close high school friends. Seated next to her, in purple, is her best friend, Duriya Farooqui. Photo courtesy of the author.

For his part, F made sure the windows of his Corolla were covered with tinted film. That way no one could tell who was inside or what they were doing.

The day of our first date was the longest school day of my life. The bells marking the end of each fifty-minute period seemed to be late all morning. After recess the opposite effect occurred: time began to whiz by, and my insides knotted up. When there were ten minutes until the last bell of the day, I told the teacher I was feeling sick and she let me leave early. I ran down the flights of stairs, across the dusty, sun-scalded grounds of the school. When the dismissal bell finally rang, I was already at the gate and I could see him standing next to his burgundy car. My face was ablaze, and my body was wired from adrenaline. Ebullient, I crossed the road, my backpack bouncing on my back, past the rows of school buses and lined-up cars. I opened the back passenger door and got inside.

We did not get caught that time or the time after that. Once we had met, and we saw that meeting was possible, we wanted still more of each other, and all the time. We began to take big risks, and then bigger risks. I pretended I had to stay after school for extra physics and math lessons. We managed to steal an hour together, and then two hours, but still we wanted more. We consoled ourselves by reminding each other that very soon we would be older and then we could be together all the time.

New ways of meeting had to be devised. On the evening before my fifteenth birthday, he parked his car across the street from our house. I stood at my darkened bedroom window, watching the orange ember of his cigarette light up as he inhaled, then exhaled, his silhouette dimly lit by the single streetlamp. We stood there until it was midnight and I turned fifteen. Before he left, he got out of his car and let a thin, long box fall over our garden wall and into a flower bed. I would retrieve it later and open it to find a beautiful gold chain and a pendant with my initials. I couldn't wear it, because people would notice, so I kept it hidden in my bra, close to my heart.

It was not our love that would eventually betray us; it was other people. At the time we met, F's father had been serving in the federal government in Islamabad and traveling between his official lodgings there and the family home in Karachi. As his four-year term came to an end, he made the decision to move his family permanently to Lahore, where F's parents were from and where the family had growing business interests. The decision was likely also owed to his belief that F sometimes ran with the wrong crowd in Karachi. While F himself was clean, it was true that he had friends who had been tempted into Karachi's thriving drug culture. Late one evening, when F returned from hanging out with his friends who were part of Karachi's underground party scene, his father told him that he would be moving to Lahore.

We were devastated. For hours and hours, we had talked about our future—but the parameters of it had now suddenly changed. Late at night, after everyone had gone to sleep, I would sneak into my father's study, unplug the phone, unscrew the plastic plug, and fold in the wires so it would appear to be plugged in when it wasn't. It was only then that I could go downstairs into the darkened formal sitting room and call him without worrying that my parents would awaken, pick up the extension, and overhear our conversation. These pre-moving calls were all the same: I wept, and he stoically stayed quiet. We said "I love you" over and over again.

By then, my parents could tell something was amiss. They had both seen the same burgundy Corolla with the same boy in it every time we went to the shops. F now had to borrow his friends' cars if he wanted to see me; if he didn't, my parents would spot his car and abandon shopping altogether. By the time we learned that F would have to move, my mother suspected that I was complicit in some way with his recurring appearances. The telephone bill gave credence to her fears. Thankfully, the Pakistan Telecommunications Corporation did not, at that time, list the telephone numbers of outgoing phone calls. Even so, the phone bill had nearly doubled in the last several months. My father began to lock the door to his study. A tiny padlock was used to lock the rotary phone and my mother kept the key. Within days of this new arrangement, I learned to pick the little lock on the sitting room phone with a bobby pin. If my grandparents inquired, I would tell them I was discussing homework with a school friend and that my mother had unlocked the phone for me before she left. I would call F and talk to him until I heard my parents' car in the driveway. Then I would lock up the phone and run upstairs, where I pretended to be studying.

F and I had come up with our own plan to stay in contact despite his moving away. The telephone line that was installed at our home was of a sort that did not support outgoing long-distance telephone calls, which meant that after he moved, I would have no way to call him directly—and if he wanted to call me, he'd have to guess when I'd be able to pick up the phone. It was F who came up with a solution: When I could talk, I would call T, one of F's close friends in Karachi—one I had seen because he lived adjacent to my aunt's house. T would then call F in Lahore and tell him to call me. It was a reassuring arrangement. When F eventually moved, we put the plan into motion. Our love would conquer all.

This certainty was short-lived. One afternoon during the fasting month of Ramzan, my mother suggested that she and I go to my grandmother's house. The suggestion itself was strange; my father had decided to come home after just a half day of work and my mother was never allowed to go off to visit her mother when my father was home. But I loved going to my grandmother's house, where my aunts and cousins also lived, so I agreed immediately.

An odd scene unfolded there. My eldest aunt was serving an extensive lunch to her husband and A, a young man I had never seen before. Instead of being told to go upstairs to my grandmother's bedroom, as was usually the case when any young men were around, I was encouraged to linger in the dining room. I learned that the young man was my aunt's nephew by marriage. He was finishing medical school in the United States and had come to Pakistan to do an elective rotation at a Pakistani hospital. He spoke barely any Urdu, so he spoke to me in American-accented English, asking what music I liked, what I was interested in studying—questions no man had been permitted to ask me before.

That evening, after we returned from this visit, I told F what had happened. I knew even then that the only reason my family would be introducing me to a man was to marry me off. F laughed. "You're fifteen years old," he said. "They can't possibly be thinking of marrying you off." I laughed, too, but I was not so sure.

I turned sixteen and began my final year of high school. One ordinary evening, as we sat watching television, my grandfather suffered a heart attack. There are no state-provided emergency services in Pakistan that can respond to medical crises. My brother and father managed to lift him into the car and drove him to the hospital, but he died in my brother's arms before they got there. In an instant, my brother and I were lurched out of our childhood faith in happy outcomes. My brother began to spend even more time outside the house. I stayed home, hoping to be able to talk to F in faraway Lahore.

Sometimes our arrangement with T as middleman worked, and we managed to have hurried, furtive conversations, assuring each other that our love was still alive. F's world had also been transformed. In Lahore, he was expected to put in long hours learning the business, which involved spending time in the textile mills that his family owned. When we spoke, he was tender, always the easygoing antidote to my highstrung self. He still teased me and he still made me laugh, refusing to be morose or serious even as we both mourned being separated. I tried not to complain about the days when we were not able to talk, the afternoons when I waited by the phone while my parents were out shopping after having called T to relay the message to F. I am a very impatient person and as a teenager I was even more so.

Since I could not talk to F every day, I began to write to him. I wrote letters that described my day, or what was happening at school, and of course how much I missed him—his voice, his touch, his jokes, even his teasing. I had no way of mailing these letters; mail service in Pakistan was (and is) sketchy and unreliable, and even if it were not, mailing a letter required a trip to the post office, money to buy stamps and mail letters, and all these were impossible hurdles for someone who was never allowed to go anywhere alone. When I was done pouring my heart out, I would tear up the letter and throw it away.

The letters were how I got caught. One afternoon after school, I came upstairs to find my mother livid, her pretty face reddened in anger. She drew me into her bedroom and shut the door and locked it. I knew then that something was about to happen; closed doors signaled trouble in our household.

Then I saw what was in her hand. My mother had found tiny torn pieces of a letter I had written to F and put them together with long strips of Scotch tape.

"Who is he?" She glared.

"Who is who?"

"Who is this boy you are writing to?"

I still do not know how much my mother knew then, how much she had read. Did she know that we had been meeting outside school? Did she know his name? Did she know that we were in love?

I denied everything. The letter was imaginary, I insisted. I had written it just for fun and because I was bored. She did not believe me.

"If you are in love with some boy, then you know what your father will do if he finds out," she whispered angrily. "He will make our lives a living hell."

Then she opened the door and walked away, taking with her the taped-together fragments of my love letter.

My favorite aunt, the eldest of my mother's three sisters, had just returned from a summer trip to the United States. Traveling to the United States from Pakistan was a big deal in the '90s, and when people returned, you visited them to welcome them back home. That is what my mother and I were doing that late summer afternoon. My aunt had made a photo album of her travels. She had stayed mostly in Connecticut, where her hosts—her husband's brother and his wife—lived. The pictures showed my aunt posing in their sitting room, their dining room, and even by the Jacuzzi in their palatial marble bathroom. The home was gorgeous: modern, contemporary, and set on the banks of a river. Clearly, her brother-in-law and his wife had realized their American dream.

I was unprepared for the last few photos in the album. These were not of my aunt at all.

They were graduation pictures of A, the man who had been having lunch in my grandmother's house a few months ago. My aunt, I now realized, had been visiting his parents.

MICROINTERVIEW WITH LING MA, PART VII

THE BELIEVER: Do you often read criticism of your work?

LING MA: I do skim it sometimes. When *Severance* was initially published, I was much more into keeping up with reviews. But it's like staring directly into the sun. You'll screw up your vision in some way. What I've learned is that the reviews or criticism where someone really sees your work, even if they're critical, are very rare. I don't feel like I'm missing out.

BLVR: Have you seen the Apple TV show *Severance*?

LM: I have not.

BLVR: The premise of the show is that employees who work at a company called Lumon agree to have a chip implanted in their brains to separate their domestic and work selves—what the show calls "outies" and "innies." It's a dark satire of corporate life.

LM: I want to watch it. People assume that I would get mad about how the TV show has the same name as my novel, but I borrowed the title from a *Mad Men* episode called "Severance." ★

"He just graduated from medical school," she told me pointedly when we got to those last photos, "and they're coming to Karachi in December."

It all came together in my head—the strange lunch where I had been introduced to a strange man, my aunt's visit to his parents' house and now his parents' imminent visit to Pakistan. I had just been told that my marriage was being arranged, without anyone actually saying the words.

My parents took forever going to sleep that evening. Hour after hour, I could hear their muffled voices, stopping and starting and mixing with the sound of the television. The theme of their conversation was what you would expect: Was their daughter too young? Was this the best marriage proposal they would get? And, of course, the unanswerable: Were they doing the right thing? It wasn't until after midnight that the house was finally silent. I followed the usual process to ensure the phone line's privacy, then I tiptoed into the sitting room and dialed T's number. He answered groggily. "Can you call him?" I begged. "It is so late, Rafia," T grumbled. I hung up. Staring at the sitting room clock, I watched the minutes tick by, hyperalert so I could answer F's call at the first tiny ring.

Ten minutes passed, and then fifteen. It was a warm night, and the sitting room with its stuffy furniture was even warmer. Dripping with sweat, but afraid to turn on the fan, I waited. That night there was no call. I went back upstairs and cried myself to sleep.

F called a day later. We were all at dinner when the phone rang—a pet peeve of my father's. I sprang up to answer it, feeling my mother's eyes following me out of the room. I had only minutes to tell F what I thought was going on. Before he could respond, I heard someone coming toward the sitting room. Afraid of being caught, I hung up.

"I am only twenty. I am not going to be able to convince my father that we should get married." F and I were arguing about what to do if my parents agreed to the match that was being arranged with the doctor from Connecticut. "And if they do ask you," he pleaded, "you just have to be brave and say no."

These conversations, even when we could have them, were not reassuring. It was becoming harder and harder for us to talk. Now, nine times out of ten, when I called T, there would be no return call from F. Sometimes T would call back instead and tell me that F wasn't answering or that he wasn't home. Bereft, I would confide my fears to T instead. "Does he not love me anymore?" I would ask poor T again and again. He would listen and give the same answer every time: "I don't know… I just don't know."

I began to feel neglected. It would serve him right if I were married off to someone else, I would threaten in a whisper, before I heard steps approaching the sitting room and had to hang up. In my teenage passion, I always assumed that while I was constrained by my parents, F was free to do anything he pleased.

T believed me when I told him I suspected that my marriage was being arranged. T was understanding about anything I told him—and he always took my phone calls. Ours was a platonic friendship, one that grew out of necessity. Our phone could not connect me with the man I loved, and T was there to listen, always.

It was a conversation with T that changed the course of my life. One evening, as I indulged in my usual dissection of F's waning attentions, I asked T's advice on the choice that I sensed I would have to make. If he were in my shoes, I asked, would he wait for F? His answer left me reeling: "F will not marry you," he said. "You should listen to your family." I believed T. I felt he had no incentive to lie.

The days that followed were a blur of rage and self-destruction. Now that I was confronted with the loss of the man I loved, the accrued guilt and shame of the past two years engulfed me. I had been a bad daughter and a bad sister. I had lied and I had cheated.

It was time to stop, I scolded myself as I prayed and prayed with a newfound piety.

It was time to repent for all the deception I had heaped on those who loved me the most, whose honor and expectations I had nearly dashed to bits.

I stopped calling T, not wanting to seem even more pathetic and desperate for the attentions of a man who did not love me and did not want to marry me. Instead, I medicated myself, stealing the Valium that had been prescribed to my grandfather when he was still alive.

December is a beautiful month in Karachi. The muted winter sun is kind and inspires a seasonal gentleness in everything else. December is also the month of weddings, the cool air an encouragement for guests to gussy themselves up in finery and head to banquet halls. There were a few weddings in our family that December, and my mother had ordered new outfits to be made for me. I remember one of them especially well: it was a long tunic of deep burgundy velvet with antique gold embroidery, which my tailor had recycled from an old tunic of my mother's from when she was about to get married.

It is what I was wearing when I met the people from my aunt's photo album. It was an intentional meeting that everyone involved pretended was a chance encounter. A's father, a jovial psychiatrist, made corny jokes as we all sat around a table. His mother, a woman who had gone to college only after her children were grown, wore blue silk and diamonds and assessed me openly, without embarrassment. My aunt and her husband were also present, to ensure that the conversation ambled along smoothly. The groom-to-be, now in his first year of residency, had not been able to make the trip.

I watched all of it happen with some detachment. The loss of F had left me numb. I had surrendered, fueled by the warped logic of heartbreak, and with a near masochistic acquiescence. I had tried to choose my own fate, my own love, and I had failed. If others wanted to take over now, I would let them. If F did not want me, then anyone who did want me could have me.

Before the week was over, A's parents showed up at our home with a marriage proposal, accompanied by my aunt and her husband. For several hours, the grown-ups sat and discussed the future A and I would have, were we to get married. I eavesdropped from the top of the stairs. My parents were concerned about how young I was, younger than any previous bride in our family. A's mother dismissed these concerns with her own promises and assurances: they would allow me to go to college after marriage; she herself had been a sixteen-year-old bride, and her life had turned out just fine. After several hours, the visitors left. It was not an immediate yes; my parents still had some concerns. But everyone appeared to be in a positive mood.

On December 31, we were all invited to my aunt's house for a celebration of the imminent nuptials. I was at home, getting ready, when I saw my father's car pull into our driveway. He came bearing terrible, shocking news. My aunt's husband, a man I had known my whole life, had died of a heart attack on his way home from work, at only fifty-two years old. My aunt, only forty-four, was now a widow.

The tragedy meant that the arrangement of my marriage had become a dead man's final wish—unfinished business that had to be completed so his soul could rest in peace. Even if I had had the courage to say no to the proposal before, I certainly did not have it now. My shame at having fallen in love with F goaded me to accept my fate. I had thrown myself at a man who did not love me. I could ask Allah for forgiveness and pay for my sins by agreeing to marry the man my family had chosen for me.

In saying yes, I believed, I would achieve moral deliverance, become a "good" girl rather than the defiant and deceptive one I had been. My heartbreak did the rest. After all, what better way to forget about F than to marry A? But aside from all this, there was a childishness in it: this would teach F not to disbelieve what I said, not to ignore my calls. All the one-sided conversations I had with myself convinced me that F did not love me and that I had to learn to forget about him. I said yes, and preparations for the wedding began.

The last time I called F was the day I married A. I was upstairs, dressed in heavy silk bridal clothes, with henna that stretched from my fingertips to my elbows. Not long after I was engaged, the telephone line in our house had been upgraded to make it easier for me to call A. Standing in my father's study, I used the familiar phone, orange with black buttons, to dial F's number in Lahore. He answered, and for one small moment, I thought about running away. But I was prepared for it; in the months since our separation, I had taught myself to take such thoughts and shove them whole into some remote and inaccessible part of myself. There would be no running away, no reunion, no happy ending. My last words to F that day were simply "You have ruined my life."

"What do you mean, why didn't I call?" F asked me when we spoke again, twenty-five years later. I was surprised at his question. "I called T again and again and begged for you to call me," I said.

There was silence on our cross-continental telephone call—a call made easy by the fact that we both had iPhones, devices that allow us to speak to anyone anywhere.

"I never got those messages," he said, finally.

In the conversation that followed, we tried to untangle the knotted misunderstandings of our long-ago love story, slipping into a familiarity that only deep intimacy creates and leaves untouched in some forgotten corner of the heart. The truth we uncovered by comparing notes shocked us. A few months after F moved to Lahore, T had simply stopped relaying any messages between us. Instead, T pretended that he was not in contact with me at all. All the while I had confided in him, he was betraying both me and F.

In Lahore, F had concluded that I did not love him anymore. In Karachi, waiting for calls that never came, I believed that he no longer loved me.

After we realized this, the terms of our conversation changed. Perhaps we had been willing to risk a conversation with the long-ago ex we once loved passionately, because we felt safe in the assumption that the other presented no danger to the lives that we had built for ourselves since then. I felt I had become a different person from the girl who had loved him, a brave and independent woman who would never wait for a man. From his perspective, the boy who had once loved me was a distant memory, with little resemblance to the middle-aged man who headed companies and was devoted to his family and to Pakistan.

The question we faced is impenetrable. How does the alteration of one crucial detail at the beginning of a story transform everything that follows? Our mutual shock peeled back the layers of reserve and maturity that had been shielding us. Without those layers, we became vulnerable again, not unlike the teenage lovers we had been. Suddenly the answers to questions that had no longer mattered felt important again. I wanted to know why he had not tried to tell his parents, or tried to save me from being married off to someone else. F was angry that I had not been braver, had not stood up for him and waited until he was old enough to marry me. Had my parents been in such a hurry to get me married? How could I have married someone else?

The ease with which we slipped back into the people we had been so long ago was as terrifying as the revelation that we had been betrayed. First love is idealized in literature and movies and everywhere else because of its intensity, its compulsive overriding of all practical sense. Some believe that first love is the only true love, the only time we do not edit our feelings and desires to be in accord with the world in which we live. If first love is thwarted by the treachery of a villainous other, it is ennobled even further.

We opened up and told each other about our lives. A few years after I was married, his family arranged a match for him; he was engaged for a while, but then broke it off. Another failed engagement followed. Finally, a marriage was arranged with the daughter of one of the most powerful families in Pakistan. They are now the parents to three children. He has founded and managed many businesses, his latest a project to transform the way K–12 students receive instruction in Pakistan. He never fell in love again, not unusual for a man living in a society where most relationships are built on duty, and only dutiful love is considered legitimate.

I am no longer married to A, the man who was chosen for me. I endured that abusive relationship for eight years, and then one day I fled with my daughter, then a toddler, to a domestic violence shelter. I got divorced and I became a single mom, all against the wishes of my family. I went to law school and then to graduate school. I wrote books. I also fell in love again: a grown-up love that made me believe in the possibility of two independent people being committed to each other through the tumult and turnarounds of life.

One of the certainties of getting older is realizing that you will not get everything you want, that only some of life's possibilities will bear fruit, while others will wither on the vine. This is not entirely unpleasant knowledge; the endless possibilities of youth are energizing but also exhausting in their inherent uncertainty. The knowledge that comes after a few decades are behind you can be comforting in its own way.

F and I decided not to stay in touch. This was not easy at first. I believed that if I got to know him as a friend, I would be less likely to fall into the many unknowable what-ifs of our story. I had been looking for closure grounded in reality. He was not interested. In the end we did stop speaking. Perhaps we stopped because of the ease with which we had slipped into who we had been—because in that single second of our reunion, we had still wanted what we had wanted when we parted. When you coddle a mistruth as long as we had, it becomes a little more truthful. We decided, I suppose, to cling to the narrative that was familiar, that I had not loved him, and he had not loved me—leaving the fabric of the lives we had woven intact.

We let each other go. The loss of our love had injured only us and that was a victory. To attempt some resurrection, even just a bit, would have hurt too many innocent bystanders. Faced with a choice like that, we chose to hurt only each other. ✱

PLACE

McDONALD'S, 24TH AND MISSION STREETS, SAN FRANCISCO

by Oscar Villalon

FEATURES:

★ One-dollar coffee

★ Seniors in berets and windbreakers

★ A continuous, agreeable hum

About twenty years ago, Mike Davis, the grand leftist excavator of Southern California's buried history, came out with his fascinating book *Magical Urbanism: Latinos Reinvent the U.S. City*. Davis pointed out how the relative ease of international travel and affordable long-distance communication changed the way immigrants experienced life in the United States. That transnational rootedness, if you will, plays a role in how communities made up of folks from Mexico and Central America maintain some aspects of their old homes in their new homes. One significant way they do this is in how they utilize public spaces.

If you walk along Mission Street from 23rd (and sometimes from 22nd) to 24th Street in San Francisco, you'll see what Davis means. The sidewalks on either side of this four-lane street are open-air markets. DVDs in not-quite-color-correct covers. The ubiquitous bacon-wrapped hot dogs sizzling on good-enough flat-tops; plastic coolers stacked with tamales; glass carts displaying cut-up fruit arranged in blossoms. Niners and Warriors merch, unofficial and unlicensed of course. The sidewalks become the agora. And the same way you would stroll around a plaza, taking in the scene while chatting with cousins, that's how people move up and down Mission. Deliberately, eyeing the wares. What's being sold may be different from what you saw on summer visits to the madre patria, and the space to navigate is much more cramped, but the idea that part of being alive means being outside, seeing and being seen, is there.

When you get to 24th and Mission, there is a McDonald's. Across the street from that McDonald's, to its north and west, are the brick-paved "plazas" that serve as the entrances and exits for the 24th Street BART station. They, too, have regularly served as sites of public gathering, becoming informal marketplaces and also the commons for protests and proselytizing and various outreach campaigns by city agencies. In late July 2022, though, the local government decided to fence off all that space, limiting its use to getting on and off BART. There had been stolen goods for sale in these plazas, boxes of cold medicine and jugs of detergent and packets of ground coffee neatly arranged on blankets on the ground. It was deemed that there were too many of these blankets, and too much drama. The optics weren't good. The inequality that defines San Francisco was all too revealed, not just in that people had to resort to selling stolen household goods to get by, but that there were so many unapologetic takers. So now, as I write this in July 2022, the plazas are empty.

Fortunately, the McDonald's remains unencumbered. It is still the clean, well-lit place I have known it to be for at least twenty years, functioning as one of the unlikeliest oases of public life in all of San Francisco. Folks are here to linger, to meet up, to be together alone. Men and women well into their sixties sit at the four-tops, all of them nursing hot coffees, the golden paper cups resting atop their brown serving trays. It's seniors in their caps and berets and windbreakers that populate the place, their murmured Spanish and meditative silence a comfort. But there also are quiet teens who do their homework here, young smiling families that let their toddlers roam a little. Nearly everyone here is brown, as is true of the employees. Sometimes a tout will come in and interrupt a group conversation and try to move kids' clothes. And sometimes there are those who bear upon their faces and bodies the distress of neglect and illness, sitting by themselves at a corner table. Mostly, there's a continuous, agreeable hum, like an uncrowded departure lounge at an airport. What a way to be in communion with your neighborhood, in a McDonald's, where a posted sign (and how long has that been there?) reads PLEASE NO LOITERING TIME LIMIT 45 MINUTES. Olvidalo. Watch the people winding along 24th and Mission. Read your book and give them time to come inside and see all of you. ★

Illustration by Sophia Foster-Dimino

ANGEL OLSEN

[MUSICIAN]

"GETTING HURT IS WORTH IT BECAUSE YOU GET TO SEE THINGS."

Images from Angel Olsen's favorite paintings:
A woman playing the rays of the moon like a harp
A hairdo that reaches the stars
An outfit made of shells

Born and raised in St. Louis by older adoptive parents, *Angel Olsen wants something real—no-nonsense experience full of life's highs and lows rather than polite niceties; she doesn't mind if it's messy or hard, especially if it's life-altering. During Olsen's 2017 Pitchfork Music Festival performance, her band vamped while she slowly strutted her way across the stage in big sunglasses, before strapping on her black Gibson and playing a smoldering version of an early song, "High & Wild." This is a woman who once sang backup for Bonnie "Prince" Billy and plotted her revenge on the exploitative, male-dominated music industry from the back line. She tossed her sunglasses aside with effortless cool to* reveal accusatory eyes. When the song ended in a fiery rave-up, she said, "Sometimes you're out there and you just got to get a couple things off your chest. And it's hard out there being real with people, every day. Being real with them. It's hard to be real with everybody in your life." Then she laughed, and you saw that her anger, leavened by a wry sense of humor, was part of the tenacious resilience that has enabled her to step into the spotlight and command her own band.

Fast-forward to 2021: there's a global pandemic, and Olsen's come out to her parents as queer, only to have her father die within a week of her revelation, with her mother following soon after. As I was writing this interview, a friend asked me, after

Illustration by Kristian Hammerstad

listening to Olsen's new album, Big Time, *"Did she go through a breakup?" I laughed—an understatement. The record is an expansive processing of Olsen's grief that reckons with heartbreak while basking in the sunshine of new love. After playing a new song, "Ghost On," in a June 4, 2022, performance at Will Geer's Theatricum Botanicum in Topanga Canyon, California, Olsen sighed and said, "It's fine. Everything's fine. It's all real. It's all real. It's all very, very real," and you got a sense that all the turmoil captured on the record was ongoing, and while she would acknowledge the turmoil, she was moving forward because she had a show to play.*

—Adalena Kavanagh

I. GRAY-ROCKING

THE BELIEVER: You've been doing this professionally for more than ten years. Is it about ten years?

ANGEL OLSEN: Ten years for me, twelve if we count my time playing with Bonnie "Prince" Billy.

BLVR: What are things you felt went right for you in order to have the career you've had?

AO: I stood in someone's shadow for a few years before I jumped into it myself, and I learned a lot by just watching. Looking at how other people did stuff, and working as a backup singer, I got a sneak peek into this corrupt, male-driven fucking industry. When I was working for other people, I kept to myself, and I was like, I'm gonna avoid this in the future. I'm gonna do it differently. And when I have a band, I won't do this. If anything, the things that upset me or angered me ended up propelling me to create. I took whatever that anger-frustration was, and I was like, No, these are words that need to be written down, and I need to put them to songs, and then we're gonna go on the road. I was so angry. I was quietly angry. I was a shy person. As a twenty-two-year-old, I was really shy, and I didn't know what touring was, and I didn't know what the world was; I didn't have a passport, and then all of a sudden, I'm all over the world, and I'm meeting booking agents, and I'm like, That guy kind of looks weird. Why is he hanging out after the show? And I'm like, Oh, because he booked the show. Why does he get to hang out here? He needs to go. He's ruining the vibe. You know? When I started putting out my own music, I think

people were familiar with me because I was already working for someone else, which I wasn't trying to use at all as an angle. When I started out, I didn't know what would happen. I did one European tour. I literally packed my LPs in a huge rolling suitcase, and mid-tour the wheels fell off, so I was dragging the suitcase from train to train. Then I did one US tour on the East Coast right after a hurricane hit, and I thought, Well, I guess no one's gonna go to my shows, but people came and it was the first time I was like, Oh, people listen to my music. I didn't really work that hard at trying to promote my music. It was weird to me, actually, that people were there, but I guess when *Strange Cacti* came out, it was a success on the internet. I think people just got it from word of mouth, and I never toured any of the songs. Imagine never touring any of your music, and then you go somewhere and there's just people there. It's weird. I don't know what worked for me other than that I've been kind of oblivious to a lot of stuff that people calculate. I think if you are good, you're good. People are gonna know if you're good. In the beginning, I was making music for me. I think people can tell when you don't make it for yourself.

BLVR: Were you surprised by the reception you had, or were you shy but confident?

AO: I was shy, but I knew that the things I was writing about were real for me and they were coming from a place that was real. I had played shows. I think that's where I felt like I could be confident. It's so classic. You are really shy and then you get onstage… and people are like, "Wait, I thought you were shy?"

BLVR: It's like being two different people.

AO: It really is. I don't want to be a leader. I'm about to do all these things with a band that I've hired, and I love all of them, and they're really sweet, and they work really hard, but I just don't like telling people on the spot what I think all the time. It's so exhausting to have seven people ask you how you want something to go, and you have to put it delicately so you don't hurt anyone's feelings. It's just very exhausting. In the past, back in the day, it was just me and a guitar. So I didn't have to talk to anybody about it. I could change it at any moment I wanted. I think being in a band is a very different thing, and it has taught me to get out of my shell and describe things that I want more and to just be more outspoken and to feel less afraid to say, like, *Hey, I don't really think we need that guitar part there.* In the past, I would have been like [*adopting a high-pitched, conciliatory voice*], *Well, I hope they're not offended or hurt, because I really do like their playing.* I don't want to spend all this time thinking, Well, I don't want them to be upset. No! I wrote the fucking song. If you don't want to be here, don't be here.

BLVR: Do you think some of that is conditioning from being a woman?

AO: Absolutely. Absolutely. I'm trying to imagine Will Oldham being told… Oh my god, don't even get me started. Imagine me telling Will Oldham, *Can you change the tone of the guitar, because it sounds like shit?*

BLVR: Do you think being in that male-dominated atmosphere taught you how to tell people what you wanted from your music?

AO: Yeah, I think I've learned to just gray-rock it. [*Gray-rocking is a technique used to divert a toxic person's behavior by acting as unresponsive as possible when you're interacting with them.*] Like whenever a cis dude pouts like a child because I'm telling him something very simple, which if he heard it from another cis dude would be totally fine. So then I just say, "OK, well, everybody, let's just keep going." And I just kind of move forward; I move forward, and I ignore the face they're making and keep going, and I don't apologize. I don't say, *I'm so sorry I hurt your feelings earlier in front of everyone.* Because I'm like, *Dude, your feelings are hurt too easily. I'm not going to coddle you.* That's not what this is about. You're not my special star, OK? But with my current band I do have a good group of people that I can be honest with, and I think that is something I actively look for. I think the hardest part of what I'm doing, as the leader of my own band, is telling people to play less—like, play simply and play

less, because it isn't about guitar solos with my music. It *is* sometimes. There are little moments. But for the most part it's about the words.

II. "A RARE VISUAL IMAGINATION"

BLVR: As a writer, I think your music is obviously about the words.

AO: Yeah, but some people listen to music and they don't hear the words, which I find to be incredibly maddening.

BLVR: There are several schools of songwriting. You seem to use story-driven songwriting, but you also use a lot of symbolism. And then there are songwriters who write, like, postmodern novels, where the point is not to make a point, but the point is that the words are sounds.

AO: Yeah, and the sounds replicate and then you meditate on them. I love that. You know, what I love is Alabaster DePlume and listening to music that has no words. I sometimes think that's more helpful. I do think there are very different kinds of experiences when we listen to music. It is important to have musical elements *surrounding* the words, but in any given precise moment, the music doesn't need to trample over them. When the words are there, they are progressively taking up space. I feel like I tried to be a scientist about it. I'm like, It's not about the importance of the thing I'm saying. It's that there's too much going on percussively, and we can't say the thing and play it always at the same time.

BLVR: That makes sense. Have you ever considered other art forms?

AO: Yeah. I really loved making the film [*Big Time*] with Kim [Stuckwisch]. When Kim and I collaborated, we put together symbolism from both her life and mine to create this sort of surreal thing. You know, when you collaborate, it's always different from how you would have done it if you did it completely alone, which is beautiful and frustrating, but I really enjoyed working with her and I love what we made together. I learned that I don't ever want to be an actor.

BLVR: That's a question I was going to ask.

AO: I realized that when you act, you don't get to write. Kim was changing the screenplay every other day. She'd add different things, and I'd be in the middle of a table scene with everybody, and Kim would be like, "And this is the part where you say your mom died." And I was like, "But the way you've written it is not how I would have said it." I was in front of everyone, and I said, "That's not how I'm gonna say it, because this isn't just a story, actually. So I can't just be your actor right now." It was intense to do. I realized that when you're an actor, you don't get to be the writer, performer, and editor. As a musician, you get to do it all, and you get to edit it. You get to be a part of the last touches to something. There's nothing better than that. I think I have a rare visual imagination, and that is why I started writing songs.

III. RINGING A BELL FOR ROADKILL

BLVR: How did you adapt to the limitations of the new world we live in?

AO: Man, I'm still adapting. I am a decade into my career and I have stable income, whether or not I take five years off. So the pandemic didn't really interrupt anything in my income. I will say that it has emotionally affected me. I started to pay attention to politics all over the world. And every day was just a new kind of overwhelming, and it still is. But now I take breaks because I will spiral out and be like, What am I doing? I'm looking like I'm just another fuckin' white virtue-signaler on the Instagram account. Get me off of this. I need to just live my life and do the work in my life. No one needs to fucking see it, and I don't have a duty to be on here all day talking about it. That's not my duty. My duty is to fucking just live a good life and try to just do acts of kindness in my actual daily life. But I was losing it a little bit. I didn't know what was gonna happen. I don't know: there was a gift to it because it made me appreciate small things that I really do love. Like I saw everyone going on long walks again and getting back into nature and really slowing down and looking at people and listening. As far as livelihood, though, I feel like I have enough of a following at this point where I could take a break and try to do something else, and I would, in fact, like to do that.

BLVR: Does it feel freeing to have that ability to make those kinds of decisions?

THINGS THAT RODRIGO S.M., THE NARRATOR OF CLARICE LISPECTOR'S *THE HOUR OF THE STAR*, DOESN'T KNOW

* How you start at the beginning, if things happen before they happen
* If the fact is an act
* If what he's about to narrate will sound treacly
* If the action is beyond the word
* Everything that's about to come
* What awaits him
* If this whom exists
* If this is how you write
* If this is a melodrama
* If that's the way it always was
* If his breath delivers him to God
* If he needs to pity God
* If the ending was as grandiloquent as you required
* What the weight of light is
* Whether he's a monster or just a person
* If this story will someday become his own congealing
* Why he's not laughing
* Who to accuse
* If he'll find one topaz of splendor in the girl's existence
* Why clouds don't fall
* Where a crowing rooster could fit in those parched storehouses holding wholesale import-export goods
* If he should say that she was crazy about soldiers
* If using some difficult technical terms would enrich the story
* Anything

—list compiled by Ginger Greene

AO: Yeah, I mean, it's been a privilege that I have to check a lot. I remember eating rice and beans all week and going to donation yoga, and trying to write a song at the café I worked at. Now I'm like, Well, I could write a book or I could not. You know? It's so fucking stupid. I want to read something to you from my journal. Is that fucking weird?

BLVR: No, I would love that.

AO: This is just an example of what my writing would be. I went to a wedding, and this passage is about a conversation I had with someone on the way to the wedding. I'll just read a little bit.

> We discussed a myriad of topics, some gossip, some about open relationships, heteronormative structures within the queer community. And then somehow we got on the topic of moss and the book *Entangled Life* by Merlin Sheldrake, and then also on to *Bluets* by Maggie Nelson. And I rang a bell in the middle of the talk because my friend had given me a bell to ring whenever I pass dead roadkill as I drive, so I ring it most of the time. It's also just weirdly fulfilling to ring a bell. Anyways, we got on to our mutual obsession with bells, dreams about them, religious associations with them, how they sound, how they teach you to pause for breath or acknowledgement, and then I suggested to her that she write a book, not unlike *Bluets*, but all about the endless meaning of bells. And then I realized the genius of *Bluets* is that she reminds the reader not about the color blue, but to look further, to take something small and sit with it. Letting it expand, we can find deeper directions of meaning and truth. And the example of that is so important. In this life, there's possibility and intricacy and marrying truth all around us if we just sit with it and notice it.

BLVR: I love that.

IV. "THE LOOK ON PEOPLE'S FACES"
BLVR: Do you like touring?

AO: No. [*Laughter*] But I do like the feeling of interacting with people and seeing their faces. Like, Oh, they know the words to my song. I just like experiencing the look on people's faces. I like to know that what I'm doing is real, too, and that it's affecting people, and you can only really feel that when you're in front of them playing, and I like playing. I just don't like the lifestyle. I just wish it could be like there's one show a week and the rest of the time you're just getting to know everybody.

BLVR: Do you think that would appeal to you: to do a residency where you could be somewhere for a while, and people could come to you?

AO: Yeah. That would be sick. [*Laughter*] You know what I want to do? Maybe I'll do a residency in gorgeous New Mexico. We're doing a festival; we're playing on Georgia O'Keeffe's property in September. I'm so excited because Patti Smith is gonna play and Sharon [Van Etten] and Devendra [Banhart] and all these people I love. I'm thinking about staying after to just hang out. It would be sick to do a residency at a museum, or at a museum that is also a venue, so you can enjoy other art while you're there and it doesn't have to be only you.

BLVR: There has to be something like that. Museums should get on that.

AO: They really should. ⸳

V. SURREALISTS WITHOUT FREUD
BLVR: Something that comes up a lot is your interest in the 1930s, because of your parents. I thought some of the costuming in the film you made with Kim was referencing the '30s—is that correct?

AO: Yeah—my parents' parents were probably more '30s, but I've always been an appreciator of nostalgia. I think the appreciation did start with my parents, because when I was younger I would go through their photo albums and look at pictures of them when they were young to try to connect with them. Later on I got really into surrealism and women surrealists like Georgia O'Keeffe and Remedios Varo and Leonora Carrington—people who practiced surrealism that weren't Freudian.

BLVR: What's the difference between Freudian and non-Freudian surrealists?

AO: The difference is that the Freudian surrealists are just chauvinists, and Remedios Varo and Leonora Carrington are like the punk rock duo. They're like, *Fuck you. We're making our art with the occult and witchcraft and folktales. And our dreams don't come from wanting to be a muse for a guy*. Varo and Carrington were really special, and they don't get a lot of public acknowledgement. I got really into their little world of surrealism. I was obsessed with that era—the surrealist movement to the Dada movement. It was its own punk rock thing, before punk rock existed.

BLVR: You mentioned Georgia O'Keeffe, Remedios Varo, and Leonora Carrington. What are some of your favorite paintings either by those three artists or any other surrealists?

AO: When I was seventeen or eighteen, I was obsessed with the relationship between Leonora Carrington and Remedios Varo, because they were best buds and they had such a romantic friendship. Leonora passed away kind of tragically. They practiced mysticism, and stuff from the occult, and paganism, and I don't consider myself an occultist, but I find that dreams and mysticism are interesting, more interesting to me than Freudian philosophy. I also really love Leonor Fini, who was famous for living with one hundred cats, and she was just kind of the crazy cat lady. One painting I really love, that I was obsessed with forever, is called *Figures on a Terrace*. There's this figure wearing a black-and-white-striped long dress on the terrace, and I looked for that dress forever, and it just looks like Montmartre. Like all these people lounging on the top of that hill in Paris. There's another painting called *The Passenger*, which I felt really moved by for a while, and I would always go back to it. But Fini is an interesting character, because the surrealists would have these masquerade balls, and she was the one who would make all their beautiful masks and hats. It's hard to find my favorite Remedios Varo paintings, but these three are pretty good for me: There's one called *The Call*, and it's just beautiful. She often draws these

figures of women where their hair is going up to the sky, then the top of their hair swirls into the moon, and their bodies and the clothes they're wearing look like shells. So they're wearing lots of shells. Some people would sexualize that and say it looks like a vagina, but for me, it looks like there's an endlessness to the creature that's walking through this hallway. I have no idea what Varo was thinking when she was painting these things, but I get a sense that she was trying to find her way through all these dark, shadowy places in her life and this was her dreamworld. There's another one called *Dead Leaves*, and she's sitting in this one. She's sitting in a big hall where she's made herself colorful… and then there's a ball of yarn that she's holding, and she's pulling the yarn out from inside a floating man that's just a few inches away from her, and inside his stomach there's endless mirrors and she keeps pulling the string out from them. I really connected with that. And then there's one called *La tejedora de Verona*. I like how she incorporates music and chemistry into her paintings as little jokes. In *Música solar* she has someone playing some sort of instrument that is made from the light of the moon, and as the moon shines down, she plays the rays like a harp. I thought, What an interesting way to talk about music and feeling a space. It's just really dreamy and spooky. I relate to surrealists because I felt really isolated a lot of the time growing up and I had to create my own world too. I'm a very visual person. When I'm not making music, or when I hear music, I think visually. I had another interview recently where we talked about synesthesia. We tried to figure out if I was a synesthete. I think I might be.

BLVR: Do you find that surrealism is more immersive for you than minimalism?

AO: Yeah. It's also about Varo's life. These surrealists just seemed really alive during a time that was dark. Whenever you go through a hard time in any situation or relationship, you can choose to feel sorry for yourself and let it eat you alive and complain about it to everyone, but you'll only push people away. Or you can start appreciating the things you can control and that are there and that are free and that are within you. These things are in your community, and they're in the language you speak with people. Making art sometimes feels like a way of encapsulating some of those things. It's like a feelings document, like, *Here are the things that are ironic and cracking me up and making me laugh*. Every now and then I hold something up that I made, and I realize, That's not mine. This is something I enjoyed doing, and now here it is for people to see, and they can have it, and we can hold it here together.

BLVR: You make a lot of references to dreams and dreaming. Why do you bring dreams into your music so much?

AO: Because I dream a dream every day. I talked with my friend Coco about this the other day, because she dreams a lot too. I was like, "Dude, I want to do something more with dreams other than just make little videos and stuff. I want to practice remembering all the details of them." I've always just been someone who dreams a lot and has really vivid dreams every day, especially if I'm going through changes, and right now I kind of am. Since my mom passed away, I have been having a lot of time-travel dreams where she appears as, like, the lord of time travel or some shit, you know, or, like, I'll be going back to her high school. It's literally like I'll be going back to her high school that I remember from her yearbook, and she's there with her friends and she's got the belt wrapped around her books and stuff. And I'm like, Where am I? And it sounds so cheesy to talk about, but, yeah, I don't know, it's difficult to talk about those kinds of themes without overdoing it or whatever. But I have a lot of dreams.

VI. AUTOBIOGRAPHY V. FANTASY

BLVR: You said you've been going through a lot of changes. How did that affect your work?

AO: Just the events in my life, or?

BLVR: I almost think the line between

autobiography and creative work is sort of like a false thing. I think people try to hide their biography because they don't want invasive inquiries. They want to do it selectively. I just take it as a given, like, it's neither… it's not more important or less important than if it was created from complete fantasy—

AO: Because even in fantasy you're trying to tell yourself something, and you wouldn't be who you are if you weren't trying to tell yourself that thing. So, yeah, you are showing who you are always. I agree. I agree. I have a friend who's a writer. I love his work. He was like, "Angel, why are you revealing your private life so much in your work?" And I was like, "What? Don't say that to me like that. Like that. Don't say it to me like that." I wanted to flip the table. I was like, "Are you fucking serious?" This writer friend, he said, "Don't do that to yourself. Why are you doing it this way? It's so personal. You won't be able to get out of it." And I was like, You know what, no matter how honest you are about every single aspect of your life, you can count on everybody's personal lens to be put up against it and to get it wrong. And there is some fucked-up safety in that. I get what he was saying to me. He was trying to warn me to protect myself more. And I was like, Do you think I'm living to protect myself? Do you think I'm gonna go back inside now and never write about anything that's deeply touched me or hurt me? You think I'll do that? Why would you think I would do that? [*Laughter*]

BLVR: That seems like it would make music more formulaic. I mean, you'd have to have a hat, right? Like topics—all right, I'm gonna write a song about this.

AO: And, you know, I am practicing a little bit of that too. I do that. And sometimes I'm surprised by what subconsciously enters that space when I think I'm doing it in a contrived way. So, yeah, to prove your point, I think that no matter what, even if it's intentional or contrived, there is an aspect of the truth that you are revealing about yourself and everything you make. Maybe I should be more careful about it. I should definitely learn how to protect myself from narcissists. [*Laughter*]

BLVR: Yeah, I agree.

AO: I like writing. I like sharing things with people. I think you lose when you close yourself off. Getting hurt is worth it because you get to see things. But it's a lonely thing, to see things deeper and deeper, when the people around you, your peers, are not enduring that kind of shit. But when you meet someone who has, it is so fucking special.

BLVR: I agree. I noticed you said something like that in the *New Yorker* profile. You did talk about how, making your record in Topanga, you were with people that had seen shit, and that really resonated with me; it made a lot of sense.

AO: I'm glad, because you say things like that on paper, and people just read through it, you know, but it is more real than anything. It's more real even than making the art itself. I'm just so glad I could sit in a room with all those people. Like, how fucking cool is that?

BLVR: Yeah, finding your people, just the ones that get it: there's nothing better than that.

AO: It really makes me want to cry. [*Mock sentimental voice*] It's just all so beautiful. [*Laughter*]

BLVR: You say on your record, "I'm a crier." We think of tears as being a bad thing, but they're just an expression of emotion.

AO: I've cried so much during the pandemic. If I could bottle the amount of crying that I've done in the last few years… It feels so good to get a lot of that shit out. I feel for my parents' generation and the people who were never taught to access their feelings. It is interesting. I feel like Gen Z feels too much sometimes. You need to talk every emotion through, and everything is a political and a safe conversation where you use the emotional tools we were given through nonviolent verbal communication, and part of me is like, *OK, kid, get it together. That's not the world we live in. Get prepared to use the tools you were given in your private school and get out there, because the world is an ugly place, and you're not going to be able to nonviolently verbally communicate it to everyone.* I know that we should use those tools, but sometimes you've just got to say, *I'm angry. Man, I'm angry!* But in my parents' generation, someone would commit suicide in their family and they wouldn't talk about it. There's got to be a middle ground here. I love that people from Gen Z listen to words. They're really invested in words, and meaning, and multiple meanings. I think it's so fucking cool. I just wish more people also could feel that. My parents—I just had to be like, *We're never going to know each other, we're strangers on this earth, but I love you.*

BLVR: You said if you weren't yourself making the music, it might not be something you were into. Are you saying that at a certain point you make something and it no longer belongs to you? Are those two things related?

AO: Here's how I guess they're related. I am an evolving person, just like anybody else, and sometimes I write songs, and later on I'm like, Why the fuck did I feel like I needed to embrace that? And I'm like, Cool, that's theirs. And I will continue to sing it, but that's not who I am anymore. I was actually lying in my bunk today, because I was thinking about how my biggest dreams and my biggest hopes are to find a place to hide and to evolve privately without anyone watching me. Going on my endless search for meaning in my life without anyone being an audience to that, and here I am doing all the things that are preventing me from having that. God, I hate the internet sometimes, because what if I do want to change my mind about something? I just want to evolve privately, but in music you can always do it again. I can always make something again, make something different next time. My dream would be to just play this record live, and I know that it would not be acceptable among fans, and I understand why; I understand why.

BLVR: It's been three years since they've been able to see you.

AO: I do feel a responsibility to connect with people. And I also need to connect with people. Over the last few years, I haven't been able to feel like what I do is real. I want to see people sing back to me, and I want to feel like they are relating to what I'm saying. Otherwise, I'm just doing it in vain. I need people so that, at a certain point, the music ceases to belong only to me. ✶

The serial killer media industrial complex rages on, but what has it taught us?
Very little about the crimes in question, and much more about ourselves.

VIOLENT DELIGHTS

BY SARAH MARSHALL

Illustration by Bruno Mangyoku

I.

If you shoot someone in the head with a .45 every time you kill somebody, it becomes like your fingerprint, see? But if you strangle one, stab another, and one you cut up, and one you don't, then the police don't know what to do. They think you're four different people. What they really want, what makes their job so much easier, is pattern.

—*Henry: Portrait of a Serial Killer, 1986*

Did you know, Helen, that more books have been written about Jack the Ripper than Abraham Lincoln? It's a sick world, isn't it, Helen?—*Copycat, 1995*

Girls be like "this my comfort show" and it's a netflix serial killer series
—@ihyjuju, Twitter, 2022

When I was in high school, I would lie in bed at night and think about how to outsmart a serial killer. The odds of my ever needing to do this seemed pretty slim, but I spent a lot of time thinking about it anyway. My plan, honed over many sleepless hours, was to talk to the killer enough to get him to see me as a person, or at least to distract him enough to hesitate and give me a chance to escape. Now I think I would have been better off focusing on learning to drive. I wanted freedom of movement, a chance to experience the world as if I were something other than a sweet treat waiting to be consumed, which was how I had been taught to see myself and everyone else: the two genders, eater and eaten. I wanted to feel like I could protect myself if I needed to, so I thought about how I could pacify the serial killers I would encounter, because as far as I knew, the only route to the things I wanted or needed was through soothing and circumventing an angry man. I was raised by an anxious mother and a domineering—see me avoiding the word *abusive*—father, and I grew up understanding that I was kept home and away from the world because it was full of men who wanted to hurt me; and that home was the domain of my father, a man who, at times, wanted to hurt me. And, as you can probably imagine, I have been confused ever since.

II.

In the fall of 2019, news outlets breathlessly announced that the FBI had identified a new serial killer, the most prolific in American history. His name was Samuel Little, and he had given up his story to a Texas Ranger named James Holland, who interviewed him after theorizing his connection to a cold case in Odessa, got a confession, and kept going. Little spent forty-eight days drinking Dr Pepper, eating pizza, and describing his murders to Holland. Then Holland described Little to the world: He was smart. He had a photographic memory. He had confessed to ninety-three murders. And he had evaded detection for so long, Holland told *60 Minutes*, because "he was so good at what he did."

I first heard about Samuel Little through this *60 Minutes* segment, which introduced him, for anyone who lacked context, as the man who had committed "more [murders] than…Ted Bundy and Jeffrey Dahmer combined"; a "cunning killer" who "preyed upon…women he believed the police wouldn't work too hard to find." He drew portraits of his victims, and the FBI made them public in the hopes that they could be connected to more cold cases.

And I guess my first question—before I ask whether killing people within the wide swath of humanity that the police don't care about actually means you're smart, or means you're just lucky because you're gambling in a casino with the best odds in the world;[1] before I ask why we seemed to be so excited to have found not just a new serial killer but the *most* prolific one; before I ask why we use the word *prolific* so unthinkingly in this context, as if some serial killers are like J. D. Salinger and others are like Stephen King—my first question, still, is this: How are we even to know that Samuel Little had a photographic memory if almost all the women in his drawings look so much like one another? Why do

---

1. It's hard to think of a serial killer who isn't remembered as smarter than they really were. There is probably no more extreme example of this than Ted Bundy, a mediocre law student who defended himself at his own murder trial, where he managed only to convince the jury that he was definitely a murderer, though he is remembered as a mastermind because he had a nondescript face and a lot of preppy clothes. He *looked* like a lawyer, which is what the photographs of his trials still convey.

so many of them have the same almond eyes, the same smokey eye makeup, the same face shape? Why did the seventy-nine-year-old man who happened to be the most prolific murderer in American history also happen to have one of the most impressive memories in American history? And if you've committed just a handful of murders—an unremarkable number, one that won't even get you on the leaderboard—then wouldn't it be, well, not a terrible idea to confess to a few dozen more? What if it makes you into something special, and helps the police close unsolved cases all over the country, and makes a great story for the people on TV, who will all want to talk to you now?[2]

Watching the first days of excited Samuel Little coverage, I thought: If it seems too good to be true, it probably is.

And then I wondered how the deadliest serial killer in American history could fall into the category of "too good to be true."

III.

In the last few years, millennials have been accused of "killing" mayonnaise, diamonds, American cheese, "education as we know it," milk, malls, cars, lunch, golf, napkins, and—in a fit of overachievement—both marriage *and* divorce. After all this killing, which is the only way headline writers are allowed to express that Kraft Singles saw a 1.6 percent decline in sales in 2018, it's remarkable that there was anything left to destroy. But somehow, we managed. ARE AMERICAN SERIAL KILLERS A DYING BREED? a *Guardian* headline wondered in 2018, and to me, the answer was clear. Millennials killed the serial killer.

In this context, "killing" means either to be less interested in a product or lifestyle than previous generations, or simply to be unable to afford it. Economically, this is murder. And along these lines, I have joked for years that maybe we see fewer serial killers these days because millennials just can't afford it as a hobby. To be a serial killer, you tend to need a house with a basement or garage, or at least a car. You need a job that pays well enough to let you waste gas driving around and looking for victims, and one that doesn't eat up so much of your time and energy that you just want to sleep on your rare days off. The millennial serial killer probably has one of those floral day planners that says HUSTLE on the cover in gold. The millennial serial killer wonders how his dad did it. This is the joke I tell, but is there any truth to it? Are serial killers harder to find, and if they are, does it have anything to do with the economy? Fewer homeowners equal fewer murder basements?

"There could be thousands of serial killers that we don't know about," one professor says, rather hopefully, in the *Guardian* article, "and for some reason we're not identifying [them] today as well as we did in the '70s, '80s and '90s." But most people quoted in the piece—and most people I talk to lately—agree with true crime writer Peter Vronsky that "there seems to be a decline in American serial killing." First manufacturing, and now this.

People suggest a lot of possible explanations: There are more security cameras now, so it's much easier to find a recorded image of a person or their car. Cell phones track our movements, and, to a great extent, our thoughts. DNA evidence makes it easier to link crimes and solve cold cases; advances in technology—some, like ViCAP, inspired by serial killers themselves—mean the authorities have the advantage. Sentencing is harsher than it once was, so serial killers are now less likely to be paroled after committing violent crimes, or a single murder, which means they don't have the chance to mature into what they would once have become. Or if they do, they now get caught after two or three murders instead of after a dozen. People who would have been serial killers in the past are now mass shooters. People aren't as trusting now; we have learned from the serial killer stories of the past, and are less likely to be easy victims. True crime has wised us up.

Of all these theories, the last one is the hardest for me to take seriously: the idea that people can educate themselves out of victimhood seems, like Samuel Little, too good to be true. I don't think Americans have suddenly evolved to be less murderable, and I don't think you can give the police too much credit either: despite the vast technological resources now available, the homicide clearance rate was 54 percent in 2020, and 77 percent of the homicides for which data was available involved

---

2. There is precedent for this behavior, perhaps most instructively in the case of Henry Lee Lucas, who confessed to hundreds of murders in the 1980s, many if not almost all of which he appears to have had nothing to do with. His continued confessions did, however, earn him cigarettes, strawberry milkshakes, and celebrity. I know this because writer Rachel Monroe told me about it on an episode of *You're Wrong About*, a podcast I host and which sometimes lands firmly in true crime territory, which is why I can't be too moralistic about the whole thing.

firearms. In 1976—during what we now call "the golden age of the serial killer"—the homicide clearance rate was 82 percent. The homicide rate that year was 8.8 per 100,000 people, and in 2020 it was 7.8 per 100,000. Crime statistics are bound to be imperfect, but if these ones are to be generally trusted, it's worth pointing out that 82 percent of 8.8 is 7.2, and 54 percent of 7.8 is 4.2. The police have not gotten better at solving murders, but they have managed to create the illusion that they did. Today we understand that we are constantly surveilled, and feel that we therefore must be safer than ever. It would be unthinkable to surrender your freedom and get nothing in return.

IV.

Maybe the question we're really asking is not where all the serial killers have gone, but where we can find the *interesting* ones. Plenty of people will tell you that they love watching serial killer documentaries, but the genre they're describing is more specific than its name suggests.[3] In *Lady Killers: Deadly Women throughout History*, Tori Telfer notes that "some say Jack the Ripper was England's first serial killer,

but that's only because others have been forgotten. About forty years before Jack came along, England suffered through a terrible spate of murderers… They were poor, migratory, and desperate. They did it for the life insurance, or to have one less mouth to feed. They got caught. They were women."

One of the best ways to go unnoticed as a serial killer, it seems, is to be a woman. For as far back as there is a recorded history of serial murder, women have been doing it too. And yet, Telfer observes, as late as 1998,

FBI profiler Roy Hazelwood—who theoretically should have known better—claimed that "there are no female serial killers." Aileen Wuornos might have been able to erroneously capture the title of America's first female serial killer because she killed like men did: she went out and found her victims on the road, and she let us tell a story where sex and murder went hand in hand. Much more often, women kill a string of people who are dependent on them as caretakers: nurses, mothers, wives. This also has also tended to disqualify them from the FBI's definition of the serial killer, which for decades referred to someone who murdered at least three strangers, with cooling-off periods in between. In 2005, around the time *Criminal Minds*[4] started airing, the FBI's Behavioral Analysis Unit hosted a Serial Murder Symposium, where, among other activities, they streamlined the definition of *serial murder*, scaling it down to "the unlawful killing of two or more victims"—because "a lower number of victims would allow law enforcement more flexibility in committing resources to a potential serial murder investigation"—and removing the condition that the victims must be previously unknown to the killer. This means that the number of serial killers in the world actually increased dramatically over the course of four days at a Sheraton in San Antonio. So where are they when we need them?

V.

Sometimes I think it's all a matter of what we pay attention to, and what we pay attention to is a matter of what we allow ourselves to fear. The murders we hear about for our entire lives—the

---

3. Over the past few years, amid the lucrative flowering of true crime podcasts and TV, many people have observed that the genre is having a moment. If that's true, then the moment is an exceedingly long one. Crime stories have always compelled us, and it used to be much harder to get a clear picture without actually smelling the blood. In *The Invention of Murder: How the Victorians Reveled in Death and Detection and Created Modern Crime*, Judith Flanders writes that after the murder of the Marr family—including their baby—in 1811, "visitors traipsed through the gore-spattered rooms, peering not only at the blood splashes… but also at the bodies themselves." If you didn't want to visit the murder scene, or simply couldn't, you could always

attend the victims' funerals. And before there were grocery store paperbacks and cable TV, there were broadsides and penny bloods and theatrical productions. One dramatic depiction of an infamous 1823 murder tried to edge out the competition by offering audiences a chance to see the very furniture that had been at the scene of the crime. Before the widespread use of photography, you could privately contemplate a murder scene by looking at a Staffordshire pottery diorama of it—if you could afford one. If not, you could take after the boy shown in a cartoon first printed in *Punch* in 1845, who asks a news vendor for "a nillustrated newspaper with a norrid murder and a likeness in it." And if none of that satisfied, you could always buy a piece of the murderer's clothes, or a section of the rope used to hang him. "Such was the excitement over" the execution of a convicted murderer in 1827, Flanders writes, that "it was reported that [the hangman] had sold off the rope sections at a guinea an inch." But the owners of this memorabilia still showed great restraint compared with the anonymous "gentleman" who intended to have a book about the trial bound in the murderer's own skin, which he was able to acquire from the hospital where he was dissected.

It also appears that for as long as true crime media has existed, it has served as a marker of class and race. Victorians fretted over how penny bloods and theatricals would corrupt members of the working class, especially children. To consider yourself able to consume crime media as a spectator who can only be shocked by the killer, rather than influenced to become more like him—whose nature is not regarded as intrinsically violent—is to feel secure of your place in a social class generally held above suspicion.

70

4. *Criminal Minds* was a CBS police procedural that premiered on September 22, 2005, and aired its 324th and final episode on February 19, 2020. (You may also know it as the show your parents always watched because it came on right after *Jeopardy!*) It depicts members of the FBI's Behavioral Analysis Unit (BAU) as they hunt down a new serial killer each week, zooming all over the country (or at least the parts that look like the greater LA area) in a Learjet. The team was initially led by Senior Agent Jason Gideon, played by Mandy Patinkin, until Patinkin left the show early in its third season and was replaced by Joe "Joey Zasa" Mantegna, who stayed on as Agent David Rossi until the final episode. Years later, Patinkin told *New York* magazine that agreeing to star in *Criminal Minds* was "the biggest public mistake I ever made… I thought it was something very different. I never thought they were going to kill and rape all these women every night, every day, week after week, year after year."

Which gives you a pretty good feel for the show, but let me give you some more. *Criminal Minds* began its life as one thing and ended it as another, and it's worth trying to track that progression. Because I can't expect you to go off and watch all fifteen seasons (even though I do recommend it), here is a highly abridged yet still overwhelming selection of the show's Wikipedia synopses, which will take you chronologically through all of *Criminal Minds*, and most of the twenty-first century so far. What follows is the lazy girl's homage to Carmen Maria Machado's "Especially Heinous," a piece of beautifully imagined fantasy fiction about *Law & Order: SVU.* These synopses imagine nothing. I'm just telling you what happened on TV:

Season 1, episode 1, "Extreme Aggressor"
When a Seattle, Washington woman goes missing and authorities connect her disappearance with three unsolved murders, the FBI's Behavioral Analysis Unit sets out to apprehend the killer and rescue his latest victim. Unit chief Aaron Hotchner is assigned to determine whether veteran profiler Jason Gideon, called out of medical leave for this case, is fit to return to duty permanently.

Season 1, episode 4, "Plain Sight"
When six San Diego, California women are raped, murdered, and posed with their eyes glued open, the BAU sets out to profile a killer who evades the authorities by striking in broad daylight and blending into the neighborhoods he targets.

Season 1, episode 10, "The Popular Kids"
When a high school student's body is found near Massanutten Mountain and his girlfriend is

ones we may even call "iconic," whatever that means or is trying to mean—don't cut through the noise of the rest of the world just because they are uniquely awful, or uniquely revealing of human nature. In real life, as far as I can tell, unendurably sad or cruel crimes are around almost every corner, but they're rarely committed by masterminds; often, they're committed by cops. And sometimes a crime can be spectacularly, giantly cruel and still not break into America's Top 40, because… why? Why did *Xanadu* flop? Because no one can predict a sure hit, not really. This is show business, kid.

Case in point: a crime I think about often is the 1987 Christmas massacre committed by Ronald Gene Simmons, which I bet you've heard of only if you watch Oxygen a lot during the holidays. But in case you haven't: Over the course of five days, Simmons methodically killed his wife, his children, his children's spouses, and his children's children, including the seven-year-old girl he had fathered by sexually abusing his oldest daughter, Sheila, when she was a teenager. Simmons had controlled and abused his wife and children for decades, and tightened his chokehold when, fearing suspicion about Sheila's pregnancy, he moved the family to a thirteen-acre tract in rural Arkansas. After three of his older children—including Sheila—left home, became independent, and started quietly making plans to help their mother escape as well, Simmons decided to kill them all. When he was done, he spent a day at home drinking beer, watching TV, and eating raw onions and cheese. Then he drove into town and started shooting, less methodically, at people he felt had wronged him, killing

two and wounding four. Among his family, there were no survivors.

In all, Simmons murdered sixteen people that day, fourteen of them family members. And if you like superlatives—and true crime, like figure skating, is all about superlatives, the firsts and mosts and bests—it was also the largest recorded mass murder of a family in American history. So why don't we hear about this story more often? Where's the hastily assembled Netflix documentary? If it were a question of sheer numbers, you'd think we'd talk about this guy—this tiny Jim Jones—at least as often as we talk about David Berkowitz, who killed six people and wounded seven. And if it were a question of evil, however you define it—or at least of how shocking the crimes were—then isn't it slightly more shocking to murder your own flesh and blood one by one than it is to gun down a stranger?

Of course, we have to acknowledge here that mass murdering commands a different kind of media attention than serial killing does, especially before the internet and the twenty-four-hour news cycle come into play. As the Son of Sam, David Berkowitz got to hold New York City hostage for months. Simmons, on the other hand, had kept his family in such profound isolation that no one learned of their deaths until he gave himself up to the local police. And rural Arkansas is not a great city, like New York or Los Angeles, where millions of lives are altered by one man's crimes, and it is not a place too famously wealthy or idyllic or white to admit murder, like Boulder, Colorado, or Scarsdale, New York, or Beverly Hills, California. Simmons didn't look particularly *not* like a murderer, so there could be no creepy delight in contemplating the distance between his family man mask and his murderous soul. The murderer had been the family man all along, but no one had noticed, no one had bothered to notice—and if they had, the assumed right of a man to exert total control over his wife and children might have been enough to make them look away.

What I have come to believe is that Ronald Gene Simmons never made it into America's murderer hall of fame because the story of his crimes didn't provide what we needed most, and what we make people into icons for giving us. He didn't give us the foil-biting pleasure of learning the details of something terrible that was happening beyond daily life, and beyond the family. What can you do with the story of a hell that was hidden in plain sight? Stories like that ask us to see our world differently, but serial killer stories—or at least the ones we tell and retell—make the light of home seem warmer and brighter, and the world beyond seem darker and scarier and less worth going out into.[5]

On May 7, 1972, after years of cruising the areas around Santa Cruz, California, and dreaming of killing and possessing women, Ed Kemper picked up two Fresno State students, Mary Ann Pesce and Anita Luchessa, who were hitchhiking from Berkeley to Stanford.

---

5. Of course, there are also plenty of exceptions. Simmons avoided becoming a national obsession, but others don't: Scott Peterson and Chris Watts are perhaps the most recent, and striking, examples. "The husband did it" stories are also a staple of true crime TV, and they're much more abundant on Oxygen than they are in the national news, which doesn't cater to a majority-female viewership.

Pesce tried to talk to Kemper, to ask him about his problems; to get him to see her, maybe, as human. He murdered them both, later saying he "felt that they were old enough to know better than to do the things they were doing… out there hitchhiking, when they had no reason or need to. They were flaunting in my face the fact that they could do any damn thing they wanted, and that society is as screwed up as it is.

"So that wasn't a prime reason for them being dead," Kemper continued. "It was just something that would get me a little uptight, the thought of that, them feeling so safe in a society where I didn't feel safe."

VI.

I am woman, watch me grow, see me standing toe to toe / as I spread my loving arms across the land / but I'm still an embryo with a long, long way to go / until I make my brother understand
—Helen Reddy, "I Am Woman," 1972

You know if someone came in here, they wouldn't believe what they'd see? You and me with long faces plunged into despair because we found out a man didn't kill his wife. We're two of the most frightening ghouls I've ever known.
—*Rear Window*, 1954

Me: brutally murdered and found dumped on the side of the highway

Two 35yr old women with a podcast: ok murder muffins we got a real oopy goopy spoopy story for you today!

Squarespace ad: ARE YOU LOOKING TO EXPAND Y
—@randyshart, Twitter, 2022

reported missing, the BAU attempts to determine whether or not the crimes were committed by a Satanic cult. Reid confides in his teammates about his battle with a series of recurring nightmares.

Season 1, episode 15, "Unfinished Business"
A notorious Philadelphia, Pennsylvania serial killer seemingly resurfaces after an eighteen-year absence, but with differing methods and older victims, and sends a taunting letter to retired FBI profiler Max Ryan. The BAU struggles to determine if this is a copycat, or if the killer has resumed his killing spree.

Season 1, episode 22,
"The Fisher King, Part 1"
When each individual BAU member receives a mysterious message while on bureau-mandated vacation, the team suspects they have become pawns in an elaborate fantasy game and sets out to identify a budding serial killer with a deadly fixation on Arthurian legend.

Season 2, episode 7, "North Mammon"
When three Pennsylvania teenage girls are abducted on the night of a pep rally, the BAU finds themselves forced to profile an entire town. JJ struggles with personal demons and the team continues to reel from Elle's abrupt departure.

Season 3, episode 2, "In Name and in Blood"
With Gideon missing, Hotch transferring, and Prentiss resigning, Strauss and the remaining members of the BAU set out to track down a Milwaukee, Wisconsin spree killer who cuts women's hearts out with a chisel.

Season 3, episode 19, "Tabula Rasa"
When a suspected Roanoke, Virginia serial killer wakes up from a coma and insists he doesn't remember the crimes he committed four years earlier, the BAU relies on brain fingerprinting to determine if his claims are true.

Season 4, episode 8, "Masterpiece"
When a narcissistic psychopath (Jason Alexander) obsessed with the fibonacci sequence confesses to killing seven people and claims that five more will die, the BAU attempts to locate his latest victims before time runs out. Meanwhile, Todd struggles to deal with the fact that the team does not yet trust her.

Season 4, episode 13, "Bloodline"
When a Harvest, Alabama couple is stabbed to death in their home and their daughter is abducted, the BAU determines the crime was

committed by a Romani family enacting a ritual aimed at acquiring wives for growing sons.

Season 5, episode 5, "Cradle to Grave"
When three Albuquerque, New Mexico women are abducted, impregnated, and strangled to death minutes after giving birth, the BAU sets out to track down a serial killer with an unusual motivation. Meanwhile, Hotch starts giving Morgan additional duties after receiving a surprise visit from Section Chief Strauss.

Season 5, episode 6, "The Eyes Have It"
With Morgan officially replacing Hotch as Unit Chief, the BAU sets out to profile and track down an Oklahoma City, Oklahoma serial killer who removes his victims' eyes and keeps them as souvenirs.

Season 6, episode 14, "Sense Memory"
The BAU returns to Los Angeles, California, to determine a serial killer's bizarre agenda after three women are abducted, drowned in methanol, and found with a piece of skin removed from their right foot. Meanwhile, Morgan notices a drastic change in Prentiss' behavior.

Season 7, episode 2, "Proof"
When two Durant, Oklahoma women are sexually assaulted and blinded with sulfuric acid, the BAU searches for a killer determined to exact revenge against a face from his past. Meanwhile, JJ confronts Reid about his recent behavior and Rossi organizes a team cooking lesson.

Season 7, episode 20, "The Company"
When Morgan's older sister gets into a car accident while attempting to follow a woman who eerily resembles their presumed-dead cousin Cindi, the BAU juggle reopening the case into her disappearance and tracking down a sexual sadist involved in a sadomasochistic ring.

Season 8, episode 16, "Carbon Copy"
When two Philadelphia, Pennsylvania nurses are found exsanguinated with their eyelids removed, the BAU suspects the crimes were committed by "The Replicator" (Mark Hamill) and sets out to prevent him from striking again. Meanwhile, Blake struggles with her personal demons after learning Strauss wants to make amends for her past actions.

Season 8, episode 24, "The Replicator"
When "The Replicator" hacks into Garcia's computer system, kills Strauss by breaking into her hotel room and forcing her to drink ecstasy-laced wine, and leaves Hotch a taunting message, the team juggles mourning the loss of one of their

"What a remarkable creature," Dr. Elliott Leyton writes in *Hunting Humans: The Rise of the Modern Multiple Murderer*, "was Edmund Emil Kemper III"; and this is certainly one way to put it. Kemper was remarkable, Leyton goes on, "not only in that his murders combined two usually separate homicidal themes—killing both relatives *and* young women—but also in his personal attributes. He was immense… Yet this was no deranged Frankenstein's monster, for his IQ measured a gifted 136… His mind perceived the world clearly and conventionally… We must pay serious attention to Kemper."

This was the passage that finally made me realize what Leyton's breathless tone has been reminding me of: the satirically imagined murder "connoisseur" who narrates Thomas De Quincey's "On Murder Considered as One of the Fine Arts." The essay, first published in *Blackwood's Magazine* in 1827, could have been written today. Addressing an audience of his fellow enthusiasts, De Quincey's speaker muses that "the truth is… relatively to others of their class, both a thief and an ulcer may have infinite degrees of merit. They are both imperfections, it is true; but to be imperfect being their essence, the very greatness of their imperfection becomes their perfection."

This speech is being delivered to us in the luxurious quarters of a Regency-era gentlemen's club: the kind of place where, as a London city guide put it a few decades later, the upper crust went "to lose a fortune at a sitting, and the next day enjoy a dainty dinner, drink their three bottles each, and afterwards make great speeches in the House of Commons." At White's, perhaps the best-known and most exclusive of all the clubs (and one that remains in operation, and refuses entry to women, to this day), "Lord Carlisle lost £11,000 in one night, and another gamester actually lost £34,000, but going on, recovered the greater part. The members betted heavily on everything—how long an old gentleman would live, whether a beauty of the day would be married within a certain period, or whether she would make a faithful wife when she was married. One member was mad or drunk enough to bet £1,500 that a man could live twelve hours under water, and another member was mad or drunk enough to take the bet. A reckless sot was induced to make the experiment; of course he died, the bet was lost, and nobody was hanged for this playing at murder."

The members of De Quincey's club don't seem to be up to anything quite so sinister. Rather than betting on the lives of the poor, they are gourmands of the murder story, and they acknowledge that they possess extremely refined taste. "People begin to see," De Quincey's narrator says proudly, "that something more goes to the composition of a fine murder than two blockheads to kill and be killed—a knife—a purse—and a dark lane. Design, gentlemen, grouping, light and shade, poetry, sentiment, are now deemed indispensable to attempts of this nature." This is also the voice, I think, of the modern true-crime enthusiast: the countless tweets and memes and merch that people use to proclaim their "love," ha ha, of murder. Consider the following tweets:

> if I'm ever murdered, I don't want a candlelight vigil. i want

two hilarious friends to make a podcast about it

If they want me to get Disney+ Mickey better start solving some cold cases real quick.

Hear me out a party bus but it picks up other moms and we get to sleep while it drives around playing true crime podcasts and nobody talks to us or asks us for anything

At any free moment, I am watching true crime documentaries or listening to death podcasts. In unrelated news, my husband said he's uncomfortable disagreeing with me.

What feels new, maybe—although it isn't—is not true crime media as a whole, but this kind of self-awareness about it: to call a podcast *My Favorite Murder* is to show that you understand the ghoulishness of your own interest. But to point it out is also to forgive it, or at least to find solidarity in that common ground. The women who now feel comfortable celebrating their love of true crime seem also to be finding comfort in the idea that they know what kind of story they are in, and understanding a story means you can follow its rules. And I'm not trying to exclude myself from this mindset, this way of existing. I understand it because I do it, because I grew up doing it; because even now, if I am with a friend and we agree to split up and meet back somewhere in an hour, I think: *And that was the last time she was seen alive.* Sometimes I think it about myself, sometimes about my

friend, sometimes about both of us. I think it not because I believe it will happen, but because if I think of it first, it can't happen; because if I understand the story, I can beat it. I can outwit the serial killer. I can see to the final page. And it would all work perfectly if I really did live in a true crime book. But I don't.

It's hard for me to condemn true crime fandom, and not just because it's been such a huge part of my own life. It feels like condemning the desire to eat Triscuits. And as gross and voyeuristic as it can get, the female-consumer-driven true crime media of today has never grossed me out nearly as much as books by male authors like Elliott Leyton, which sometimes reveal much more about the author than his subject. In one passage, Leyton describes the (now largely forgotten) serial killer Christopher Wilder, who "abducted eleven beautiful and elegant women" and "[subjected] them to electric shocks and other tortures before killing them," but whose "motivation," Leyton argues, "was only sexual."

This is the kind of passage that makes me wonder if men actually know what sex is, and if their own fascination with serial killers has to do with the fact that they see themselves in them. To say that Wilder could have satisfied his urges by frequenting sex workers, as Leyton helpfully suggests, seems like a misreading of either sex or Wilder or both: if you abduct women, torture them, and kill them, you're getting something you can't access in a consensual encounter. You are getting—I think—the experience not just of dominance but of ownership, of ultimate control. You own a woman.

own and identifying the motive behind the stalker-turned-serial killer's twisted spree.

Season 9, episode 18, "Rabid"
When three sets of human remains are excavated from a shallow grave outside Milwaukee, Wisconsin, the BAU attempts to track down a killer who infects his victims with rabies and films them as their symptoms worsen. Meanwhile, Garcia and Reid juggle preparing for an upcoming fitness test and keeping their plans secret from Morgan.

Season 10, episode 6, "If the Shoe Fits"
When two Missoula, Montana college students are stabbed to death, the BAU sets out to track down a female serial killer who believes she is an iconic fairy-tale character. Meanwhile, JJ struggles to come to terms with her suppressed feelings about a family tragedy.

Season 10, episode 15, "Scream"
When several Diamond Bar, California women are abducted and tortured, the BAU sets out to catch a killer who witnessed profound abuse as a child. Meanwhile, Kate becomes concerned when her niece Meg makes a date with a boy she met online.

Season 10, episode 23, "The Hunt"
When Meg and her best friend are abducted while preparing to meet who they think is a teenage boy, the BAU hunts for a predator connected to an online human trafficking ring that caters to serial killers.

Season 11, episode 10, "Future Perfect"
The BAU returns to Florida after two people are found dead in St. Augustine and find themselves profiling a killer who performs gruesome medical experiments on his victims in an attempt to find a cure for a mysterious disease. Meanwhile, Garcia grows stir-crazy as the search for the hit man network continues.

Season 12, episode 5, "The Anti-Terror Squad"
When three of the four members of a family from Winona, Minnesota are gunned down in their sleep, the BAU sets out to determine if the sole survivor was behind the killings or if she was deliberately spared. Meanwhile, Garcia attempts to find the perfect gift for Alvez's dog.

Season 13, episode 17, "The Capilanos"
When a Guymon, Oklahoma man is stabbed to death during a home invasion and his seven-year-old son claims a man dressed as a circus clown killed him, the BAU attempts to determine if the child's statement is true or not.

Season 14, episode 7, "Twenty Seven"
When three people in the Washington metropolitan area are hospitalized with life-threatening injuries after being attacked with a machete, the BAU works with the local field office to track down a pair of spree killers driven to take a life every twenty-seven minutes.

Season 15, episode 1, "Under the Skin"
When mutilated bodies appear in the Washington [DC] metropolitan area, Rossi becomes convinced they are the work of Everett Lynch (Michael Mosley), otherwise known as "The Chameleon," the serial killer who nearly killed him and then disappeared. Meanwhile, Reid and JJ struggle in dealing with an awkward situation.

Season 15, episode 6, "Date Night"
When a father and daughter are kidnapped in Washington, DC, Reid is forced into another confrontation with hit woman Cat Adams (Aubrey Plaza), which threatens his date plans with Maxine.

Season 15, episode 10, "And in the End"
With Reid in the hospital from a brain injury caused by the BAU's standoff with Lynch, the rest of the team continues their hunt for Lynch, which leads to a violent and climactic final confrontation. Meanwhile, Rossi contemplates retirement, while Garcia makes a life-changing decision that will alter the course of the BAU's future forever.

What I notice when I read through this list—aside from the fact that the person or persons responsible for writing these synopses is extremely fond of the word *juggle*—is how the show started off as a fairly straightforward police procedural, and gradually turned into a prime-time soap opera set in a world where every fifth person is a serial killer. It's weird to call the show's first episodes "realistic" or "low-key": even the pilot ends with Gideon running into an active serial killer because he happened to stop for gas on a scenic drive (Inigo Montoya has one nemesis; Jason Gideon has dozens). But something interesting happens after the first season: the writers seem simply to have run out of actual serial killers to use as inspiration.

As the seasons progress, *Criminal Minds* moves away from the stories that true crime is generally stuck with—the man who sexually tortures woman after woman for reasons he never really tries to articulate—and into a gory wonderland. Simply murdering strangers is not enough. Like Las Vegas casinos, every killer has a theme: the eyeball guy, the Fibonacci guy, the rabies guy. The serial killers in *Criminal Minds* make me think of the monologue from *The Kids in the Hall* where

And it's hard to think that serial killers like Wilder came up with this idea all by themselves. America has never quite accepted the idea that women aren't a commodity, or that a man's ability to attract and control women isn't essential to his validity as a man. To say that a man abducts and possesses women because he wants to have sex is to say that sex is possession, or that sex is indistinguishable from rape. This kind of writing worries me more than anything said by an actual serial killer.

True crime media made for or by women rarely reveals this kind of absurdity; it reveals other absurdities instead. Regardless of its actual demographic, mass-market true crime seems aimed almost exclusively at white women, and rarely mentions any other kind of victim. You can't understand the rules of the story if no one bothers to tell a story about you. True crime tells middle-class cis white women in particular that we are in danger, but that our murders, if they happen, will matter to someone, will leave a tear in the fabric, will seem *unfair*. It reassures us that we are endangered: that we are, still, the real victims here—not sex workers, not trans women, not women of color—even if nothing has happened to us *yet*. It reminds us that men see us as possessions, and lets us forget that Black Americans were literally defined as less than human by the law, and in many ways remain so. To identify as a victim, or as someone defined by your potential to become one, is also a handy way of erasing your own power. Or maybe, even more meaningfully, it's a way of confessing that there is only one form of power you believe you will ever have.

VII.

He was not inconsequential. Not anymore.

—*William Goldman, No Way to Treat a Lady, 1964*

Jack the Ripper became a legend by offering a gold mine to journalists; the Son of Sam terrorized New York City during a tabloid circulation war, and was considerate enough to generate even more coverage by writing to journalist Jimmy Breslin. The letters that we think of when we think of Jack the Ripper—"They say I'm a doctor now, ha ha"—could have been written by the killer, or, as many have theorized, by a journalist trying to gin up a story. (Looking beyond the ones commonly attributed to Saucy Jacky, the vast majority of them must have been: the police and the press received hundreds.) There was nothing new about Jack the Ripper's murders, but there was novelty in his apparent interaction with the press. Ever since, we have loved stories of serial killers who seem, in a way, to be killing *for us*: to be motivated not by their own unavoidable compulsions but by a desire to shock the public, to terrorize a city, to outwit the police, and to bring us together.

In the stories we tell, serial killers are driven by a desire for celebrity and power, but relatively few seem to have fixated on this kind of transaction—killing for headlines—as a significant motive. In our fictional serial killer stories, we have avoided learning much about our subject, and instead told on ourselves. We have revealed the easiest way to get our attention.

I don't know if someone who would

have been a serial killer a few decades ago would be a mass shooter today; I don't think that's knowledge any of us can have. But it's hard to think of the shift between then and now without thinking about Eric Harris and Dylan Klebold, the perpetrators of the Columbine massacre, who, Rachel Monroe writes, "had no intention of being ciphers," and spent "their final days… [debating] which director would film the story of their lives, Quentin Tarantino or Steven Spielberg." On the morning of the attack, Monroe relates, Harris left a recorded message for his parents: "People will die because of me. It will be a day that will be remembered forever."

The most haunting thing about all this, to me, is that Harris and Klebold were right: they, too, understood the rules of the story they were in. Their code phrase for the day of the shooting was *NBK: Natural Born Killers*. This wasn't a reference to a movie about a mass shooting, a concept that barely existed at the time, and of which there are still, comparatively, very few fictional depictions. It was a reference to Oliver Stone's movie about a pair of serial killers in love, and the media obsession they inspire. We show our own hand in the stories we tell, and in the '90s, we told story after story in which the reward for killing was attention, fascination, and a kind of immortality. We imagined serial killers being motivated by the desire for fame, and few of them seem to have been. But this behavior seems remarkably widespread among mass shooters, and they didn't figure it out all by themselves.

VIII.

Investigators / and forensic experts / unravel my life, / Assemble / the be-
ginning, / Middle, / End, / Assuring / that all will / be / Remembered, / told, / shared.

You tell me / hands and other / weapons wait, / but there are rules / I can follow— / park close / to the door, / buy mace / to spray / in the determined eyes / of ursine men, / step my runs / in zigs / and zags— / you are / Scheherazade / weaving beautiful / Tales that keep / me coming / back for the beginning, / for the middle, / for the end, / in a world without beginnings / without middles, / with endless endings.

—Amelia Tenne, "Ode to the Murder Show"

When you guys pick and choose that stuff, it demeans the work. What's important was, there were people getting killed, and you saw some breasts.

—Danny Steinmann, director of *Friday the 13th Part V: A New Beginning*

Samuel Little died in prison, of COVID, in December 2020, and the truth of whatever he did is now gone too. In retrospect, the news of his alleged crimes broke at perhaps the last moment that serial killers could be imagined as a statistically meaningful risk to American life. In the time of COVID, the right to invite death into your home and to spread it around to others became, somehow, the context of a presidential election. As far as I can tell, Americans love killing one another, and always have, but serial killers make us look a little better. The United States was built on the bones and blood of endless murder, of slavery, and of genocide; crucially, the FBI's

David Foley plays a burned-out serial killer having a tea break: "The funny thing about killing—after the first time you've killed, the second time, it's easy. The third time you start to get cocky, so you've gotta be careful… and oh, by around the seventh time, you're likely to feel like you're in a bit of a rut, want to get artistic with it, you know. Start cutting off the middle toe of each victim so you'll be known as 'The Middle Toe Murderer.' But at that point, I don't know, I think that's showboating. You know, you've got to ask yourself: Who am I doing this for? Am I doing it for myself, or the press?"

The hugeness of the American serial killer demographic in the world according to *Criminal Minds* becomes apparent when, at the end of season ten, we learn that serial killers are abundant enough to create a customer base for a sustainable human trafficking business. And it's also important to point out, I think, that this story line asks us to imagine a world—as Showtime's *Dexter* and NBC's *Hannibal* did around the same period—where serial killers are not maladjusted loners who often seem to feel they have very little ability to connect with other human beings, but actually form a hidden social class, visible all around us, if only we care to look.

I grew up doing my math homework while watching *Copycat* on TNT, which seemed to air it about four times a week between 2001 and 2005. It's a movie that seems deeply silly to me now, but was everything I wanted when I was fourteen. In it, Dr. Helen Hudson (Sigourney Weaver)—a serial killer expert who has been agoraphobic ever since a serial killer (Harry Connick Jr.) almost killed her after she delivered a lecture on serial killers—helps San Francisco detective MJ Monahan (Holly Hunter) catch a serial killer who is imitating other serial killers in the order in which Helen named them in her lecture on serial killers. The movie assumes two things, both of which I found extremely comforting: (1) you can make a good enough living studying serial killers to afford a San Francisco apartment so huge that you won't even notice when one of them is hiding in it; and (2) serial killers are a learnable, knowable, and ultimately totally predictable group. They are utterly different from normal people, so normal people can master them as a field of knowledge and taxonomize them accordingly.

The great dream of criminal profiling—which *Criminal Minds* uses in a much more restrained way than many actual experts in the field—is to be able to study a crime scene and envision the person who left it behind. In reality, the efforts of both FBI profilers and criminal profilers are sometimes breathtakingly accurate and sometimes utterly useless, or even disastrously misleading. The *science* in *Behavioral Science Unit* (*science* became *analysis* in

1997) was developed by FBI agents Robert Ressler and John Douglas, who interviewed thirty-six serial killers in the 1970s. "The more they learned," Malcolm Gladwell wrote in a 2007 *New Yorker* article, "the more precise the associations became. If the victim was white, the killer would be white. If the victim was old, the killer would be sexually immature." The methodology Ressler and Douglas developed based on these interviews is used by criminal profilers to this day. But, Gladwell argues, someone trained in this discipline could produce a profile of a killer that seems accurate in the same way that horoscopes do: "so full of unverifiable and contradictory and ambiguous language that it could support virtually any interpretation." When the BTK Killer was still at large, Gladwell writes, "the best minds in the F.B.I. [gave] the Wichita detectives a blueprint for their investigation. Look for an American male with a possible connection to the military. His I.Q. will be above 105… He won't be comfortable with women. But he may have women friends. He will be a lone wolf. But he will be able to function in social settings. He won't be unmemorable. But he will be unknowable. He will be either never married, divorced, or married, and if he was or is married his wife will be younger or older. He may or may not live in a rental, and might be lower class, upper lower class, lower middle class or middle class." And this description, as vague as it was, still managed to get a lot wrong.

All of which makes sense if you think about it. The hard part is thinking about it. When I was a teenager, watching *Copycat* and *The Silence of the Lambs* and reading Ann Rule, it never occurred to me to question the wisdom of a system that involves a guy taking a good hard look at a crime scene and throwing out some guesses. But the guesses are made into something more real by the office he represents, and by the fact that we want to live in a world where someone, somewhere, just *knows*.

The fact is, *Criminal Minds* was made for people like me: teenage girls who trusted authority a little too much, and who had their friends over to watch *Snapped* marathons on Oxygen. (Finally, a show where husbands are murdered *by* their wives, instead of murdering them!) Oxygen, for what it's worth, has had an interesting trajectory as well: in the beginning, it was simply marketed as "Fresh Television for Women" (*Kate & Allie* reruns, *Inhale Yoga with Steve Ross*)—something a little cooler and more Gen X–focused than Lifetime, "Televison for Women," which was a gallery of TV movies about women alternately stalking and being stalked, murdering and being murdered. Remember the one where Tracey Gold almost dies of anorexia? Remember the one where Tracey Gold is murdered by Courtney Thorne-Smith?

current classification of a serial killer stipulates "unlawful" killings, because otherwise, a lot of cops and federal agents would be serial killers too.

Before it hunted serial killers, the FBI busied itself with projects like trying to blackmail Martin Luther King Jr. into suicide, and to call that anything other than attempted murder seems pretty academic; to look at the FBI's collaboration with the Chicago Police Department in the killing of Fred Hampton and call it anything other than murder would just be a lie. That I grew up thinking of the FBI as the good guys who caught serial killers, rather than as the organization that tried to stamp out the civil rights movement, is the result of many things, the limits of my own education chief among them. But serial killers—both the ones who were caught and the theoretical ones we could imagine were still out there—had a lot to offer the FBI, and the American legal system as a whole. David Schmid writes in *Natural Born Celebrities* that the serial killer is "the figure that, in a sense, [was] the FBI's greatest ally." A champion needs a monster to fight.

These are real crimes, and so are the people who commit them; what I wonder is why we focus so relentlessly on just one corner of the picture, as awful as it may be. In America, the most common cause of death for pregnant women is homicide. Isn't this just as horrifying? Isn't it worse? But to develop a cultural fixation on men who kill their pregnant partners is to acknowledge a problem bigger than a few inhuman specimens, born beyond redemption. It is to acknowledge that serial killers terrify us not because they are so different from normal people,

but because they are so similar to normal men. They exonerate "normal" American violence because they will always be worse. They drive women back in from the open road and into the arms of a more probable killer.

"The golden age of the serial killer" coincided almost exactly with the rise and fall of women's liberation, and the killers whose victims we paid the most attention to were the ones who killed, and usually sexually assaulted, "nice girls": pretty, white, middle-class college students, the exceptions to the general rule that women are disposable. Their continued deaths or disappearances looked bad for the police, which made the idea of the serial killer as a mastermind more attractive: you can't blame yourself for failing to take down a genius, or someone motivated by an evil so pure it seems like its own kind of protection. This is the serial killer we're talking about when we wonder where the serial killers have gone: the kind whose activities we notice because we care about the people they kill, even if we care about them largely as the prized property of the ruling class. These are the specimens we can imagine as truly inhuman, and they changed us forever, perhaps because we allowed them to, because they gave us so much in return. Serial killers proved both that women couldn't survive alone in the world and that prisons were too comfortable, sentences too light, and trials too biased in favor of the defense. None of these things were ever true, and the latter beliefs have gotten much less true since the 1970s. Serial killers helped us learn to see prisons as places that sealed their inhuman evil away from the rest of the world, and forget that they contain human beings.

Are there fewer serial killers than there used to be, or are we playing that old trick on ourselves and remembering the past based on what we paid the most attention to? We do catch serial killers today, and sometimes they even make good copy: Israel Keyes fit the methodical-mastermind role better than most serial killers ever have; Shawn Grate got his clueless girlfriend to clean up a victim's blood, then used the same victim's ring to propose. This is, by any metric, fantastically cold-blooded, but I had never heard of this story before I researched this piece, and I bet you hadn't, either.

Keyes and Grate are white, but many of the serial killers who were discovered or apprehended in the past decade or so have been Black, and that feels related too. We love nice white girls as victims, but we love nice white boys as serial killers even more. White America loves masterminds, but we seem to think only white people are capable of playing this role; a Black serial killer is—to quote *Veep*—as useless to us as a forty-year-old woman. Samuel Little was Black, as were many of his victims, and the cynic in me says that the only reason any of them were scooped out of obscurity is because he vaulted to the top of the victim count podium. The most dramatic serial killer collar in recent memory was that of Joseph DeAngelo, a retired cop who Americans know better as the Golden State Killer. But the drama of his capture, meaningfully, was connected not to any recent crimes, but to murders and sexual assaults he had committed through the '70s and '80s. Were these men so compelling to us not because their identification made us any safer, but

because they seemed like remnants of a lost time?

If America loves serial killers, and I think we do, we love them most when they feel a little far away, something to joke about or stuff our real fears beneath. Maybe we want to believe that we have hunted them to extinction, that all the money we keep funneling into law enforcement and incarceration really *has* made us safer, and this is the proof: the extinguishing of a raging inferno that never really was. "By the 1980s, with the encouragement of the FBI," Scott Sayare writes in another *Guardian* article, about a French serial killer expert who turned out to be a fraud (and a bit of a serial killer fanboy), "the American news media had begun to speak of an 'epidemic' of serial murder, one that claimed thousands of lives each year. After pushing this theory for several years, however, the bureau quietly withdrew its claims: serial killers are now thought to account for less than 1% of homicides." This feeling of a precipitous change, in other words, is connected not to serial killers themselves, but to the world we learn to imagine we live in.

The numbers we now have, as much as we can trust them, do suggest a downward trajectory, but not an exponential one. Mike Aamodt's serial killer database shows 1987 to be the year with the most active American serial killers: 189. In 2015, there were 30 active serial killers. Which is fewer, but not none. And, without hazarding a guess that thousands of serial killers are quietly at work, it's worth pointing out that whether or not a serial killer is active in a given year is sometimes in the eye of the beholder. How many serial killers currently go unnoticed because they

Remember the one where Tracey Gold blinds a college administrator so she can keep using the scholarship of the girl she murdered? What I'm saying is, "Television for Women" has a history of turning into the true crime channel. Recent Oxygen shows include *Florida Man Murders*, *Framed by the Killer*, and *The Real Murders of Orange County*. *Snapped* is still going strong.

In *Savage Appetites: Four True Stories of Women, Crime, and Obsession*, her book on true crime and the women who both shape it and are shaped by it, Rachel Monroe describes a trip to CrimeCon, the fan convention that Oxygen started organizing after it officially became a true crime channel in 2017. "Oxygen shows feature a stable of authoritative crime experts," Monroe writes, "mostly men with handsome-haggard faces and law enforcement experience. They're real people, but they always seem half in character… There seemed to be at least one of them on every true crime show, these inexplicably sexy cop-dads. One of them, former FBI profiler Jim Clemente, wearing a cowboy hat, strode out onto the stage to a round of huge cheers." Clemente also worked as a consultant on *Criminal Minds,* doing so, his website says, "because it was an opportunity to teach; he says the collaboration works well, creating an accurate picture of the BAU for the public." At CrimeCon, Clemente addresses the audience of "a couple thousand women and a smattering of men," asking: "Why are *you* here? Do you love the genre? Do you want to solve a cold case?… I have a theory. You want to learn so you can protect those you love. It's a very altruistic goal." Later on, an Oxygen employee offers Monroe a different insight into the audience for true crime TV. "People leave it on all night," he tells her. "They fall asleep to it. People tell me all the time that they find these shows soothing."

I am one of the people who fall asleep to these shows, specifically to *Law & Order* and *Forensic Files*, but *Criminal Minds* can do the trick as well. This is the same show that Mandy Patinkin said he had to leave because "it was very destructive to my soul," and it remains to be seen what it's doing to *my* soul: What does it do to a person to watch women being raped and murdered "every night, every day, week after week, year after year"? What does it do to a country?

Maybe my favorite episode summary, out of those I've listed above, is the one for "Proof," the second episode of season seven: "When two Durant, Oklahoma women are sexually assaulted and blinded with sulfuric acid, the BAU searches for a killer determined to exact revenge against a face from his past. Meanwhile, JJ confronts Reid about his recent behavior and Rossi organizes a team cooking lesson." "When… Meanwhile" is a are "smart" enough to kill Indigenous women, Black women, brown women, poor women, trans women, and sex workers? How many of them don't even bother to kill women, despite the cultural consensus that this is their job?

Something almost too obvious to notice may be at work here, too: true crime media is, by definition, about the past. If it were about a present danger, it would just be called the news. Americans first started hearing about "serial killers" in the 1970s, but it was only in the 1990s, after the massive success of both Jonathan Demme's adaptation of *The Silence of the Lambs* and Dr. Robert Hare's *Without Conscience: The Disturbing World of the Psychopaths among Us,* that serial killers took over the entertainment industry. 1991, the year *The Silence of the Lambs* became the fourth top-grossing movie of the year—before going on to sweep the Oscars—was also, revealingly, the year Jeffrey Dahmer was apprehended in Milwaukee, after one of his victims, Tracy Edwards, escaped his apartment and got help. It was, yet more revealingly, the second time this had happened: the first victim who got away, fifteen-year-old Konerak Sinthasomphone, ran into the street, and, with the help of two Black women, found the police, who gamely returned him to the custody of his killer. There had been no ongoing manhunt for Dahmer before he was caught. The police hadn't been bothered by the disappearances of his victims, few of whom were white and many of whom were gay. No one had been looking for him. But he was, it seems, the last of the serial killers we lament the disappearance of: the last of the household names.

After Dahmer, the most famous serial killers would be, for the most part, fictitious. And perhaps this was also because, by the end of the '90s, no real person could live up to the myth. To be a serial killer, fiction suggested, you had to be a genius (*The Silence of the Lambs*) and a philosopher (*Se7en*); it helped if you owned an actual dungeon (*Kiss the Girls*), but a portfolio of fabulous San Francisco real estate would do (*Basic Instinct*). You couldn't just go out there and follow your instincts: you had to meticulously plan your murders and perhaps pay homage to your mentors (*Copycat*) to get ahead. By the time NBC's *Hannibal* rolled around, audiences had spent so many years with the serial killer as arty mastermind that it didn't seem ridiculous to have a serial killer who posed preserved human bodies in a massive "mural," or one who lobotomized her victims and filled their skulls with beehives. ("Who am I doing this for? Am I doing it for myself, or the press?") At a certain point, I think, actual serial killers got left behind by their fictional counterparts. And maybe that's a good thing. The real serial killers of the world are as human as the rest of us: damaged, dangerous, and often pretty boring. They aren't prophets. They have no wisdom to share with us. All we can learn from them is how a human psyche can produce the compulsion to kill; and how the killers who escape society's notice can reveal not their own genius, but our deepest flaws.

If we have moved on from truly fearing the serial killer, though, then maybe it's because we have so much else to be afraid of, and can finally focus on the enemies we need to fight. The past few years have seen the political rise of undisguised white nationalism in America; have shown us that our country is unable or unwilling to do anything about mass shootings; have shown us police officers that make serial killers look like amateurs. These forces, these killings, were always present, always happening, always there for white Americans to see. But there were so many serial killers; we were so busy, and so endangered, that we couldn't look away. Can we look away now, or will we just keep retelling our fictions? ✱

---

poetic form akin to the haiku, and by this point in the show's run, we know how it's working here, and how it will let us fall asleep. When serial killers torture and murder their victims, BAU agents appear and stop them in their tracks, and meanwhile have little adventures, tell jokes, cook, laugh, and bond. Every week there's a new serial killer, but that's to be expected, and over time it becomes background, the everyday existence of the characters we love, whom all this is really about.

Something that's hard to explain about *Criminal Minds*, and that the discordance of these summaries shows—sulfuric acid, cooking lesson—is its sweetness. We get inured to the unsubs, the stabbings, the flayings, the dungeons, the rabies, the baby farming, and the hearts cut out with chisels, through sheer repetition; this is the world we live in, just like these are the characters we identify with. We get to hear two things we apparently want to be true: The world is a terrifying place, evil beyond all hope of redemption, but we can still have love and joy and friendship in our own little world. And even if a serial killer abducts you or frames you for murder—both of which happen to poor Spencer Reid—your friends will help you get through the trauma. In an era of prestige TV shows that take pride in killing off fan favorites, or keeping audiences guessing until the end, the finale of *Criminal Minds* is about Agent Rossi deciding to retire from the BAU, throwing a party where everyone says goodbye, and then deciding not to retire after all. Then Garcia decides to leave the BAU and everyone gets to say goodbye again. A serial killer from Rossi's past returns, and the team handily defeats him, then goes straight back to talking about how much they all mean to one another. The show's writers thought about killing off a character in the finale, but couldn't bear to get rid of anyone, so they blew up the team's Learjet instead.

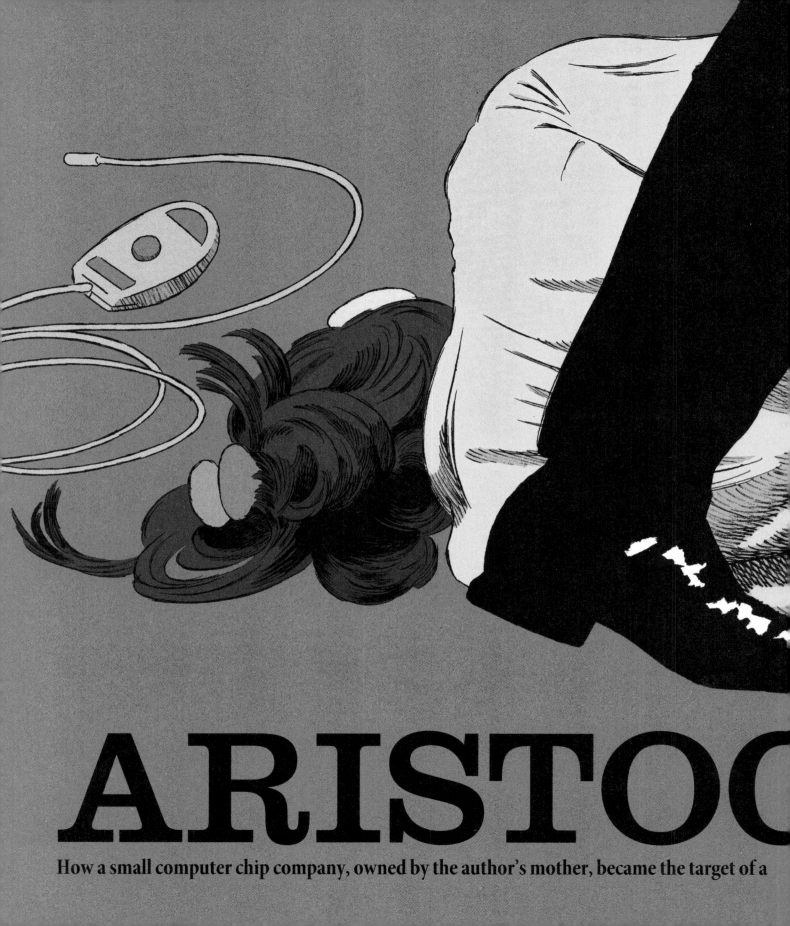

ARISTOC

How a small computer chip company, owned by the author's mother, became the target of a

RAT INC.

sprawling pan-Asian crime ring that operated throughout Silicon Valley   BY NATALIE SO

ILLUSTRATIONS BY *Andrea Settimo*

1.

On a Wednesday morning during an unbearable late-summer heat wave, I sat in the back seat of my mother's car, my three-month-old baby beside me, as we cruised along the 85, which runs from San Jose up to Mountain View. My mother was at the wheel, and we were on our way to pick up an assortment of Taiwanese snacks—taro cakes, red bean rice cakes, green mango sorbet, and shao bing—from an outpost of a Taiwanese specialty store called Combo Market. Outside, on the freeway, the tall, yellowed grasses and perennially faded shrubbery looked prehistoric, as if they had been there for decades unmoved.

We decided to take a short detour before picking up the food. My mother made her way toward the 237, and then exited onto Lawrence Expressway in Sunnyvale. "Mumu Hotspot," she murmured to herself, as we passed a new hot pot restaurant. We pulled into the parking lot of a nondescript one-story complex: a group of bitonal buildings, cream on top and taupe on the bottom. Each office was marked by a sign whose formatting must have been mandated by the property managers, because the company names were in all-caps, uniformly rendered in a bland and unstylish serif font. I looked around to see what types of businesses were here now: LE BREAD XPRESS, KINGDOM BRICK SUPPLY, BIOCERYX TECHNOLOGIES INC. One would not have guessed we were in Silicon Valley.

There was only one office that appeared empty, with a company placard that was blank. The door to that office was emblazoned with the numbers 1233 in white. When I peered in, I saw no one, no furniture, nothing. It was a small room that might have been a reception area once, with brown carpet that appeared at least a decade old. There were two closed doors adjacent to each other, one of which had a sign that read EMPLOY-EES ONLY. An ominous white camera blinked on the floor in the far corner, likely a deterrent for grifters and interlopers.

2.

Eight years ago, I began researching a story that took place at this very office in August of 1995. It was a story I'd heard many times as a child, though in far vaguer terms than are delineated below. The story went like this:

On a Friday morning, a Hong Kong woman named Grace arrived at work. Grace was tall and extremely thin, with a jutting chin and frizzy, permed, shoulder-length black hair. It was around 9:00 a.m., and two of her coworkers, a husband-and-wife couple named Irene and Paul, were outside the office waiting to be let in.

After Grace unlocked the office for the two of them, she realized she'd left something in the car. Upon approaching the office door a second time, she noticed two men in suits coming out the door of the neighboring company, Freshers Soft Frozen Lemonade, a wholesale distributor for ballparks and stadiums. They were also Asian, but darker-skinned than she was. As they approached her, one of them said, "We're here to see Steven." Grace told them that Steven no longer worked at the company. "Then can we see your boss?" they asked. They were insinuating that they were familiar with the company by giving Grace a name, but Grace was suspicious. Clients never showed up this early. "Could you come back later?" she asked.

One man pushed her into the back room, a warehouse-like space where all supplies and inventory were kept.

Instead of answering, the men moved closer to her—so close, in fact, that Grace noticed a large, distinctive mole on one man's chin, as she would later testify. They pushed her into the reception area of the office. The mole-marked man opened his suit jacket, pointed to what appeared to be a gun in the inner lining, and said to her, "You know what I want."

And she did—Grace had heard of things like this happening recently. People had been kidnapped. A man had been killed. Just a few days ago her coworkers had joked about getting robbed. These events were occurring with such frequency that at times they seemed banal, but even then, she had never imagined it would happen at her own workplace. Grace's boss had recently installed a new alarm system and distributed panic buttons to all her employees, but the men had cornered her so quickly that she'd had no time to act. "Don't do anything stupid," the men said. "This robbery is going to be covered by your insurance, anyway." Now Grace, Paul, Irene, and another coworker named Anna—who had arrived at the office shortly after the men confronted Grace—all lay face-down on the floor. Soon they would have their wrists and ankles bound with zip ties.

Except for Anna, because she was the only person besides their boss who knew where all the inventory was kept. This was a precaution taken in the event of a worst-case scenario—the kind of scenario that was happening now. One man pushed her into the back room, a warehouse-like space where all supplies and inventory were kept. Anna was a petite Taiwanese woman who spoke broken English. Later, she would recall that she was scared, but on instinct did not think these men were evil. They did not shout or scream or even raise their voices. Instead, they spoke in calm, measured tones. They were peculiar, she thought: more like businessmen than criminals.

Anna pulled out box after box as the man watched (the other stayed with the rest of the employees). These robbers knew exactly what they were looking for, because they had been scouting this office for days. They'd even made an appointment with the wholesale lemonade purveyor next door under the guise that they were interested in purchasing lemonade, so they could keep an eye on this very place. They knew a shipment had come in just a few days ago, and if they could find what they were looking for, they'd be making off with hundreds of thousands of dollars' worth of goods. After all, pound for pound, the loot they were after was more valuable than either heroin or cocaine.

The man who was watching Anna seemed frustrated, and he made a phone call. Anna heard him listing the items in the stockroom, a litany of model names. Not wanting to linger too long, the men grabbed several boxes and then left through the back loading dock, where a getaway car was waiting.

What in Silicon Valley at the time was so valuable, so hotly desired, that even gangs accustomed to trafficking drugs had started to take notice? What was at once easily transported, concealed, disposed of, and virtually untraceable? There was only one thing, which the Santa Clara deputy DA would later call "the dope of the '90s": computer chips.

Not until twenty years later would I learn just how frequently these robberies were taking place. Even though millions of dollars' worth of computer chips were stolen, this era of Silicon Valley would largely be forgotten. Computer hardware would eventually give way to the dot-com bubble, after which social media, the cloud, big data, and later, Bitcoin, NFTs, and other increasingly intangible technologies would come to the fore. But for a time, the boom of personal computing transformed Silicon Valley into the Wild West, a new frontier that drew every kind of speculator, immigrant, entrepreneur, and bandit, all lured by the possibilities of riches, success, and the promise of a new life. The Silicon Valley of the '90s was in many ways an expression of the quintessential American story, but an unexpected one: one that involved organized crime, narcotics trafficking, confidential informants, and Asian gangs. It is also part of my family history. Grace, as it turns out, is my aunt. And the company being robbed? It was my mother's.

3.

In 1989, Jim McMahon was a thirty-five-year-old mustachioed street cop working the Police Personnel Unit at the San Jose Police Department. He was also the only officer who brought his own laptop to work. The Toshiba T1000 in his possession consisted of a rectangular screen no taller than six inches and a plastic keyboard with cream and gray keys. When closed, the laptop could fit into a briefcase. The IBM Selectric typewriters that the police department used were slow and clunky. With the Toshiba, he could make corrections without white-out.

A captain named Ken Hawks took notice. One day, he called McMahon into his office. "We notice you carry a computer," he said. In Hawks's view, McMahon was tech savvy in a way the rest of the police department was not. If he owned a portable computer, how could he not be? Hawks's assumption was right in some sense. The son of an engineer employed by Lockheed, McMahon had grown up in nearby Cupertino, a few miles from Apple's headquarters. As a young boy, he had taken a keen interest in electronics. Shortly after he joined the police force at the age of twenty-one, he bought his first computer, a Radio Shack TRS-80 Model 1. He was what people now call an "early adopter." He had even taught himself to program and tinker with computer parts.

Hawks needed someone to run the High-Tech Crimes Detail, a one-man department that had never been particularly effective. Then, that one man transferred to a different division, looking for a retirement opportunity. This unit was not one McMahon had ever intended to work in. Among police cadres, it did not have the same cachet as, say, the Homicide Squad, the department McMahon had initially set his heart on. To his knowledge, there were no serial killers to catch or whodunnit mysteries to solve when dealing with high-tech crimes.

But unbeknownst to him, here in the heart of Silicon Valley in the late 1980s, computer-related crime was on the rise. Criminals were beginning to use computers for embezzlement and fraud, and pedophiles and pornographers had begun to digitize their operations as well. A July 1989 memo published by the US Department of Justice about computer crime investigations noted, "Police say they arrive at the scene of these criminal networks and discover computers in operation."

Captain Hawks gave McMahon no choice. If someone was going to investigate computer-related crimes, it should be the guy carrying the laptop—the guy, in McMahon's words, who "could speak 'tron." McMahon was given his pick of a partner and

two desks in the fraud unit, where he began fielding calls.

At the time that McMahon was conscripted to join the High-Tech Crimes Detail, the police department's understanding of computers was so poor that its officers often could not identify when a technology-related crime was being committed. Shortly after McMahon was transferred, he got a call from a patrol officer who had pulled over a man at a traffic stop. When asked what he was carrying in his car, the man said "paperweights." McMahon asked what was written on them. "'Hewlett-Packard' or something. It's 'twenty megabyte,'" said the officer. When McMahon arrived on the scene, he turned to the patrol officer and told him they weren't paperweights—they were hard drives.

Soon the number of calls to McMahon increased. An average day might consist of breaking into a suspect's encrypted computer or driving to the airport to help customs officials identify technological cargo coming in. There were thefts—many of them. People broke in to electronics stores; stockroom employees swiped extra disks and resold them. At one point, several hundred laser-jet printers went missing from Hewlett-Packard—millions of dollars' worth. McMahon later discovered that they were being packed into 18-wheelers by a prison gang, driven down to Los Angeles, and resold for fifty cents on the dollar. The high-tech crimes evidence room at San Jose police headquarters was beginning to fill up, littered with piles of stolen computers, hard drives, SIMM strips, and microprocessor chips.

Through the crimes that were being reported, McMahon started to

learn what was valuable—what thieves wanted to steal and what they could resell, which at that point was almost any piece of computer hardware. In the early '90s, computer hardware was the bread and butter of Silicon Valley, and global demand for it was starting to surge. In 1989, around 21 million personal computers were sold worldwide. Over the course of the '90s, that number would more than quadruple. By 1998, worldwide sales would reach 93 million.

In November 1993, McMahon received a call from the FBI. Four years after being assigned to the High-Tech Crimes Detail by Captain Hawks, McMahon had developed a reputation among law enforcement for his technological know-how. Most police departments did not yet have high-tech crime units, nor did the FBI. There had been a big robbery up in Tualatin, Oregon, on Halloween night, and the FBI wanted McMahon to investigate.

The site of the robbery was the manufacturing facility of OKI Semiconductor, a subsidiary of Japan's Oki Electric Industry Co. Five robbers in matching blue coveralls, masks, and balaclavas, armed with revolvers and automatic rifles, had entered the premises and attacked a security guard. They tied, gagged, and blindfolded twelve employees, and according to McMahon, they also pistol-whipped a few of them. After they took what they had come for, they fled in a van.

Upon arrival, McMahon noted how organized the robbery was. It looked as though it had been carefully orchestrated and executed, like a paramilitary operation. The thieves were, in his words, "pretty slick." Not only did they already know where the goods were located on site, but they were also familiar with the cargo, transport, and storage systems that OKI used. They didn't pilfer blindly, like men who had decided to rob the factory on a whim, but rather, they took specific items, a strategy that could have been deployed only with foresight and technical knowledge. An abandoned van found near the crime scene had been sprayed down with WD-40, precluding the collection of fingerprints or DNA. These robbers were not amateurs, McMahon deduced.

As was the case in the theft in Sunnyvale, the robbers had come for one thing only: computer chips. At the time of the robbery, law enforcement guessed that approximately $2 million worth of goods had been stolen. Later, they would discover that this number was closer to $9 million. (In 1993, this amount of money could have bought eighteen houses in Palo Alto. Now maybe just one.)

In many ways, computer chips made for the perfect plunder. They had an insanely high dollar-per-pound ratio, and were in heavy demand everywhere. The path from manufacturer to consumer was long and convoluted, often crossing an expansive gray market, with opportunities for interception all along the way. Criminal punishment for selling stolen property was far less severe than for drug dealing, thereby making computer parts a less risky enterprise. And, as Jim McMahon discovered when he joined the High-Tech Crimes Detail, police officers often lacked the technological fluency to recognize computer chips to begin with.

It wasn't the first time that McMahon had been called to investigate a computer chip robbery. By then, chip theft had become fairly common. But the kinds of theft McMahon was accustomed to seeing were either one-off burglaries or cases of missing inventory—the accumulation of many small petty thefts, likely by employees. This chip heist was different, in both scale and level of organization.

Of course, the sheer value of the stolen property was staggering. At the time, the OKI robbery was the largest theft of its kind. But it also marked the beginning of a trend in the world of technology-related crimes. Soon reports of chip heists like the one at OKI would make their way to McMahon's desk with increasing frequency, heists that were planned and executed swiftly and intelligently—almost always by gangs of Asian men.

4.

My mother heard about the OKI robbery shortly after it happened. In 1993, she was thirty years old. She ran a small company called Aristocrat Inc. that bought and sold computer chips, routing surpluses from suppliers to companies that needed them. She was married and living in Cupertino, just a few streets away from where McMahon grew up. In June of that year, she had given birth to a second daughter. I was two at the time. From the outside, there was nothing extraordinary about her: she was just an Asian immigrant working in the technology sector in the Bay Area.

Working in the computer industry had been a matter of time, place, and opportunity for my mother. Unlike her husband, my father, who was an engineer working on inkjet printers at Hewlett-Packard, she was not among the class of highly educated immigrants that accounted for nearly one-third of the Bay Area's scientific and engineering workforce in 1990. Those immigrants, like my father, had come to the States in the '80s for grad school, after which they were routed directly into tech companies in Silicon Valley. This was a fairly common, if not archetypal, route to ensuring a steady and often sizable income, which could then fulfill the promise of upward socioeconomic mobility.

My mother, on the other hand, was not an engineer, and in many ways was the antithesis of the stereotypical straight-A-earning Asian student. She had scored abysmally on the SATs and majored in studio art at Cal State, Long Beach. She was vocationally unequipped in a way that made any version of the immigrant success story seem completely out of reach for her. But by 1993, her knowledge of computer chips had swelled to an encyclopedic level. She knew the exact makes and models of the new chips on the market and how much they were worth. She knew where to buy them and where to sell them. And, most important, she knew how to make a profit off them. My parents always joked that my father was book-smart, but my mother was street-smart. While my father ruled by logic and reason, my mother led with intuition and honed instincts.

My mother is a petite woman at five feet, three inches tall. A friend who recently met her described her as "smiley and effervescent." For my entire life, she's maintained the exact same haircut, one that is somewhat universal among Asian moms: a chin-length bob with the ends curled in, always parted on the left side. Her hair—which is jet-black like mine, thick, with very few grays even now, at fifty-nine—frames full, youthful cheeks and dark, almond-shaped eyes, whose lids are tattooed with permanent eyeliner (for the sake of convenience, she has said). Her demure appearance belies the fact that she possesses the kind of boldness, persuasiveness, and doggedness that make her a force to be reckoned with, both as a mother and as a person of the world.

As a child, I was embarrassed by those traits. At airplane ticket counters and in restaurants, she could talk her way from clerk to manager, never afraid to ask for the impossible. In foreign countries she approached strangers for directions without pause and could curry the goodwill of a bus driver with whom she did not share a language, solely through gestures and charm. Once, when I was stuck in Florence, Italy, during a terrible snowstorm, all the taxis had stopped running, and I was left without a ride to the airport. I phoned my mother. Hours later, she called back: a middle-aged Italian housewife was on her way to pick me up in a minivan. In a culture that portrayed Asian American women as docile, passive, and shy, my mother was an anomaly. She had the daring of a free climber and the savviness of a salesperson. Who's to say if this was constitutional or the developed character of an immigrant trying to survive?

Born in Taipei, Taiwan, in the '60s, my mother moved to Orange County in Los Angeles with her family when she was sixteen. In 1971, the United Nations had voted to admit the People's Republic of China, thereby ousting Taiwan from its cohort. This worried my grandparents, who feared that China might try to take over Taiwan. Around the same time, her brother, Richard, had been expelled from several Taiwanese schools for bad behavior; immigrating to America was a last-ditch effort to reform him. Richard was my mother's Irish twin, born 356 days before her. My mother attributes her fearlessness to him; as an uber-athletic, ultra-mischievous child, he would coerce my mother into scrambling over fences and sneaking into neighbors' yards to steal their fruit.

When my mother arrived in America, she spoke little English. There were no ESL courses at her school, so instead she was held back a grade and put in a class with the delinquent kids, the ones who, according to her, showed up to class barefoot, blasting music from their portable stereos. After school, she washed dishes and chopped raw meat at her uncle's Chinese restaurant in exchange for her family's room and board. "You are the girl. You have to stay in the kitchen," she remembers being told. "I was very isolated. It was a very lonely time." In Taiwan she had wanted to be a journalist, but in America that dream was no longer tenable. Instead, while she was in college at Cal State, Long Beach, she heard about a part-time job as a receptionist at a company called Delta Lu Electronics in Cerritos. My mom didn't care what the job was. She needed the money, so she applied.

In 1984, the year my mother started at Delta Lu, the PC industry was on the rise. The year commenced with Apple's launch of the Macintosh computer during a Ridley Scott–directed Super Bowl commercial wherein a Princess Di doppelgänger in running shorts throws a sledgehammer at Big Brother to free a mass of blue-gray-garbed drones from technocratic dominance. This was Apple's proclamation that the Mac would save everyone from the dystopia rendered in George Orwell's *1984*—the irony of which should not escape anybody. That same year, CD-ROMs were the new hot technology, Dell and Cisco were just getting started, and Bill Gates appeared on the cover of *Time* magazine with a floppy disk balanced on his index finger. In Southern California, an enterprising immigrant named Don Lu, eager to ride this wave of technological innovation, began importing memory chips, keyboards, graphics cards, monitors, and motherboards from Japan and Taiwan. Companies and individuals were building their own PCs and needed the parts. As his company grew, he needed a receptionist. So he hired my mother for five dollars an hour.

Delta Lu Electronics was what we might now call a start-up, and because of its fledgling nature, my mother's job description continually shifted and expanded. She was shuffled between departments, through accounting and returns, learning the ropes of the entire business as she went. After about a year she was promoted to a sales position in a new company called Byte Resources, and unsurprisingly, she became very good at her job: she was keenly attuned to people's needs and deft at negotiations. While the average salesperson might turn away a customer when

to the Bay Area, where he was starting in the Optoelectronics Division at Hewlett-Packard in San Jose. After growing up in Hong Kong and attending university in England, he'd arrived in California to get a PhD in electrical engineering at Caltech. Now he was working on semiconductors in Silicon Valley. In the middle-class suburbs where I grew up, many Asian parents, mostly Taiwanese, Chinese, and Indian, did the same. They worked at companies like IBM, Intel, and AMD, and sent their kids to the best public schools in Cupertino and San Jose.

My parents moved into a seven-hundred-square-foot apartment on Homestead Road in Cupertino, a large boulevard dotted with strip malls and unremarkable one-story houses. While my father was at work, my mother, jobless, passed each day in a state of ennui, waking up at two in the afternoon only to lie in bed and page through whatever newspapers were lying around. She felt lost and directionless, like she was in a foreign country. The feelings were familiar—she had felt the same way when she first moved to the United States. "It was so boring," she told me. She had no friends and nothing to do. But not long after the move, the phone began to ring. Her former colleagues at Byte Resources were calling. Her customers were asking for her, they said. They urged her to start her own company. My mother considered the suggestion—it was not a bad idea.

Gigabyte was the name my mother chose for her company, which she started in December 1987 with two accountant friends. She was in charge of sales and purchasing, while the other

they didn't have a part on hand, my mother never did. Instead, she'd say, "Let me see what I can do for you," and would call around to suppliers until she found exactly what the customer needed. Then she'd smartly quote a higher price and make a sale. She wasn't the type of person who needed permission, and in her eyes, anything was possible with a little extra effort.

My parents got married in August of 1987, after meeting at a party in Long Beach. My mother was twenty-four, my father twenty-seven. After a year and a half at Byte Resources, my mother quit her job to move with her new husband

▲
Hawks needed someone to run the High-Tech Crimes Detail, a one-man department that had never been particularly effective.

two processed orders via fax machine and managed the books. The PC business was booming now, and the company did well. But after a year, unable to resolve an argument about salaries and commissions, the three decided to part ways. My mother, not one to back down, was confident she could survive without their help. "I'm not a quitter," she said. "It never came to my mind that I should quit." In fact, the more challenges that arose, the more she felt compelled to persevere. Undeterred, she decided to start over again, by herself. This time, the company was called Aristocrat Inc. My dad picked the name. When asked over thirty years later how he chose it, he said: "Don't remember, but probably from some English classic like *Monte Cristo*."

5.

When Aristocrat Inc. was robbed, I was four years old and just starting preschool. I have very few recollections of that time, except of things that were told to me later. Even so, the robbery remained a strange, vague aberration in my memory that did not square with my otherwise undramatic, comfortable, and privileged childhood. It was an incident that was referenced and alluded to by my family every so often, but rarely discussed in detail. When I began working in Silicon Valley myself, after college, at the age of twenty-one—the same age as my mother when she started at Delta Lu—the memory of the robbery came to the fore, contrasting sharply with the shiny, manicured world I had plunged into.

By the fall of 2012, nearly all traces of the Silicon Valley my mom knew had vanished. After moving back to the Bay from the East Coast, I began working for a start-up that bought and sold personal data, a concept I didn't fully understand when I signed my contract but then later discovered was actually quite morally dubious. The tech industry I found myself in trafficked increasingly in the intangible. Earlier that year, Facebook had gone public; WordPress started accepting Bitcoin in November; and I took my first Lyft ride. Hired as a marketing and PR associate, I scrambled to make Twitter, Facebook, and LinkedIn pages for the company to help fluff up the brand's online presence. Around that time, social media had begun to mean something.

The company I worked for tried hard to be a semaphore for a cool new start-up, and as such, the work environment read like a parody. The founders—two brothers from rural Illinois—were avid Burners who participated in a ceremonial, psychedelics-fueled gathering every New Year's Day to set their "intentions" for the year and were buying up millions of dollars worth of land in New Zealand. On Monday mornings, the company-wide meeting began with a "minute of mindfulness," which was often followed by a startling if well-intentioned rap by the younger brother, which he called his "flowetry." It was cute, but also not. In the morning before work, I'd take a train down the Peninsula to swim laps at a company-subsidized gym, after which I'd walk across the street and eat breakfast in the office kitchen. Occasionally I'd take a nap or do yoga in the Zen Room—activities that were encouraged by the company's "happiness engineer." The entire experience felt at once frictionless and empty, like bad contemporary art. It was a world apart from the Silicon Valley I had heard about from my mother.

The Silicon Valley in which my mother got her start was volatile, high-stakes, and frenzied. For her, there was no goal of an IPO, no fantasies about artificial intelligence or life extension—there was only survival. Hardware reigned supreme, and the technological infrastructure that today supports our one-click consumption was still in its infancy. (Amazon got its start in 1994. Craigslist surfaced on the internet in 1995. Larry and Sergey conceived of a student project in 1996 that would eventually culminate in a start-up called Google in 1998.) Companies like Aristocrat Inc. would eventually disappear as the internet became a more robust marketplace, diminishing the necessity for a gray market, and making fluid direct-to-consumer sales. But when my mother started her business, the marketplace was decentralized, and demand often outpaced supply. Frequent shortages meant that companies could not find the parts they were looking for through regular distribution channels, so they searched for components like motherboards, memory chips, and hard drives on the gray market. As a result, hundreds of small companies formed, acting as brokers or speculators. Aristocrat Inc. was one of those companies.

As a twenty-six-year-old in 1989, starting a business out of her own apartment, my mother got hold of as many computer industry trade publications as she could find (like *PC Magazine* and *BYTE* magazine) and flipped through their back pages, which were full of ads selling and soliciting computer chips. She would jot down the names of companies and phone numbers as she went along. Then she would call potential sources and clients, big and small, introduce herself, and ask to speak to the purchasing department. She was plucky and audacious, with nothing to lose. "I'm just very bold. I'll call anybody. If I get rejected, that's fine," she said. Once, she called Dell Computer Corporation, hoping she could reel them in as a client. Later on, she told me, she realized it was not conventional for a young woman like herself to call the sales department of a large, established company. But at the time she did not know that, and if she had—well, I'm guessing she would not have cared.

Aristocrat Inc. grew quickly. The margins of buying and selling computer chips were slim, the turnaround fast and the volume high. The chip industry, my mother said, felt like the stock market, with boom-and-bust cycles that led to occasional chip shortages, called "chip famines." She and her employees were like frantic floor brokers in the pit of the stock exchange. The work was high-pressure. The days were long and grueling. Silicon Valley is known for its white-collar labor, but this was not that. My mom was a businesswoman, but much of the daily work of Aristocrat Inc. was non-stop manual labor: moving inventory, packing, and shipping. She says she was lifting boxes until the day before she gave birth—both times. Sometimes she would have a glass of milk in the morning and then nothing else to eat for the rest of the day.

A normal day in the Aristocrat Inc. office began with phone calls to larger brokers and companies with excess inventory to ask for pricing on specific chips. My mother would call around until she found the best selling price. If chips were scarce, she would order them from foreign sources in Taiwan and Japan—she is fluent in Japanese, Mandarin, Taiwanese, and Cantonese, so she had a lot of suppliers in Asia. Based on the selling prices of the day, she would quote a price to her customers. She had customers all over the world, and notably in South America, where, she said, "people were buying and selling like crazy." The continent was several years behind in computer technology, which intensified the demand in countries like Colombia, Venezuela, and Brazil. In the afternoon, customers would call and tell her what they needed, after which my mother would call around again to purchase the merchandise. This was a time-sensitive game, with prices rising and dropping quickly. Once, she lost one hundred thousand dollars before the merchandise she had ordered even arrived—the price of the chips dropped drastically while they were still in the air.

My mother recalls that around 1994, chips started becoming very expensive. In July 1993, on the island of Shikoku, in Japan, an explosion destroyed a factory that produced more than half the world's supply of epoxy resin, a key material in the manufacturing of silicon chips. This disruption in the supply chain led to a chip famine, which resulted in a price hike. The market became increasingly tumultuous. There were stories of Intel employees selling contraband parts in the parking lot. People were scraping the 25 MHz markings off memory chips and reinscribing them with 33 MHz labels—they could make two hundred dollars more per chip if the memory capacity appeared to be larger.

Then, in 1995, Microsoft released a new operating system. For computer technology, this was a seminal year. *Fast Company* called it "the year that everything changed." Windows 95 was an even bigger event than a new iPhone release today, or, for those who came of age in the aughts, as I did, a Harry Potter book launch. *The New York Times* reported on the news under the headline MIDNIGHT SALES FRENZY USHERS IN WINDOWS 95, and the writer called it "a computer-age milestone." According to one tech writer, "Windows 95 was the most important operating system of all time… the first commercial operating system aimed [at] regular people, not just professionals or hobbyists." Many people were bringing computers (and the internet) into their homes for the first time. With Windows 95, the computer became user-friendly, no longer solely the domain of specialists and nerdy technologists. My mother recalls that because of this launch, the demand for chips—both CPUs and microprocessors—was skyrocketing, not just in the United States, but around the world.

"It was a risky business," my mother told me. The risk grew in tandem with the demand, and there were opportunities for huge losses in almost every part of the business. From the moment she purchased chips from manufacturers in Asia, she had to take exceptional precautions. If chips were being shipped from Taiwan, for instance, she would have to hire an expert to inspect the cargo to make sure none of it was counterfeit or stolen, then pay someone else to pack the shipment in an extra layer of wooden crates so that no one could open it in transit. Once the chips landed stateside, they were delivered by truck to the Sunnyvale office, but only if the truck was not hijacked first, which occasionally happened. And then, after the chips were repacked and shipped, robbers might target the UPS or FedEx trucks.

Once, a client ordered around $180,000 worth of merchandise. The next morning, when the shipment arrived, the client found only sheafs of newspaper and pages ripped out of a telephone book. Sometimes my mother's own employees stole from her: drivers she hired would come back from suppliers short on merchandise. Though they had insurance against these mishaps, the insurance company eventually dropped Aristocrat Inc. because the risk was too steep, and they had to find a new one. This was an industry-wide problem: by 1994, Chubb, which insured almost one-third of the tech companies in Silicon Valley, had reportedly lost $15 million from high-tech computer theft.

The stories my mother heard only grew increasingly more harrowing: Gangs tortured executives until they handed over their merchandise. A computer company employee was shot and killed in his car. A friend who worked for a module assembly manufacturer was kidnapped at gunpoint. My mother, wary and vigilant, said she purposely drove a clunky old car because she did not want to attract attention. Even so, gangs took notice of Aristocrat Inc.

6.

Forty miles north of Sunnyvale, Special Agent Carol Lee was following these stories too, from her desk at San Francisco's FBI headquarters. Lee was in her mid-thirties, with straight black hair and a broad, tanned face. She was finally starting to piece things together and make progress on a case that had dogged her for years.

In the early '90s, the FBI had learned of a Vietnamese-Chinese heroin organization that was closely aligned with Vietnamese street gangs throughout the United States. Their connections were wide-ranging, and they were loosely affiliated with the Triads (including Frank Ma, one of the last Chinese "godfathers" in New York), as well as with several other high-echelon Asian crime bosses in various American cities. But this heroin organization operated differently from the Asian gangs of previous generations.

First, they relied on two key pieces of technology: the cellular phone and the pager. They were financially and technologically savvy, and instead of being tied to one specific location, they operated a national network, with cells and confederates in various cities. Lee's boss at the time, Kingman Wong, who supervised the Asian Organized Crime and Drug Squad at the San Francisco bureau, noted one other factor that made this group distinctive: though most Asian gangs comprised only one ethnicity, this group was "somewhat of a United Nations," with several Asian ethnicities (Vietnamese, Cambodian, Laotian, Korean, Japanese, Chinese) in the mix. Such intermingling was rare. "When they see they have the same goal, they're willing to break down national barriers," he said.

Lee had spent some time deciphering this gang. To take down the entire organization, she knew she would have to go straight for the top bosses, the masterminds from whom all directives flowed. It was easy to nab the henchmen who did the dirty work—the drug handling, the physical exchange of goods for money—but they were also easily replaced. In essence, you had to lop the head off the monster. As such, buy-bust scenarios, in which law enforcement descends upon the seller as soon as the goods have been exchanged, would be futile. Lee knew that isolated transactions like those revealed almost nothing about the supply chain. And they provided little evidence for a case against the gang's upper management.

Lee's team had narrowed in on one person, a Vietnamese Chinese man in his mid-twenties. He went by at least a dozen different nicknames, but his legal name was John That Luong. He was short and had a Korean girlfriend. Since 1990, Luong had been suspected of drug smuggling and distribution, supported by a coterie of Vietnamese Chinese gang members in Boston, Philadelphia, San Francisco, Denver, and Los Angeles. The FBI had reason to believe he played a critical role in trafficking heroin between the East and West Coasts. There was also evidence that he had been involved in alien smuggling, illegal firearms sales, credit card fraud, money laundering, and counterfeit currency production. After nine months of gathering evidence against Luong and his associates for their heroin trafficking enterprise,

Lee could tell that Luong was a cautious operator. He did not trust many people, and he employed aggressive counter-surveillance techniques. Every month he switched cell phones and pagers. When he encountered law enforcement, he gave aliases and fake identification. He also used cloned phones, co-opting an unsuspecting stranger's number to make and receive calls. One FBI affidavit noted that Luong frequented mostly Vietnamese and Chinese businesses, making it "extremely difficult for law enforcement to surveil him without detection," because he blended in so well.

After years of traditional investigation—including seven different confidential informants—yielded little about his inner circle, Lee's team submitted an application to intercept all of Luong's wireless and electronic communications. In August 1995, just days before the Aristocrat Inc. robbery, a judge authorized the wiretap.

As Lee began listening to Luong's phone calls, she noticed something unusual. Often, Luong did not sound like he was talking about drugs. Luong and his associates frequently used coded language and nicknames, but Lee, who had spent years tracking Korean meth dealers in Hawaii, could easily recognize a language pattern that insinuated drugs. She also had a general idea of how much dealers paid for heroin and how much they sold it for, but the financial discussions she overheard did not seem to correlate. Luong and his men talked about "big jobs" and staffing those jobs. They talked about scouting job sites, which they often called "fishponds" or "stores." They referred to goods as "food," using different types of seafood (lobster and shrimp) to denote specific items. They talked about "tools" that were needed for the jobs, as well as U-Haul trucks, warehouses, and security. Testifying in court later, Lee's colleague Nelson Low, a special agent on the Asian Organized Crime and Drug Squad, said, "We [started] picking up some sense that maybe these guys were involved in some robberies and things of that sort."

A few weeks earlier, on July 10, a man named Tony Bao Quoc Ly, who had been jailed in San Francisco for a probation violation, told an investigating officer that he wanted to exchange information for his freedom. He said he was part of a group that was intending to rob a computer warehouse in Minneapolis of its entire stock of computer chips, worth around $1 million. The robbery, he said, was going to happen soon.

To prove he was serious, he provided these details: During the last week of June, he had flown to Minneapolis, cased a computer warehouse, picked out weapons—an assortment of Berettas, revolvers, and semiautomatics—and rented a safe house in Champlin, a suburb twenty miles north of Minneapolis. His co-participants were Vietnamese men from the Bay Area, Sacramento, and Los Angeles—most were between the ages of eighteen and twenty-one. They would travel to Minneapolis together to rob the warehouse. Ly had been assigned to drive one of the vans. After the robbery, he would take the chips to the safe house, where they would be stored before being shipped to buyers. The group would then drive to Chicago and fly back to the West Coast.

On the night of July 12, at around 9:00 p.m., four armed men confronted two employees as they were leaving the warehouse of a computer company called NEI Electronics in Blaine, Minnesota. The men tried to coerce the employees to reopen the business, but the employees said they could not—they didn't have the alarm code. The men forced the two employees—a woman and a man—into their van. During the ride, they tried to persuade the male employee to cooperate with them in committing a robbery later, but he refused. Eventually, they dropped the two employees off at a mall and attempted to make an escape.

But their escape was short-lived. The intel from Ly had been relayed to the San Francisco FBI, who then passed it on to the Minneapolis FBI. Tipped off by the Minneapolis FBI, officers from the Blaine Police Department had in fact been surveilling NEI Electronics since the early evening. The police followed the vans and eventually arrested the men. Inside the vans they found bolt cutters, numerous cell phones and paging devices, maps of the Twin Cities, a gun, several rolls of duct tape, plastic wrist cuffs, opaque surgical gloves, an address for a house in Champlin, and the address of NEI Electronics.

The robbers were held at Anoka County Jail, where they made several calls. An FBI agent in Minnesota would later tell the San Francisco FBI that the individuals were involved with a man in California called Ah Sing—his name was mentioned frequently during the phone calls. Ah Sing, it turned out, was one of Luong's many nicknames, which also included Thang, Johnny,

Tony, Duong, and John Dao. A court indictment would list ten in total.

Soon, Agent Lee realized that when Luong talked about going to "look at fishponds," or when he said, "The store is wide-open. The food is good. Lobster and shrimp only," he was describing computer chip companies and the parts they had on hand. Guns were called "legs" or "tools." The "front line" were the crew members performing the robbery.

In reality, Luong and his associates were not just heroin dealers. They were also businessmen who had identified a lucrative opportunity amid a fast-growing industry. They had diversified their revenue streams, and by selling stolen computer chips, they could finance their heroin operation. The intercepted conversations Lee heard were slowly starting to reveal the full scope of Luong's criminal activities. On August 6, the Asian Organized Crime and Drug Squad intercepted conversations between John That Luong and a man named Charlie about a robbery they were planning in Sunnyvale.

The FBI was beginning to make sense of things. The Luong investigation would be called Operation Bytes Dust.

7.

After the botched NEI robbery in July of 1995, Luong's gang was strapped for money. The men who were arrested had called for help from jail, and Luong paid sixty-four thousand dollars to cover their legal fees. Wiretaps around this time revealed tension among the group's top-tier leaders regarding their financial troubles. Luong and his associates started talking about the possibility of creating an emergency fund from a portion of their profits in case things went south again. To mitigate their monetary woes, they decided they should rob more computer companies. In early August 1995, John Cheng Jung Chu, a man who the FBI would later discover served as a sales broker and scout for Luong, gave the name and address of Aristocrat Inc. to two of Luong's associates as a potential robbery target. Two weeks later, on August 18, they robbed my mother's company.

My mother was running late to work that day. Her parents were visiting at the time, and when the two men arrived for the computer chips, she was still at home, entertaining. Later that morning, she received a panicked call from one of her employees, Irene, who told her what had happened. My mother told Irene to stop kidding around—it was not funny. But Irene was not joking.

On September 3, 1995, the Stockton police arrested a man named Chhayarith Reth. He was also known as Charlie—presumably the Charlie that the FBI had overheard speaking to Luong just days before the Aristocrat Inc. robbery. Reth had a distinctive mole on his chin, just like the man who had first approached Grace on that Friday morning. Aristocrat Inc. employees had picked his face out of a photo lineup.

Like Tony Bao Quoc Ly, Reth told the police that he had information to give, for a price. A true negotiator, he wanted to be released from jail, and he demanded plane tickets to Cambodia for himself and his fiancée. He also asked that he not receive a sentence greater than five years for any criminal charges. The police said they could not promise him anything. But on the advice of his lawyer, Reth decided to talk anyway.

In front of an audience of police officers from San Jose and Stockton, Reth painted a portrait of an organization that was run like a business, with a hierarchical structure that delineated responsibilities for each individual involved. There was a direct chain of command and an established process for conducting robberies that allowed the group to do so with tactical precision.

At the top of the group, Reth said, were four bosses,[1] whom he called "the main men." They had started the operation with the help of a Chinese store owner in the Bay Area. Three lived in or near Sacramento, and the fourth lived in Los Angeles. One, he said, was a gambler, and another, named Mady, had two wives. The main men essentially performed the duties of CEO, CFO, and COO, devising strategies, issuing directives, and handling financial affairs. They commissioned armed robberies and paid attorneys' fees and bail for their crew members—a kind of workers' compensation that they had the foresight to set aside as an operating expense. Though they were rarely present for the robberies themselves, they coordinated over the phone, occasionally meeting for dinner at a Chinese restaurant to discuss their plans. Reth said he worked mostly for one boss, a man whose name was transcribed on

---

1. The court files offer varying accounts of how many bosses there were. Some documents claim there were three; others suggest four or five.

the police report that day as Donovan Wong—likely a mondegreen for John That Luong.

Reth himself was a "crew leader" (also called "crew chief"), one level below the bosses. Crew chiefs conducted surveys of potential targets, recruited crew members, and obtained rental vehicles, weapons, safe houses, and motel rooms for participants. They also supervised the robberies. Reth said that he was one of the most trusted among the multiple crew leaders, with more responsibilities, privileges, and knowledge than the others. Each crew leader had a preference for the ethnicity of the crew they used. Dung employed mostly Vietnamese men; Mark liked Chinese and Italians; Peter used Cambodian and Chinese men; and Vanthieng worked exclusively with Cambodians.

Below the crew chiefs were the "crew," the soldiers who participated in the armed robberies. The bosses sometimes referred to them as "the little ones," as many were in their late teens and early twenties, just barely out of high school. They performed the dirty work, holding employees hostage and transporting the stolen merchandise—this was the role Tony Bao Quoc Ly would have played in the NEI Electronics robbery. The crew was composed of "freelancers," commissioned on a job-by-job basis. For one robbery, Reth said, each crew member was paid two thousand dollars. According to Ly, the bosses received 40 percent of the robbery proceeds and the crews received 60 percent.

To find robbery targets, the bosses worked with "sales brokers," who had "the inside information." Reth called these men "connections." They were the liaisons to the computer industry, and they often ran legitimate businesses of their own. John Cheng Jung Chu, who told the bosses about Aristocrat Inc., was one of these brokers. Because of their established connections, they were also able to assist in the sale of stolen merchandise (for which they received a 10 percent commission). Unsurprisingly, most of the robbery targets they identified were owned by Asian Americans—these were the people they networked with the most. By providing a "shopping list" to the bosses—a list of the parts most desired by buyers—they could ensure successful sales. In some ways, these brokers' jobs were not so different from my mother's.

Once a robbery target was identified, crew chiefs and members would scout the site, often multiple times, up to a month before the robbery. During these visits, they would learn as much as they could about the security systems and identify the best time of day to conduct the robbery. Sometimes, in order to get a better look at an office, they would create a ruse and go into a company asking to use the bathroom or for a job application. Once, during a reconnaissance, they noticed that the employees were wearing headphone-like contraptions, whose communication capabilities, they feared, could thwart a robbery. It was too risky. They decided not to proceed.

The FBI would later learn that the group referred to itself as the Company—an apt moniker—and had more than four hundred members spread throughout the United States. The bosses formed a kind of family business. One of the bosses, Huy Chi Luong, a.k.a. Jimmy, was John That Luong's cousin, and another boss, Mady Chan, was Huy Chi Luong's brother-in-law. It was possible there were even more bosses than Reth mentioned. The FBI believed there was an older man in the shadows who oversaw them all. The bosses called him Dai Lo, or "Big Brother"—his real name was Son Quoc Luu and he lived in Stockton. Assistant US attorney Elizabeth Lee, who would eventually prosecute the criminal case against the group, would call the Company "a powerful alliance of criminal associates… [that] knew no limits. The Company was designed to make money for its leaders—and it did."

Back at the San Joaquin County Jail, a detective asked Reth for information about several computer companies that had been robbed: Centon Electronics, Micro Distribution Center, International Memory Source, ASA Computers, CMC, Valtrix, PC Team, MA Labs. He knew them all. Not only that, but also his knowledge of the robberies was detailed, though he claimed not to have participated in any of them. The Centon robbery, he said, was committed in eight minutes, with twenty people involved. During a one-month surveillance, the robbers had made videotapes of the business and learned its security schedule. A twenty-one-year-old, he said, had rented a U-Haul for the job. At ASA Computers, the crew took mostly hard drives. International Memory Source was a small take. Valtrix was hit twice in two months. When MA Labs was robbed, the owner, terrified, had jumped out the window.

8.

With Reth's arrest, and Lee's team still on the wiretap, the Company was becoming more vulnerable. The bosses spoke about Reth's arrest over the phone as Lee and her team listened in. On one call, Luong spoke about the Aristocrat Inc. robbery, later translated as: "That case, there is no evidence. The only unfortunate thing is the mole on the face." Luong worried that if their group did not bail out Reth soon, he could decide to cooperate with law enforcement and disclose a lot of valuable information. They were unaware that he had already done so.

The Company's financial troubles intensified, with lawyer and bail fees starting to pile up. Wiretaps revealed that during the fall of 1995, the main men appeared to be fighting over a large sum of money, somewhere between $480,000 and $750,000. "There were a lot of money problems at that time… It caused a lot… of friction amongst the leaders," Agent Nelson Low later testified in court. As a result of that friction, two of the bosses pulled out of the operation for the time being. Another sensed that something was going awry—he thought he was being followed, so he told the group he was going to lie low for a while.

But their troubles were only beginning. The cell phone, the very technology that had allowed the Company to operate so efficiently and expansively, would ultimately be their downfall. They did not know that the FBI had begun to preempt their robberies via wiretap. Less than two weeks after Reth was arrested, another four crew members were arrested after a failed robbery at a computer store called Qualstar in Reseda, California. In early February of 1996, the FBI intercepted conversations between Luong and his associates in which they spoke about planning some robberies before the Chinese New Year. Exactly a week before the holiday, eleven men attempted to rob PKI Computers in Torrance, California. Luong had spent the week prior to the robbery in Los Angeles, tailing the owners of various computer chip companies. On February 12, when the robbers arrived at the PKI warehouse, they were met by police and arrested.

Meanwhile, on the East Coast, the FBI continued to employ undercover agents in heroin deals with Luong's affiliates. On March 4, a courier flew into Newark, New Jersey from Phoenix, Arizona. He was picked up by a man named Bing Yi Chen, who often worked with Luong. Chen drove the courier to a Burger King, where the courier sold seventy thousand dollars' worth of heroin to an undercover agent in the bathroom.

The bosses were becoming desperate. "If I could only complete one good job, we could get a lot of the guys that are in jail out quickly," said Luong over the wiretap. Luong and his cousin Jimmy were both running low on money, so they asked Mady Chan for "seed money" to finance the next robbery. In March, they began scouting warehouses for a series of robberies they were planning in Los Angeles.

On a Friday evening in March, just as the workweek was winding down, an employee of ACE Micro in San Diego was leaving his office when he was ambushed by five armed Asian men, some of them wearing ski masks. They forced the employee back into the office and then bound him with cable ties. They took seventy thousand dollars' worth of computer chips and parts with them. Afterward, Luong received a call from a man who said that it had been "taken care of." Luong instructed the man to transport the goods to his house in Sacramento. But first they would meet at the Walmart near Elk Grove Boulevard.

When Luong arrived at Walmart the next morning, around 7:00 a.m., he saw police searching a U-Haul vehicle and questioning two Asian males, who were then arrested. When the police searched the truck, they found computer chips and five thousand dollars in cash.

The next day, Lee's team overheard Luong talking to Jimmy, wondering how the men had gotten arrested. They couldn't think of a good reason and speculated that the men had hit a parked car. They did not know that the FBI could hear everything they were saying, and that Lee's team was closing in.

9.

On the morning of April 11, 1996, Luong took his girlfriend, Gina, out for a driving lesson. She had an appointment for a driving test later that week. A little while later, they pulled up to Connie's Drive-In, a small roadside restaurant owned by his brother Paul and sister-in-law Winnie that served sandwiches, burgers, and hot dogs. According to Luong's lawyer, Luong and Gina had a shift at the restaurant that morning, but when they noticed several police cars, they drove away and went to their friend Tuan Phan's home, in the suburbs of Sacramento. An hour later, around 11:00 a.m., as Luong was sitting on the backyard patio talking to Gina, he suddenly stood up, took a step, and chucked his cell phone over a brick wall that bordered the yard. FBI special agent William Beck had just rounded the corner of the house. Luong was arrested that day, along with hundreds of his associates across the country.

Luong was only twenty-four years old when he was arrested—my mother's age when she started Gigabyte. He was five feet, six inches tall and weighed 165 pounds, with a stocky build and black hair. For at least three years, if not more, he had run what amounted to a successful, though illegal, business that spanned the country, without any college education. He had not been in America for even a decade when he was arrested.

Born in Saigon City, Vietnam, Luong was the third youngest of eight children in a lower-middle-class, ethnically Chinese family. His parents had spent their lives continually fleeing from communism, first from China, and then from Vietnam in 1986. Before they immigrated to the States, they spent eight months in refugee camps.

When they arrived in San Francisco, Luong's uncle picked up the family and drove them to Sacramento, where the family lived with Luong's grandfather for some time. Luong was fourteen years old, two years younger than my mother was when she immigrated to the States. The entire family took up menial jobs to survive. Luong's older sisters worked in doughnut shops and grocery stores or as chambermaids in hotels. His older

brothers worked at restaurants, just as my mother had. In high school, Luong did well in his math, science, and physics classes, but poorly in English and social studies. This is an oft-forgotten but typical backstory for many Asian American immigrants—the antithesis of the well-to-do Asian, the one who fulfills the model-minority myth.

In 1990, Luong was involved in a car chase, and a warrant was put out for his arrest. He fled to New York City, where he lived under an alias for a few years, before returning to Sacramento with Gina to live with his mother. Later, Luong would be linked to the *Pai Sheng*, a ship that smuggled more than two-hundred Chinese aliens onto a pier near the Golden Gate Bridge in 1993. He was paid $650,000 for his help. According to his lawyer, when Luong returned to the Bay Area from New York, he enrolled in a continuing education class and began working at Connie's Drive-In, earning $5.50 an hour. He and Gina had a daughter in 1995.

I learned of Luong's origin story from a single document submitted by his lawyer that still resides in the court files of this case. It was a plea for leniency, given his background. His history was not unfamiliar to me—the escape from communism, the limbo of resettlement, the construction of a new life from nothing at all. But even though Luong and my mother both arrived in this country as immigrants, with little grasp of the language, his circumstances were encumbered by the cruelties of far more recent traumas, which perhaps accounts for the different trajectory of his life. In the end,

they both became entrepreneurs, seizing opportunities in an industry in which they were underdogs. Where business was booming, both did whatever they needed to do to survive.

10.

In 2012, as memories of the Aristocrat Inc. robbery surfaced as a reaction to the strange workplace in which I found myself, I began to search for a chapter of Silicon Valley history that seemed to have been lost, written over, and completely forgotten. Google searches turned up a smattering of mostly local news articles about the thefts from the early-to-mid-'90s, but the information available online was scant, and everyone to whom I told my mom's story—mostly friends in their twenties and thirties—was shocked to hear it. For them, as it did for me, it created a sense of fracture and cognitive dissonance in their understanding of Silicon Valley.

How was it that I had grown up here, with immigrant parents who worked in technology (and with classmates who were mostly the children of Southeast and East Asian immigrants who also worked in technology), but still perceived Silicon Valley to consist of the Steve Jobs and Mark Zuckerbergs and Elon Musks of the world? Who writes the Silicon Valley story? And who is excluded from it? Maybe I had been too naive, glomming on to the narratives that were presented to me and consequently lionizing only the achievements of these lauded white men. Or was it merely that Asian Americans had been left out of the history and hidden away, as they have been since they first arrived stateside?

When I realized that the Silicon Valley I had landed in was focused only on the future, making obsolescent anything and anyone it did not mythologize, I became obsessed with unearthing the past: the Silicon Valley that my mom—and thousands of other immigrants like her—had been a part of. I called my mom frequently with dozens of questions. I talked to my aunt Grace, and my mom's employee Anna, and the couple of FBI agents who spoke to me very reluctantly. I visited courthouses in San Francisco and San Jose, where I sat in small, windowless rooms paging through thousands of pages of undigitized court files, trying to take photos of important transcripts underneath a desk, where the court clerk could not see me. After several hours, I'd go for a quick lunch, slurp down a bowl of phở, then return and try to get through as many files as I could. It struck me that all the details of these robberies and investigations had been preserved and stowed away in their analog form behind closed doors, in a manner that made them nearly impossible to access. They'd been relegated to a dusty corner, familiar only to those who knew they were there.

I never did interview John That Luong, even though I wanted to. I felt an urgency to bring this story to the fore and a sadness that so many details were lost to the private memories of individuals I could not find, but I was wary, too, of reviving a past that had once been dangerous for my family. I didn't want John That Luong to remember my mom. It's a stereotypically Asian way to be, not wanting to draw too much attention to ourselves. But that, too, is how we let ourselves be forgotten.

▲

At the time I had seen only the surface of things. I was too young to understand the kinds of rigors and tribulations my mom was facing.

11.

For my mother, who is a deeply religious woman, the robbery played out as a series of "small miracles." She counts herself lucky that she was late to work that day. She had heard that company owners often suffered the brunt of the raid. Their families might be held hostage, or they themselves might be tortured. An industry acquaintance, Paul Heng, CEO of the chip manufacturer Unigen, was the target of a kidnapping attempt in 1995, in which armed robbers ambushed his car as he was nearing his house. As he frantically reversed his car, the robbers shot at him. One bullet went through the car radiator.

All in all, the value of the goods stolen from Aristocrat Inc. amounted to around sixty-one thousand dollars, and the majority were returned merchandise, later reimbursed by the company's insurance. But still, the robbery shattered an illusion of invincibility that my mother had previously possessed. The business of computer chips had always been financially risky, and though she had heard the litany of stories about robberies and kidnappings, the danger had still seemed abstract and distant. When Aristocrat Inc. was robbed, the precarious nature of the industry suddenly became tangible. A robbery was not only possible—it had, in fact, happened. Fearing for our family's safety, my mother would move us into the foothills of the Santa Cruz Mountains a year later. She bought the house with the money she had made at Aristocrat Inc.

The robbery was, in a way, a wake-up call that forced her to consider her own mortality. "I was dragged into the business and the business was booming. I just couldn't stop. There was no time to think. It was the robbery that made me stop and think," she told me. The momentum of the early Silicon Valley computer craze had swept her up, and she had profited from it, but at what cost? After the robbery, she thought about what she would do if she had only one month to live, and she began to realize that running the business was not it. Doing so had caused her a great deal of stress. After dropping me off at school in the morning, she would arrive at the office around 9:00 a.m. In the evening, after bringing me home, she would drive back to the office without eating dinner, and she would often work until 10 p.m. or midnight. When my sister started day care, she'd often be the last child to be picked up. After the UPS shipping deadline of 6:00 p.m., my mom would speed over to get her, but never fast enough to avoid the ire of the day care lady. "I realized there was something more important to me than the company," she said. "If I were more ambitious, I could have made it bigger. But I'm content with what I have."

Shortly after the robbery, my mother began thinking about dissolving Aristocrat Inc. But the business was still doing well. Then, as luck would have it, in 1996, an acquaintance offered to buy the company from her. She sold Aristocrat Inc. that year. She would work part-time as a consultant for two more years before leaving the industry entirely in 1998. It was good timing, she later told me: right before the dot-com boom rendered companies like Aristocrat Inc. irrelevant. "It was the beginning of a different era," she said.

Both my parents were an integral part of the immigrant labor force in the technology industry, but they worked in entirely different parts of Silicon Valley—my father in the more genteel, privileged, and intellectual sector that is typically conjured when thinking about the technology industry; my mother in a rougher, more brutal, and less visible line of work. Luong, on the other hand, did not formally operate in any sector at all but rather in the merciless, dark underbelly of Silicon Valley that is little known to this day. This stratification of Asian Americans along class and ethnic lines continues to abide in the Bay Area and in the United States, where they are the most economically divided of any racial group.

Even knowing this, I was surprised—though I shouldn't have been—to hear that the underbelly Luong was a part of still exists. In 2011, fifteen robbers stole more than $37 million worth of computer chips from Unigen, the largest chip robbery in the history of the business, and a sum almost twice as large as the biggest bank heist in American history. It was the same company whose owner, Paul Heng, had been ambushed in his car in 1995. When I started reporting this story, my mother urged me to speak to him, and he told me that the very first time he had a gun put to his head was in 1988, even before he started Unigen, when the electronics broker he was working for was robbed. Since Unigen's founding, in 1991, Heng's company has been robbed more than six times, most recently in July of 2019. Still, he said, the 1995 incident (the same year that Aristocrat Inc. was robbed) was the most terrifying. When I asked him if he was ever deterred by the robberies, he said no. "Either you go small and quit, or you grow bigger," he said.

12.

On April 9, 1996, a federal grand jury issued a six-count indictment charging John That Luong with racketeering, RICO conspiracy, conspiracy to interfere with commerce by threats or violence, and conspiracy to distribute heroin. (RICO, or the Racketeer Influenced and Corrupt Organizations Act, was originally created to go after mobs and has since become the prosecution of choice against any form of organized crime.) The court trials were long and drawn-out, and Luong did not receive his sentence until 2010: life in prison plus eighty years. For the alien smuggling case, he was sentenced to forty-five months in prison in 1998. He faced a separate indictment for laundering money and stolen cars.

My mother, for her part, does not know John That Luong's name. Nor is she familiar with the intricacies of the Company or of the FBI operation that led to his capture. Luong was just one leader among several gangs that stole and trafficked computer chips, and my mom was but one small-business owner among hundreds whose companies were robbed. He was no El Chapo, and she was no Sheryl Sandberg. But it was in part because she was also an Asian immigrant that Aristocrat Inc. became one of Luong's targets.

Kingman Wong, the FBI agent who supervised Operation Bytes Dust, told me that Asian criminals targeted Asian-run companies because they saw the commonality as an advantage. They were more likely to share a language, and the gangs often knew people who worked at these companies—it made their jobs easier. At one point during our conversations, my mother offhandedly told me that the son of a Chinese nanny that babysat me back in 1992 had been part of the gang that robbed a company called Wintec Industries in 1998, during which one of the employees was shot and killed. What I infer from this is that when immigrants prey on their own, they assume the consequences will be less dire, or even nonexistent. Though Luong ultimately received a severe punishment for his crimes, most of the reporting about these computer chip robberies has been buried. If these crimes had been perpetrated against white people, would they have been covered, and remembered differently?

13.

The neighborhood my parents live in now is quiet and bosky, with multistory houses shielded by tall deciduous trees that turn red and gold in the fall. Their house is on a cul-de-sac at the end of a windy, hilly road. A majority of their neighbors have been there as long as, if not longer than they have. Many of them are part of the old guard of tech, like the man two doors down who was a marketing manager at Apple in the early '80s; he later started the ad agency that created an early iteration of the eBay logo. When my parents moved to this house, so that Luong's people would not be able to find them, their address was unsearchable on Google Maps. The trick was that you had to use MapQuest—that was the only way to route yourself to their house.

The day we drove to the old headquarters of Aristocrat Inc. in Sunnyvale was the first time my mom had been back to her old office in two decades—and mine too. When my mom described her working days to me before, I'd had a hard time picturing the place where the robbery had gone down, but upon pulling into the parking lot, I suddenly remembered I'd been here before. In my mind's eye I could see the room where all the office workers sat, desks parallel to one another. That room opened up into an expansive, high-ceilinged warehouse, with cold concrete floors and tall metal shelves filled with boxes. I remember how delighted I was when I got to visit my mother at her workplace, mystified by the abundance of packing peanuts and the seemingly endless rolls of pink bubble wrap, which I'd pull out and pop one by one. In that office, I had perceived a magical, grown-up world full of office accoutrements like staplers and mini receipt-printers and large plastic calculators whose buttons clacked when you pressed them.

At the time I had seen only the surface of things. I was too young to understand the kinds of rigors and tribulations my mom was facing. Back then, and for a long time thereafter, she'd just been my mom, who'd worked for a while, and then stopped, and that was it. But part of becoming an adult is beginning to see your parents as distinct and separate humans, and as this story unraveled, my mom slowly began to appear differently to me. I'd always admired her, but now I felt a kind of awe.

My mother seemed indifferent to the sight of her old office; if she felt otherwise, she did not show it. Maybe she'd never had a sentimental attachment, or else it had waned, and now the place just represented a bounded time in her life that had come and gone. She stayed in the car with my baby—her grandson—as I stepped out and looked around. A couple of bespectacled workers in their late twenties or early thirties, both women, walked by me, plastic bags in hand—they must have gotten burritos or Nepalese momos from the food trucks nearby. The entire complex looked like a relic of the '90s, much of its facade and coloring unchanged. "It looks about the same," said my mom. ✦

ALAN ALDA

[ACTOR]

"MY ADVICE IS TO TRY TO NOT GIVE TOO MUCH ADVICE."

Appliances built by Alan Alda in his childhood:
A five-way can opener
A lazy Susan designed for refrigerators
A malted milk machine fashioned from spare parts

Alan Alda needs no introduction. You just don't need to introduce someone who has been a fixture on television for sixty-four years. He first appeared on The Phil Silvers Show in 1958, then slowly built a career in TV, movies, and TV movies, before landing what, for a lesser actor, would have been the role of a lifetime—playing the sardonic, seen-it-all military doctor Hawkeye Pierce on M*A*S*H. He played Hawkeye for eleven years and then just kept going, earning accolades for his roles on 30 Rock and Ray Donovan and as a politician on The West Wing.

Alda is a six-time winner of both the Emmy Award and the Golden Globe Award. He's directed four movies; written three books, including the evocatively named If I Understood You, Would I Have This Look on My Face?; and spent over a decade hosting PBS's Scientific American Frontiers. That last role turned out to be transitional for Alda, moving him into the position of science translator, breaking down complicated theories into easily digestible media for the masses. Building on that experience, in 2009 he helped create the Alan Alda Center for Communicating Science at New York's Stony Brook University, with a mission to teach scientists, engineers, and medical professionals to communicate clearly and vividly. The phrase "clear and vivid" has become a sort of mantra for Alda's latest chapter.

Illustration by Kristian Hammerstad

At eighty-six years old, Alda is fully engaged in a third (or is that fourth?) act in his career. As a podcaster, he has hosted more than two hundred episodes of Clear+Vivid with Alan Alda, *in which he gently presses authors, artists, scientists, and luminaries—including Yo-Yo Ma, Mel Brooks, Stephen Breyer, and Madeleine Albright—about their fields of study. He even has an all-science offshoot podcast called* Science Clear+Vivid. *Both showcase Alda's natural curiosity and eagerness to learn through listening.*

—Melissa Locker

I. INBOX TEN THOUSAND

ALAN ALDA: While we talk, I'm going to email my office and let them know I'm on it so they don't get nervous.

THE BELIEVER: Well, that's good. Are you a good multitasker?

AA: I have a special way to multitask: I don't think about anything while I'm doing other things.

BLVR: So… is that multitasking?

AA: Not quite multi, but I get a lot of things done.

BLVR: That's always useful. It seems like you do have a lot of things you need to be getting done lately.

AA: Yeah, I'm always pretty busy, but I haven't been this busy in a long time. I have a really long list of things I have to get done, and they're all—almost all—urgent. I just think about the most urgent one and don't think about the rest until I get that done.

BLVR: I suppose that's good as long as you're able to prioritize. I feel like I'm bad at prioritizing.

AA: Yeah, you kinda get drawn to the one that's the squeakiest wheel, but that may not be the one that needs priority. Also, it's good to get a head start on something that's coming up a long time from now so it doesn't weigh on your mind. Just get a head start and then put it away for a while.

BLVR: So does that mean you've done all your Christmas shopping already?

AA: I— Well, I take care of that by not doing any Christmas shopping.

BLVR: None?

AA: No!

BLVR: I guess that is one way to just make sure it never pops up on your to-do list.

AA: Yeah, I'm not that good at prioritizing—I've got about 120 flagged emails in my inbox right now.

BLVR: How many emails do you have in total?

AA: Oh, tens of thousands that I have to answer.

BLVR: [*Gasps*] So you're not an inbox-zero person, then.

AA: Once in a while I get to that point, but people have to wait for a while.

BLVR: I'm a firm believer in it. Every time I get an email, I answer it right away.

AA: The trouble is, I get too many emails that ask me to read something or analyze something, and you can't just do that while you're in the back of a taxicab.

BLVR: Well, you could…

AA: Well, you could if you give it no thought whatsoever. Which is also a good strategy. Or you can give one-word answers like "yes," "no."

BLVR: You've been on a mission recently to enhance global communication and explore the way we communicate with one another. Do you think that taking the time to properly answer an email is part of that?

AA: I think it depends on what you're answering and who you're talking to. If somebody is OK with a one-word answer, because they're in constant touch with you and they appreciate a brief answer, that's fine. If some head of a university writes you a five-page email and begs you to accept an honorary doctorate, the word *no* is probably rude.

BLVR: You should just respond with an emoji, right?

AA: Yeah, well, I think emojis are a hopeful sign, because they're an indication that at that moment in your message, you're thinking about what the other person might misunderstand. You stick in an emoji to make it clear you're not being snarky or sarcastic or rude, but that you mean what you said as a lighthearted thing. And that's an indication that you're thinking of what the other person's thinking.

BLVR: Right, because it gives context to the words that you're saying.

AA: Yeah, you're aware of the other person's thought process, and that's the first step in communicating. Communication is often thought of as crafting the best message—a message that best expresses what you have in mind. But what good is the best message if it doesn't land on the person you're aiming at? You gotta know where they are, where their mind is, and craft your message according to that.

BLVR: Because you put this kind of importance on emojis, do you feel like you are an expert-level emoji user?

AA: I wouldn't say I'm at an expert level. I just have a couple of favorites that are fun—the guy with his tongue sticking out with one eye closed.

BLVR: Yes, that's an important one.

AA: Sometimes I can't make out what they're saying. But that's OK, because if one emoji expert is talking to another emoji expert, then they probably understand each other fine. It's important that there's a place for jargon.

II. REASONABLE TALK
FOR SERIOUS PROBLEMS

BLVR: You have a podcast and you're a Twitter user and you have obviously been on TV shows and so many things. Do you find that your personal communication style changes depending on the nature of the platform?

AA: Well, obviously you can be more expansive on the podcast than on Twitter because Twitter limits the number of characters you can use. But the approach remains always the same: to be clear and vivid. It's important no matter what—in fact, it's a little harder but more important when you have character limits. I see a lot of tweets that could mean a lot of things because they're not thoughtfully constructed.

BLVR: Has "clear and vivid" been sort of a mantra for you for a while?

AA: Yeah, it grew out of the work that we did at the Center for Communicating Science, which I started over a decade ago.

BLVR: What are you most proud of that has come out of the center?

AA: I think it's the impact we've had on scientists, doctors, and other medical professionals. Some of the senior scientists say they understand their own science better because they learned how to communicate it better to the public. They get an overview of their own work that they didn't have before, and it helps them in their own work, which is surprising and very satisfying. Another really surprising thing that led to the book about communication I wrote, and that led to the podcast, was a scientist telling us, "This training is saving my marriage." Then I began to realize in concrete ways that it's not just for scientists and doctors: it's for everybody. That's the point of view that I wrote the book from. And, of course, that's the point of view in the podcast, because I have conversations with people in every conceivable field.

BLVR: You've interviewed everyone from Itzhak Perlman to Judge Judy. That's quite the range!

AA: Yeah, Sarah Silverman, Itzhak Perlman, and Judge Judy—you don't often find them together in the back of a taxi cab.

BLVR: No, but I think it would be a fun taxi to be stuck in! So how have you been choosing the guests for the podcast?

AA: People who I think will have interesting and insightful stories about relating to other people and communicating. So far, everybody has had a really interesting story—stories,

I think, are very important. And also people who can have a good conversation: not pontificate or do a little media lecture, but have a real conversation where the ball goes back and forth.

BLVR: I feel like social media has made so many conversations one-sided. Twitter and Facebook posts are just like monologues, without any conversation. Do you feel like that's true?

AA: Yeah, I do. I think it's much more engaging for a listener to hear a good conversation than to hear a monologue. And a conversation that sounds like a conventional interview is not a real conversation. I'm really much more interested in a conversation that expresses my own curiosity about the other person. I don't know what I'm going to ask the other person until I hear them tell me something. I go in with a couple of things I know I'm going to want to ask, but I don't have a list of questions that I go down point by point, because

---

DOG-NAME SUGGESTIONS FROM A 1905 HOUND-BREEDING MANUAL THAT SOUND LIKE DATING APPS

* Active
* Blossom
* Bouncer
* Bounty
* Chaser
* Chaplet
* Charmer
* Custard
* Damsel
* Dandy
* Driver
* Fetish
* Gameboy
* Giddy
* Guiltless
* Linkboy
* Listless
* Locket
* Lonely
* Nectar
* Nipper
* Primate
* Rambler
* Redrose
* Saucy
* Sociable
* Tractive
* Truelove
* Trusty
* Wallflower
* Worthy

—*list compiled by Ginger Greene*

all that does is make the other person give me their little set pieces—that's boring. You don't hear two people having a dance together.

BLVR: As someone who does a lot of interviews, I find that people who just recite what they want to recite and don't actually engage with you—

AA: Yeah, that's right! They've decided they have the perfect way to express what they are selling or what their ideas are. And regardless of what you say to them, they just want to tell you in that perfect way and they don't want to really get into your head. They just want you to be a stenographer for them, and that's not fun! That's not fun to listen to.

BLVR: It's funny for me to hear you say that, just because I feel like Aaron Sorkin is kind of responsible for a lot of the monologues you get in pop culture these days. Like he has fed into this monologue culture that we live in now.

AA: Well, it's true. I don't know if there's less listening than before, but I think the problem facing good communication has always been listening. I don't know if it's worse now, but the country is split politically and the sides don't listen to each other. I don't see how we're going to get anyplace if they don't.

BLVR: I was rewatching *The West Wing*, and while it's obviously a fictional show, the interaction between Republicans and Democrats seems *so* civil and reasonable and rational, compared to what we have now.

AA: I don't know if it ever was a picture of reality so much as a dramatic presentation of what could be. But it was uplifting to see the opponents have a rational talk. But that sure couldn't happen in real life. There was a time—they all tell me there was a time—when they would argue on the floor heatedly and then go out for a beer together and find out about one another's families. And when you do that, it's hard to demonize the other person. But, boy, demonization is rampant now.

BLVR: Well, yeah. I mean, every day I feel like there's a new walking evil…

AA: "Walking evil"—that's good.

BLVR: I was really struck while watching a scene in *The West Wing* with your character [Arnold Vinick] and Jimmy Smits's character [Matthew Santos], where you're having this very intense conversation and you're obviously in rival political parties and you're going against each other and you're so civil and nice and reasonable. I know it's fictional, but it also just made me nostalgic for a day when that seemed possible, because now I feel like that's a fantasy even more than fiction.

AA: It's very hard now. Everybody seems to be convinced that everybody else is lying, making up facts, and it's hard to have a discussion when you can't agree on basic things. But knowing the other person, knowing who you're talking to, plays into that again. I'm finding on my podcast that when you bring people together who were fierce enemies, trying to kill each

---

AN INCOMPLETE LIST OF *SATURDAY NIGHT LIVE* SKITS WITH DANCE NUMBERS

✶ "King Tut," season 3, episode 18
✶ Patrick Swayze, season 16, episode 4 (two dances)
✶ "Lunch Lady Land," season 19, episode 11
✶ "Spartan Cheerleaders at Tryouts," season 23, episode 2
✶ "Janet Reno's Dance Party with Rudy Giuliani,"
   season 26, episode 10
✶ "The Demarco Brothers' Audition," season 26,
   episode 19
✶ "Omeletteville," season 29, episode 2
✶ "Single Ladies," season 34, episode 8
✶ Joseph Gordon-Levitt's monologue, season 35,
   episode 7
✶ "Les Jeunes de Paris," season 36, episode 4
✶ "Boy Dance Party," season 39, episode 5
✶ "Haunted Elevator (feat. David S. Pumpkins),"
   season 42, episode 4
✶ Jimmy Fallon's monologue, season 42, episode 18
✶ "Diner Lobster," season 43, episode 20
✶ "Late Night Battle," season 44, episode 2

—list compiled by Abigail Walker

---

other, and get them to have a view of each other as people, to know about their families, their childhood experiences, things like that, they are able to talk more reasonably with each other and solve serious problems. Like, I had a conversation with George Mitchell, the former senator who negotiated the agreement in Northern Ireland between people who had been killing one another for decades. And I talked with Letty Cottin Pogrebin, who organized groups of women, half of them Israeli and half of them Palestinian, and had them visit places that were important to them and their culture. They had a softened view of one another as a result of that.

BLVR: So do you believe the idea that once you get to know someone else's story, it's hard to hate them?

AA: It might not work every time—like the guy who's in jail in California for all those murders in the '70s. What's his name?

BLVR: Manson?

AA: Manson. Yeah, I doubt that if I heard his life story, I'd have more sympathy for him. But in the broad range of people, not an extreme outlier like him, it does make it harder to hate someone when you see how similar they are to you.

III. "I'M DOING EXACTLY WHAT I OUGHT TO DO"

BLVR: Who do you wish you could sit down and talk to? Who are your dream guests?

AA: So far, pretty much everybody has said yes.

BLVR: Really?

AA: Yeah, Michelle Obama. It'd be fun to talk to her because so many people respond to her, on all sides. And it's interesting to see what a person understands about the response to them. I've always wanted to talk to this scientist in Switzerland who has done functional MRI studies and discovered that the reward centers in the brain are activated when someone is punishing someone else for what they perceive as a transgression of some kind. The idea that we feel good when we're punishing somebody is a really interesting discovery, I think.

BLVR: So is this sort of like a Milgram experiment?

AA: I forget. I probably read how he does the experiment, but I doubt it's a Milgram-type thing, because I don't think they can do that anymore.

BLVR: Well, if it's in Switzerland, who knows what the rules are?

AA: Yeah. Maybe in Switzerland it's different. I don't know. But I think you can set up a situation where you punish somebody in a mild way, and it's not like the Milgram thing, where you punish them to extremes. The thing that really interests me is: What does that mean for how we communicate? When someone says something we disagree with and we correct them strongly, was it really important to correct them for the sake of the discussion, or were we just getting off on it?

BLVR: Does that mean we're all secretly sadists or at least have, like, sadistic tendencies?

AA: I see what you mean. I see that it could sound like that. I don't know. There's probably some survival benefits from it, but like all benefits, you have to modulate it so it doesn't do more harm than good.

BLVR: Have you always been a science nerd?

AA: Since I was a kid, I was always interested in how things worked. I was an amateur inventor when I was a kid.

BLVR: What did you invent?

AA: I invented a five-way can opener. There were five different functions, and I put them together in one device. It wasn't much of an invention, but—

BLVR: It sounds like you invented a Swiss Army knife but just for opening cans.

AA: Well, one thing that I invented that really was not a bad idea was a lazy Susan in the refrigerator, so you didn't have to reach to the back to get things: you could just turn the turntable. And about a year or two after I thought of that, a refrigerator company [General Electric] actually came out with one. And then a year after that, they stopped making them. Like, there were bottles of ketchup flying around kitchens all over the country.

BLVR: Too bad you hadn't patented it, though. You could've made a little money.

AA: Well, at the age of ten, I didn't know about patenting.

BLVR: So you invented a can opener and a refrigerator lazy Susan. Are all your inventions food-related?

AA: That's funny; I never thought of that! Maybe so. I didn't invent a malted milk machine, but I did make one out of spare parts.

BLVR: How do you make a malted milk machine?

AA: Well, you get a tube and you solder it to a motor and stick it over a glass.

BLVR: OK, maybe I don't know what a malted milk is, because I thought it was like a milkshake.

AA: Yeah, it is, it is. But the machine is just a thing to electronically stir. It was really just for the fun of it, making something; it really wasn't anything.

BLVR: So why did you let acting distract you from your obviously brilliant career in invention?

AA: My brilliant career as an inventor! My father was an actor, and from the time I was about two and a half or even younger, as far as I know, I was standing in the wings watching him perform. So there was no other life I even considered except writing. I wanted to be a writer even before I wanted to be an actor.

BLVR: So you just dabbled in invention?

AA: Yeah, I was an inventor on the side. It was just fun. You know, it's always been fun. In my twenties I really started reading about science seriously, and I kept at it. Not because I had some urgent need to understand it; I was just curious, and it was extremely entertaining to me to find out what people had figured out about nature.

BLVR: You've played a doctor several times in your career. Were you able to use any of the scientific knowledge you've gleaned in your roles?

AA: I don't think so.

BLVR: That is too bad.

AA: I just play what's in the script.

BLVR: And it sounds like maybe in a different time, you could've been the next Elon Musk.

AA: Well, I think we have one of those.

BLVR: Yeah, but you could've been a better one. With fewer weird pastimes.

AA: No, I'm doing exactly what I ought to do. And it's only because I followed my nose and kept looking for what was interesting to me. I wanted to be a really good writer, and I never stopped trying to figure out how I could do that. The same thing with acting. And that curiosity about science led me to do the television series *Scientific American Frontiers*, which I did for eleven years. I learned an awful lot about science, but I didn't realize I was learning about communication at the same time.

BLVR: So when did you realize that it was all about communication?

AA: Well, when I got off the show, I realized that the successful interviews were conversations and that they involved improvising, which I had studied as an actor. They were like the experience of two actors on the stage, where they have to listen to each other in a rich way. Otherwise, it doesn't look like real life. It isn't real life; it's just dueling monologues. And I thought: Wouldn't it be interesting if we could train scientists to have that relationship with whoever they're talking with?

So that's when I started experimenting, teaching scientists improvisation. That expanded into using improvisation to learn the basics of crafting a message. We found that it doesn't matter if the person is physically in front of you—they could be distant in time and space, the way they are when you're writing for an audience—but if you're thinking about who you're writing for and their mental process, you can apply those same techniques to writing. It sounds odd. I mean, the techniques are based on recognizing body language and other clues that you get from the voice and the face of the other person. But you can still think of what they're going through, even if you can't see them.

IV. CAKE TALK

BLVR: It's interesting that you've been so inspired by improv and have kind of extrapolated it into this entire communication methodology, because in my experience, improv is usually the thing somebody invites you to on a second date and you really don't want to go.

AA: Well, that's curious, because if it's the second date, they should already have enough clues from the first date to know you wouldn't want to go to improv. Sounds like poor communication to me. They're not paying attention to you.

BLVR: So you're saying most bad dates come down to poor communication?

AA: I would probably say slightly more than 100 percent of the time. I mean, I haven't been on many dates in my life. I've been married over sixty years! But first dates are usually, I would imagine, so filled with anxiety that you could be picking up on a lot of information, a lot of data on the other person. If you don't pick up on it and if you don't feel you can comfortably respond to that, then I would guess there shouldn't be a second date.

BLVR: I feel like sometimes you don't realize they're not picking up on the information until you go on the second date, and then you realize they didn't listen to anything you said on the first date.

AA: Oh, I see! Yeah, some people are good at the listening pose—the pose that says, *I'm really listening with fascination.*

BLVR: Maybe that's what Rodin based his sculpture on. But you've mentioned you've been married for sixty-one years now, and I've heard that you guys met over rum cake. Could you tell me that story?

AA: Well, at the risk of doing a monologue, I will. The first time we met was brief. Arlene was playing chamber music at a friend's house—Arlene was a clarinetist when we met, professional. The second time we met, we were invited to the same apartment for dinner. The woman who had invited us had made a rum cake for dessert, and she had it up on the top of the refrigerator in the kitchen to cool during dinner. But the refrigerator was an old Philco refrigerator—they don't even make them anymore, I think—and it had a rounded top and it shook while it worked, and during dinner the rum cake slowly made it way to the edge of the top of the refrigerator, and then it went *splat* on the floor. And Arlene and I were the only two people who got up with our spoons and ate it off the floor. So when that happens, you know destiny is talking to you.

BLVR: Yeah, I mean, it's hard to find two people who believe in the five-second rule!

AA: I've read a scientist who reported on that. They actually studied it, and they said microbes move a lot faster than five seconds. So if it's on the floor at all, you're picking up microbes. But we didn't eat the bottom part; we ate the top part, which didn't touch the floor. Do you think we were crazy?

BLVR: How many other cakes have you guys shared off the floor in your lives?

AA: None, but we… On our fiftieth anniversary we served everybody rum cake for dessert, and we were really tempted to have the waiters drop it on the floor. Instead of eharmony and all those dating sites, all you have to do is toss a piece of rum cake on the floor and see who goes for it. Especially if someone's been laughing at your jokes throughout dinner like Arlene was. Oh, I was ready for the rum cake experience.

BLVR: Is rum cake your favorite kind of cake, then?

AA: I love rum cake, and partly for the memories, but I don't eat it much.

BLVR: No? What do you tend to eat instead?

AA: What do I eat instead? I eat, like, carrot cake.

BLVR: Carrot cake, huh? Honestly, if we just talked about cake for the rest of the time, I would be thrilled.

AA: Well, it doesn't have much appeal for me, but whatever you want to talk about.

BLVR: So you don't have much of a sweet tooth, or just the topic of conversation doesn't appeal to you?

AA: Oh, well, it doesn't seem fruitful as a topic of conversation.

BLVR: What if we talked about fruitcake: that would fruitful.

AA: Actually, I like fruitcake. It has such a bad reputation because most fruitcakes are passed around. After a few years they become inedible, but a fresh fruitcake isn't bad. You know what's really, really good? Panforte. It's fruitcake-like. Isn't it good?

BLVR: It is delicious. You know, at Prince Louis's christening they served seven-year-old fruitcake.

AA: Seven-year-old? You'd have to eat it with a hammer.

BLVR: Apparently it was Kate and Williams's wedding cake, and they saved a slice to serve at his christening.

AA: So could your teeth make a dent in it?

BLVR: I don't know; I assume. I don't know. Maybe they gave everyone, like, tiny hacksaws.

AA: English toffee is good too.

BLVR: Oh, yeah, you can't go too wrong with that.

V. "I JUST DID IT BECAUSE IT WAS FUN"

BLVR: That's enough sweet talk for someone without a sweet tooth. What led you to start a podcast?

AA: To spread this idea and to bring in some income for the

Center for Communicating Science, because all the income that we take in from ad sales goes to support the Center for Communicating Science.

BLVR: So you've decided that podcasting is the way to fortune?

AA: Well, no. It's just one way. I'm busy raising money in conventional ways for the center too. I give talks around the country on the lecture circuit. And all the money from those talks goes to the center. So that helps a lot.

BLVR: Were you inspired by any podcast in particular? Like, do you have favorites?

AA: No, I think I was more inspired by all the work I've done over the last twenty-five years. And the producer of the podcast was the producer of *Scientific American Frontiers* all those years ago. He also worked for a couple of years at the Center for Communicating Science, so we've been working together for two and a half decades. And the idea is to get a really interactive conversation going, a true conversation. And hopefully with good stories coming out of it and some

---

EXOPLANETS IN THE HABITABLE ZONE

✵ Proxima Centauri b, 4.25 light-years from Earth
✵ Kepler-186f, 580 light-years from Earth
✵ Gliese 667 Cc, 23.62 light-years from Earth
✵ Tau Ceti e, 11.9 light-years from Earth
✵ Gliese 581g, 20 light-years from Earth
✵ TRAPPIST-1b, 40 light-years from Earth
✵ 55 Cancri e, 41 light-years from Earth
✵ HD 80606 b, 190 light-years from Earth
✵ 51 Pegasi b, 50 light-years from Earth
✵ 70 Virginis b, 60 light-years from Earth
✵ WASP-33b, 383 light-years from Earth
✵ Wolf 1061c, 13.8 light-years from Earth
✵ K2-296b, 519 light-years from Earth
✵ TOI 700 d, 101 light-years from Earth

—list compiled by Abigail Walker

---

fun, you know: some laughter! I listen to other podcasts, but I haven't heard one quite like that.

BLVR: What's on your podcast playlist?

AA: I like *Freakonomics*. And I think Marc Maron does a terrific job. His conversation with Barack Obama was amazing, I thought. I interviewed Marc Maron on the show. He was a good conversationalist. Very honest, very straight. And Sarah Silverman was too. I was so impressed with the story she tells about that guy who insulted her on Twitter and how she turned his life around just by being thoughtful and caring about it.

BLVR: Yeah, and I feel like you don't hear that story very often when it comes to people we consider trolls.

AA: Well, if you treat them like a troll, they'll probably act more like a troll. But that doesn't mean that what she did would work with everybody. When she looked at his profile, I think she probably thought she had a chance to connect with this person. Maybe she wouldn't have reached out to him if she hadn't had that feeling.

BLVR: Do you listen to *The West Wing Weekly*?

AA: Did you say "wrestling"?

BLVR: No, "West Wing."

AA: Oh! No, but I do catch wrestling as often as I can.

BLVR: Do you really? Are you a wrestling fan?

AA: No! I don't think there is a podcast for that.

BLVR: There probably is—there are a lot of podcasts.

AA: No, I didn't know there was a *West Wing* show. What do they talk about? *West Wing* is all over.

BLVR: Joshua Malina and Hrishikesh Hirway watch the show and talk about it. Well, it's something to add to the playlist.

AA: Well, I'm kind of busy making them now. I don't listen to them that much.

BLVR: Yeah, I think that's actually one of the biggest problems—there's so much content these days, it's hard to keep up. Especially if you're a content creator. You don't have time to watch everything or read every scientific article, every science book, and listen to all the podcasts. How do you balance?

AA: I skim a lot. But you can't do that with the podcasts.

BLVR: You can if you listen on one-and-a-half speed.

AA: Oh, yeah, but then it sounds like Porky Pig is talking.

BLVR: What do you have planned for the future? You have a podcast and the center and an incredible acting career. What do you want to do next?

AA: I don't make plans about the future.

BLVR: Oh, really?

AA: Yeah. I think five-year plans tend not to work. I tend to make a new one every year.

BLVR: How long have you been not making plans?

AA: Probably since I was born? Yeah, I just go—follow what interests me. And that really works. I know there are people, even in my business, show business, who have

a planned future: *I did this and now I should do that and then I should do this.* I think when you make plans in my field, the world is so uncertain, you can't stick to that plan. You gotta adjust to the uncertainties. So it's more like an improvisation, and that's more comfortable for me, and I'm happy dealing with uncertainty. For example, in the town where we have a country place, there's a wonderful concert festival every summer, and for the last three years I've taken part in the opening concert. I write a story based on the correspondence of the composer with people important in his life, and each part of the story is connected to one of pieces they are playing. Last night—and tonight is the second performance—it was Fanny and Felix Mendelssohn, brother and sister, and I just did it because it was fun.

BLVR: Well, fun is a good reason to do things.

AA: While I was busy doing the podcast and promoting it and raising money for the center and helping work out management problems and things like that, I was reading hundreds of letters between Fanny and Felix Mendelssohn and trying to find a story and then getting up and performing it with the octet, who are brilliant musicians, some of the best in the country. And that—I just did that because it interested me and it opened up a world to me. I did it with Mozart last year and the year before that. No, last year was Schumann and Brahms, and before that it was Mozart. And it's exciting to accomplish something even when it's far afield from what you've usually done or what you're known for doing. And I didn't plan to do that; I didn't have in my mind for three years that once a year I was going to write and perform a piece about a famous composer.

BLVR: And yet here you are. So, yeah, I guess if you planned too far in advance, maybe it wouldn't have happened.

AA: Yeah, I would be doing something else, which maybe I wouldn't be enjoying.

BLVR: OK, so your advice is never make plans and always communicate your lack of plans clearly.

AA: My advice is to try to not give too much advice. It works best for me. ★

BEING

ONFIM, THE ETERNAL BOY

by Annie Rauwerda

In the city of Novgorod, in the thirteenth century, a seven-year-old named Onfim drew mythical creatures on birchbark. Nothing about Onfim's drawings are world-shattering. That is why I love them. He was a little boy, living in what is present-day Russia, who grew bored of his school assignments. His self-portraits look a bit like tadpoles or perhaps Mr. Potato Head, like the people I drew as a kid (and you probably did too): smiling ovals with sticks for limbs and a random smattering of fingers. It's the same style of drawing you affixed to fridges or drawn on the sidewalk in chalk. They are a developmental rite of passage and endearingly human.

One drawing features a catlike creature and the words "I am a wild beast" in the Cyrillic alphabet. Onfim also wrote "Greetings from Onfim to Daniel," suggesting that he passed his masterpiece on to a friend. Another scrap of paper shows that Onfim abandoned his alphabet practice after just eleven letters, instead opting to draw a knightly figure on horseback, piercing an enemy on the ground. He plastered his name above it, appearing to label the heroic figure as himself. On another piece of paper, Onfim drew a stick figure boy fighting a bizarre multiheaded creature (kind of a Hydra): "Lord, help your servant Onfim," he wrote, as if requesting divine intervention in his imaginary battle against the monster.

Onfim taps into some magical maternal instinct in me, and I could practically cry because I love him so much. Unlike the billions of kids whose drawings and daydreams have washed away into oblivion, Onfim's seventeen preserved scraps of paper have given him a sort of eternal life. It's possible that he became a grandfather or a scribe, or fulfilled his dream of being a famous warrior, but to us he's forever a little boy who dreams of knightly valor while being stuck memorizing the Psalms. He captures something indescribable—his work feels like a rage comic, or a goofy *Calvin and Hobbes* saga. Onfim is the eternal boy, and one can only imagine how much he would have loved to drive a go-kart or play *Minecraft*.

Beginning in the ninth century, Onfim's city of Novgorod became a bustling medieval trade hub. Its people appear to have had unusually high rates of literacy, and its wet low-oxygen soil (dubbed "archeological gold") has given us many fossilized relics: more than one thousand birchbark documents filled with the unmediated voices of ordinary people have been discovered there since 1951. Around 1380, someone named Boris sent a note asking for someone named Nastasia to send him shirts he'd forgotten to pack on his journey. There are requests to buy barley, a reminder to hire a carpenter, a note in which a father tells his son the current price of salt. Sometime between 1280 and 1300, a man named Mikita proposed marriage to a woman named Anna, writing, "I want you, and you me."

As long as there have been behaviorally modern humans—for at least the past forty thousand years, maybe longer—there have been imaginative little boys daydreaming about wild beasts. A few people wrote laws and dealt with the other boring affairs that tend to get classified as "history," but the rest were falling in love or cooking dinner or doodling in the margins. There were probably knights who told corny dad jokes and medieval peasants who doubled over while laughing about some stupid inside joke. They weren't brutish; they weren't simple. Onfim's drawings are a reminder of their intricate interiority. ✶

Illustration by Hartley Lin

MEDIEVAL DEMON BABIES

1370–1450	1454–1465	1470–1480	1480–1500	1500–1625

MADONNA AND CHILD
by Paolo Di Giovanni Fei
HEAD SIZE: *substantial*
MOOD: *uninterested*

MADONNA AND CHILD
by Andrea Mantegna
HEAD SIZE: *larger than average*
MOOD: *religiously ecstatic*

MADONNA AND CHILD
by Benvenuto di Giovanni
HEAD SIZE: *average*
MOOD: *euphoric*

MADONNA AND CHILD
by Filippino Lippi
HEAD SIZE: *large, especially up top*
MOOD: *too high to focus*

VIRGIN AND CHILD
attributed to Lucas van Leyden
HEAD SIZE: *eggplant-like*
MOOD: *pure evil*

MADONNA AND CHILD
by Domenico di Bartolo
HEAD SIZE: *average*
MOOD: *aged despair*

MADONNA ADORING THE SLEEPING CHILD
by Giovanni Bellini
HEAD SIZE: *average*

VIRGIN AND CHILD
by Master of the St. Ursula Legend
HEAD SIZE: *average for an adult but not a baby*

MADONNA AND CHILD
by Carlo Crivelli
HEAD SIZE: *slightly rectangular*
MOOD: *starving for his pet bird*

MADONNA AND CHILD
by Luca Signorelli
HEAD SIZE: *abnormally large*
MOOD: *aged apathy*

MADONNA AND CHILD
by Masolino and Masaccio
HEAD SIZE: *abnormally large*
MOOD: *jaded, apathetic*

THE VIRGIN AND CHILD
by Petrus Christus
HEAD SIZE: *average*
MOOD: *deceptively cheerful*

VIRGIN AND CHILD
by Hugo van der Goes
HEAD SIZE: *average*
MOOD: *unfulfilled*

MADONNA LITTA
by Leonardo da Vinci
HEAD SIZE: *normal enough*
MOOD: *sleepily content*

THE VIRGIN OF THE CHAIR
by Guido Reni
HEAD SIZE: *average*
MOOD: *sick of posing*

THE VIRGIN AND CHILD
by Rogier van der Weyden
HEAD SIZE: slightly long
MOOD: curious

VIRGIN AND CHILD
by Rogier van der Weyden
HEAD SIZE: average
MOOD: transfixed

MADONNA AND CHILD
by Andrea del Verrocchio
MOOD: trying to go to his happy
place; not working so well

MADONNA AND CHILD
by Pietro Perugino
HEAD SIZE: above average
MOOD: longing for baby St. John

THE VIRGIN AND CHILD
by Luis de Morales
MOOD: already over being
the leader of a new religion

MADONNA AND CHILD
by Lorenzo di Bicci
HEAD SIZE: average
MOOD: unsure

MADONNA AND CHILD
by Andrea Mantegna
HEAD SIZE: average, if big-cheeked
MOOD: apathetic

MADONNA AND CHILD
attributed to Giovanni Bellini
HEAD SIZE: creepily round
MOOD: muted

MADONNA AND CHILD
by Giovanni Bellini
HEAD SIZE: surprisingly normal
MOOD: catatonic

VIRGIN AND CHILD
by Joos van Cleve
MOOD: knows he's about to get
drunk and apprehensive about it

MADONNA AND CHILD
by Sassetta
HEAD SIZE: teeny-tiny
MOOD: complete neutrality

MADONNA AND CHILD
by Giovanni di Paolo
HEAD SIZE: oblong
MOOD: slightly cheeky

MADONNA WITH CHILD
by Matteo di Giovanni
HEAD SIZE: average
MOOD: emotionally exhausted

MADONNA OF THE BOOK
by Sandro Botticelli
HEAD SIZE: a bit lumpy
MOOD: naive curiosity

MADONNA AND CHILD
by Giralamo dai Libri
MOOD: thinking of his
long lost baby love

I
f you take a survey course in the art, history, and music of Western civilization, you will learn that no painter before the modern era had ever seen a baby in real life. Every infant depicted in a pre-eighteenth-century painting falls somewhere on the spectrum of "decrepit old man" to "demon that tortures hell's worst offenders." Madonna and Child paintings best exemplify this bizarre phenomenon; the image of the Virgin Mary holding an infant Jesus has been a mainstay of Christian art since the beginning of the common era, and thus offers us a wide range of babies to inspect. Each artistic period seems to have many ugly tiny Jesuses, but the painters of the Italian and Dutch Renaissances created uniquely demonic images of the Christian infant lord and savior. I have gathered and organized them here, alongside some general impressions of their emotional states.

—Yasmin Patel

I TELL HOLLY TO GO AHEAD TO WORK. I'LL TAKE AN EXTRA "BEREAVEMENT DAY" TO DEAL WITH THIS.

THIS IS RIDICULOUS!

JESUS.

COME OUT, YOU WORTHLESS ANIMAL!!

I FIND THE URN TOPPLED OVER. BIRD DROPPINGS AND TRACKS AND GRAY ASHES—WHAT'S LEFT OF *HIM*—HAVE BEEN STAMPED INTO THE CARPET.

WHEN I MANAGE TO LOCK THE BIRD OUTSIDE, IT REFUSES TO BE FREE. IT KEEPS STRIKING THE SLIDING DOOR WITH ACID *RAGE*.

STAB
STAB

I LET IT BACK IN SO ITS HEAD DOESN'T EXPLODE.

WHAT IS *WRONG* WITH YOU?!

SQUAWK

I HERD IT INTO WHAT WILL EVENTUALLY BECOME OUR BABY'S ROOM AND LAY OUT GARBAGE BAGS. YOU KIND OF GET USED TO THE WAY IT SMELLS.

I'M GOOD IN A CRISIS. EARLY ON, I LEARNED HOW TO THIN OUT MY EMOTIONS DURING EMERGENCIES...

KARL WAS THE SENSITIVE ONE.

SOMETIMES I STILL SEE HIM AS AN 8-YEAR-OLD, PACING IN OUR SHARED BEDROOM DURING ONE OF DAD'S "MOODS." HIS HANDS BALLED UP INTO TIGHT LITTLE FISTS.

SQUAWK
SQUAWK

BUT I TRY NOT TO DWELL ON THE PAST. I START DRIVING TOWARD CANMORE... I FIGURE THERE'S A WORKABLE HABITAT THERE FOR THIS MANIC-SUICIDAL BIRD.

WHY ARE YOU SUDDENLY SO QUIET? WHAT'S WRONG WITH YOU?

OF COURSE, SHE'S RIGHT. BUT SHE DOESN'T GET THAT CALL ANYTIME SOON.

DO YOU KNOW HOW EASY IT IS TO HAVE 4 LBS OF FRESH MACKEREL DELIVERED TO YOUR DOORSTEP?

HOLLY'S NOT HEARTLESS. I ONCE FOUND HER CRYING IN THE BATHROOM AFTER MY DAD REFUSED TO COME TO OUR WEDDING. WHICH, REALLY, WAS A LOGISTICAL RELIEF...

SHE SAID SHE FELT **SORRY** FOR HIM.

THINGS FEEL DIFFERENT WHEN THE SUN RISES. THE BIRD STARTS VIOLENTLY PLUCKING OUT ITS OWN CHEST FEATHERS.

IT WON'T TAKE ANY FOOD OR WATER. ITS WINGS ARE NOW THE GRAY OF PROPERTY TAX NOTICES.

THE BIRD EVENTUALLY FOLDS INTO A DARK CORNER, WHERE IT OPENS ITS BILL FOR LONG, SOUNDLESS INTERVALS...

IT'S NO LONGER A NUISANCE. I WISH IT WAS STILL A NUISANCE.

MY DAD'S NICKNAME COMES BACK TO ME—WHAT THEY CALLED HIM YEARS AGO IN LOUD BARS. THEY CALLED HIM "*THE PHOENIX*." "HERE COMES THE PHOENIX..."

THE GARBAGE BAGS ARE CONVENIENT. SOON I'LL BE WRAPPING THEM AROUND THE BIRD.

HOW LONG IS THAT SUPPOSED TO STAY IN MY HEAD?

RICKIE LEE JONES

[MUSICIAN]

"I REALLY THOUGHT I COULD DO EVERYTHING
BY MYSELF, BUT I AM NOT MY BEST BY MYSELF."

Advice for young artists from Rickie Lee Jones:
Make yourself out of things that are not contemporary
Be prepared for the storm of public life
It has to be bigger, longer, older
It has to be true

It seems there was no choice for Rickie Lee Jones but to be an artist. Born into a troubled, itinerant family, Rickie Lee was already a runaway by the time she was fifteen, with a vagabond lifestyle and a kid's dream of liberation, illuminated by the twilight of the '60s. In the mid-'70s, she was living in Venice Beach, working as a fake secretary for a gangster and writing lyrics on his IBM typewriter. She knew she was destined for something true and artistic. At a desolate bar, she figured out what her voice could do, performing jazz while the rest of the world turned its attention to antic disco. In 1978, Rickie Lee was the object of a major-label bidding war, and her uncanny, singular, stylish debut album vaulted her into the mainstream. There she arrived, fully formed, understood as what she was and still is: an iconoclast. Dubbed the Duchess of Coolsville, she wrote unconventional songs that bent and strayed out of pop convention and doubled back through jazz phrasing and American songbook; what came out of the speakers was always Rickie, wholly and truly. Her music was a dare to go further. A pop star who was undeniably her own girl, Rickie endowed a legacy that was later taken up by Fiona Apple, Tori Amos, Sheryl Crow, and others of the "to thy own self be true" kick. Her debut "Chuck E's in Love" became part of the Top 40 canon and put her on the cover of Rolling Stone

Illustration by Kristian Hammerstad

twice in two years. She was always in her trademark beret, a sensual wild girl, divining a pure musical fate.

Landmark albums followed, like 1981's Pirates *and 1989's* Flying Cowboys, *as did a grip of Grammys, and the acclaim continued through the eclectic sprawl of* Pop Pop, Ghostyhead, *and* The Sermon on Exposition Boulevard *in the '90s and '00s. Her inimitable voice has stretched across five decades. Her songs are full of curious characters, molls and dolls, girls tossed by fate, truest lost loves, death wish abysses, humor, and heavenly connection—and all are luminous with desire and full of life. Her work is vast, gloriously unpredictable, ever-evolving, steadfast in its vision. Which is to say, Rickie Lee is a treasure; her life's work is a master class in being a free woman. Her recent memoir,* Last Chance Texaco: Chronicles of an American Troubadour, *is now out in paperback.*

I spoke with her over Zoom in the summer of 2022. She had just returned home to New Orleans, after having finished a long stretch of sessions in New York for what will be her first proper jazz album, to be released next year. Rickie Lee's reputation as a truth teller has been earned. We talked about gatekeeping, the evolution of her voice, and going to a Black Flag gig with Tom Waits.

—Jessica Hopper

I. COMING HOME TO JAZZ

THE BELIEVER: Hi! Nice to see you again.

RICKIE LEE JONES: Nice to see you. How'd your film [*Women Who Rock* premiere at the Tribeca Film Festival] go in New York?

BLVR: Oh, really well. Really well. People love it. You know you've made something good when all the girls say, "It just made me cry" and the boys quibble over genre.

RLJ: Boys need stuff like that. They're so *Gotta have A, B, C, D,* and *It has to go like that.* They need that structure so badly. Women don't thrive in it, I think, but men do. Some of them.

BLVR: No. No. We work on vibes rather than on instructions and rules. How are you now that you are home from recording?

RLJ: I'm good. Recording the album is not over yet—usually after a project ends, I get very depressed and confused. I'm still tying up loose ends, so I feel pretty good. And I'm gonna go on vacation, which is really good.

BLVR: Let's talk about the record. You are making a proper jazz record. I re-read your book again, for the third time, and I came upon that spot where you're talking about when you were younger and you were getting into jazz and, like, nobody was into jazz. What was your journey and your relationship with jazz from there to here? How has it evolved?

RLJ: Rich question. So I gotta write down my thoughts as you're saying it, 'cause the first thought is with the music. But the second thought is with the genre, which is laden with men—

BLVR: [*Laughs*]

RLJ: —who decide who gets through the door. I'm gonna answer about genre first. So when I was growing up, my dad played the trumpet and sang jazz in the fashion of his father and also what was contemporary in his world, where Frank Sinatra was the main guy. But also, coming from vaudeville, my grandfather and uncle, who were expert musicians, they're playing things like "On the Sunny Side of the Street." The old stuff, then the new stuff, [the Miles Davis Quintet's] "It Never Entered My Mind," and Nina Simone, who my dad loved. He also had Ella Fitzgerald and Sarah Vaughan records, and the pop stars—Andy Williams and, uh, Harry Belafonte. These were the albums I grew up hearing. This is the palette of my early education. Now the Beatles come and introduce me to pop, right? But it's their version of pop, which has remnants of rhythm and blues from the '50s and all the things that made them.

So in 1974, '75, when I was twenty or twenty-one and living in Venice [California], there was one club to go to— the Comeback Inn. They had a couple of acts every night. So you could hear jazz at seven and maybe a singer-songwriter at nine. I'd go there and order Burgundy wine and watch them. Somehow I got myself up onstage with one of the jazz trios and sang "My Funny Valentine." [*Singing*] "You made me leave my happy home… [*speaking*] since I fell for you." I was very emotional in my deliveries, and they took notice. And then they began inviting me up onstage. It was a big deal 'cause they were very snobby guys. And that was my introduction to how lucky I was to be invited onto this stage of people playing this kind of music.

All right, so then a couple years later, when I got my record contract, it stipulated that it all had to be composed by me. It couldn't be any covers. So when I toured for that record, I did "My Funny Valentine," and once in a while some other one. I think somebody had taught me, roughly, "Lush Life," which is really hard, and a couple other ballads, which we began to work into the live shows. And I was a very big deal! So I assumed that the larger world would know—this is just ego stuff, but I'm telling it—that I was singing jazz on a rock-and-roll/pop stage—a forbidden thing to do! [*Laughter*] And I was doing it successfully! And for years, for many years, people would say, "You were the first time I heard jazz," and I went, "Yeah [*claps*], I did it."

But the old guard of jazz players are the descendants—people like Tom Scott. The LA horn players were like, *Fuck her*. I'm not sure why: maybe imprecision or too much emotion or whatever it is they don't like about women, or don't like about women singers, or don't like about me personally. They would not let me in. Not to jazz radio, or anywhere people were gathering—it made me feel really bad—anywhere people were gathering to play jazz. I was excluded, I thought, and it hurt a lot at the time because I was thinking, I'm carrying the banner of jazz singing, exciting jazz—not, you know, like those old guys who sing it really straight.

But that's important because that's my experience with jazz. When I did a jazz record [*Pop Pop* (1991)] and Charlotte [her daughter] was like three or two or something, we did "Dat Dere" and we put her on in the beginning and we put an Argentinian instrument, a bandoneon, on. We—the producer, David Was, but especially me—tried to cover up or adorn the jazz to such an extent that maybe people would listen to it. So the *LA Times* reviewed

my record with two different reviewers—a pop critic and a jazz critic on the page next to each other. Well, guys, I'm awfully important! And [jazz critic] Leonard Feather… destroyed me. And I remember going, "Why would you wanna hurt somebody like this?" You know? Ending with the glib remark, or somewhere in there, "[Natalie Cole, you have] nothing to worry about." So this guy had been part of the club that hated Rickie Lee Jones singing jazz. All the pop singers came in with jazz albums after I made it possible. But nobody knew that, because I hadn't done a record.

So as years went by, in my work of forging new places for us to go, I became perceived by younger people as a follower. OK, that affects my ego, but it also affects my ability to make a living, because people aren't seeing me as who I am, because I didn't promote it. I thought it was understood. Leonard Feather really puts me down and the record goes nowhere and I don't do another jazz record. So it's my fortieth birthday. And the great saxophonist Joe Henderson, who played on that record—he came to my party, and he's sitting there real quietly. I went up and sat next to him and I said, "Thank you so much for coming." He said, "You know, I really liked your record… and I was disappointed that you didn't do another. I really thought you were onto something."

BLVR: [*Whispers*] Wow.

RLJ: And he just… put me right back where I was supposed to be. Like, I was chasing the unkind things people had said. In that one sentence he said, *We're musicians and we follow our little dreams and try to make something real*. For whatever reason, you know, I had stopped looking at that and went, Oh, shit, people are saying mean things about me. Guess I'm not gonna do jazz—I keep failing. I keep failing!

So all this stuff got attached to jazz and I didn't do it anymore. A couple years ago, I think, when I started writing new work and thinking about my best experiences in this studio and the best records I had made, I went, You know, it's time to call Russ Titelman again. The moment I called him [*claps*], we were one. I said, "I think I'm doing—I'm doing a jazz record." And he said, "Good. Finally." [*Laughs*] And here's the one thing I want to say about this: that when I'm with a *real* producer, whose one job is to listen, and I have his full attention, I do better than I can do by myself. It's inexplicable to me, because I really thought I could do everything by myself, but I am not my best by myself. The moment he started organizing [the process of making the album] and going, "We have to rehearse first." I haven't rehearsed in thirty-five years! What are you talking about? "We're gonna rehearse. And then we're gonna decide how to do it… just like we did when we made your first record." I didn't remember that we had rehearsed before we recorded. I didn't remember any of that. What a novel idea: preparing! We can still be spontaneous [*snaps*], but we'll know what we're doing. Ha! Fantastic.

So Russ brings the discipline that I don't have. And the love of what's possible from me. Both of us, but especially me—I have a really short attention span—I go, Oh, let's put some of that in over there, and before you know it, it's not a jazz record. It's like *Girl at Her Volcano*. It's some jazz and some rock and some pop, which, at the time, was a novel idea. People only did one discipline. I thought, Well, I'm forging ground. Because I always felt like the critics were telling us what we could do. How ironic that I ended up so squashed by those very same critics. But anyway, so that's my genre relationship with jazz.

My musical relationship has been probably just this one simple thing—that it's the best thing I sing. It's my natural rhythm. I'm so far behind the beat, and that's hard in pop music, because pop music and folk music and every other thing really would like you to sing pretty much in the first couple of beats. But I love coming in late and singing whatever I feel like singing when I get there! Jazz is the perfect place for me to do that. The thing about this year is that my voice has really aged. I discovered as I sang these songs that, yes, there's some stuff I can't do. But in place of it, or because of that, I try harder, and another sound is happening, this… it's almost like color, but it's the—not to be cute—but it's a deep patina of age that is in the voice now that's really beautiful and flawed or fragile. Little Judy Garland: Remember when her voice vibratos so much and starts to skip? It's the symptoms and sounds of a woman giving all she has, which might not happen when you're younger, because you have it all. So, yes, a lot of emotions. But this other thing that happens as this star is bursting and dying is there are these other colors that are in this record that I am so proud of. It's like I'd been away on a long voyage and [*laughs*] came home.

II. PATINA

BLVR: When you were talking, I was thinking about this Joni Mitchell quote from the '80s, where she talked about

---

MICROINTERVIEW WITH LING MA, PART VIII

THE BELIEVER: In your novel, *Severance*, Shen Fever erupts around the time of the Occupy Wall Street protests. A lot of reviewers have commented on the implicit critique of capitalism and consumer culture in the book. Why did you choose to set it around 2011?

LING MA: [The year] 2011 was nearly the present-day then. I started the novel in 2012, the first draft was finished in 2016, and it was published in 2018. The year that I finished the first draft was also the year of Trump's election. Once that happened, I thought *Severance* was a bit outdated.

What I mean by that is: if the novel was supposed to observe the absurdity of working in America, of global capitalism and the supply chains, the absurdity in American life just ratcheted up twentyfold after 2016. As a fiction writer, you're always wary of writing stories that are too on the nose. After Trump, the level of absurdity that a reader will accept in fiction is different from before Trump. Like we're in a new era of absurdity now, and the scenario sketched out in *Severance* reflects the old absurdity, which is much more muted by comparison. It would have been different if I had written it maybe even a year later. ⋆

how, you know, part of the reason she turned toward jazz was because she felt like she couldn't age in rock. That there wasn't a space where you could be a woman and age and be allowed to be a genius. Joni believed women could be *geniuses* in jazz. But that wasn't how it was in rock in 1977.

RLJ: She was forging the way in whatever genre she chose. She's the first bright star across the sky. And she forges the way for women to age in rock or pop or anything. Because she didn't die [*laughs*], and she kept recording.

BLVR: And then she was just performing again this week, and, with people being reverent about how her voice has aged, that sort of reverence about an aging voice felt new. Do you feel like your voice, in this space where you're talking about working with the way your voice has changed—has your relationship to it changed?

RLJ: No, it hasn't. No, it's still—my voice is still intact. I was just always a natural singer. And to my surprise, I got better, you know, than I was when I started. When I first started, I strained, I was still really a beginner. But as time went by, I became a better singer. My relationship with my voice is very private. Like all of us, I just like hearing the sound of my voice, like a little kid. [*Laughs*] So it hasn't changed at all. I am just in awe of how the texture of the voice tells us so much about the feelings of the person who's making the sound, whether or not it's shaky.

I mean, let's face it, if it's too aged, we're not gonna enjoy hearing it. And it's about our enjoyment. And even if it's a torn-up old voice, if it can relate the song, then we'll come and listen to it. So you still gotta be able to relate to the other person as a singer. I think that last album by Johnny Cash… they shouldn't have put that out. That guy was dying and he could hardly croak anything. So that's using his fame and his name to sell a record. And yeah, sure, we'll go into the studio as we're dying [*laughs*] if we can. I mean, I'm still on the fence about it. I just—I think that we are

always striving to be the best we can be in art. And maybe a friend will say, *Well, you think the best is refining, but it's not. It's actually when you're flawed that you're at your best.* But if you can't even hold a note anymore, should you still sing? I don't think so. I think you should let it go now… and don't let Rick Rubin make another record out of your flaws. [*Laughter*] But the good part about making a record of flaws is that it reminds people that we're, you know—in lieu of all the technical stuff, where everything is a machine and perfect—it's a response to that. And as that, I accept it. But I do think we should keep trying to be a beautiful sound. Yes, I do. Yes, I do.

That was why I wasn't a punk rocker, because punk rock didn't care if you could sing. It was about our collective force onstage. This, collectively, is the sound we're making. And I just couldn't go there. I just couldn't. And I know now that it's far more popular than Christopher Cross or—I just heard this term yesterday—yacht rock. What an offensive thing to say.

BLVR: [*Laughs*]

RLJ: But the music that people tried to make—that was their best, refined.

III. "A ROOM FULL OF MEN"

BLVR: I was just messaging with a photographer who chronicled LA punks who hung out at the Tropicana a lot. And she was saying, "We just thought Rickie was the coolest. Punks in LA loved Rickie." They could see the ways that you were outside the mainstream, your own creation. Did you go to punk shows?

RLJ: They were at the Troubadour, where I hung out. So I could slip in and see what was going on. And there was just too much spit. You might get hit with that. The behavior was hard to endure in order to hear what was happening. But I remember that Black Flag show I went in to see. And, um, who's that guy?

BLVR: Henry Rollins.

RLJ: Yes. I remember. He's hard to forget. Right. What a thoughtful and amazing guy. I quite like him. But I remember seeing these men onstage and the violence that they seemed to be perpetrating. That seemed to be the music more than any music. I just felt so much masculine [*mimicking voice*] "*Uhr-r-r-r,*" and that was hard, you know. We can set that aside now and go, *But the music and the humanity*. But if you were there at the time, you would've gone, *Let's get the fuck outta here. These guys are gonna kill us.* That's real. You know, when we saw kids coming to do punk rock shows, wearing brown shirts and those combat boots, there was no missing the Nazi thing that was floating around there. I have my own issues with the police, you know? I mean, it was like, What's happening here? This is so Aryan and… what are they doing?! Tom [Waits] and Chuck [E. Weiss] were my ambassadors to a larger kind of music I would never have even listened to, to be honest. Punk was just too… frightening to me, or the experiences I've had, to be in a room full of men, all going, "*Ruh-ruh-ruh-ruh-ruh.*" I just didn't wanna be there.

BLVR: Mm-hmm. I feel you.

RLJ: I'm really glad to hear what you say. I felt that at the time, for the first year or so of my career, that I was a floater. I wasn't this or that or that… but that makes me feel really good—really good—to hear somebody say that about how I was thought of. Thank you.

IV. "IT ALSO HAS TO BE TRUE"

BLVR: There are so many things that you can't control about who and how people see you, you know, and at that time you were on a bigger and bigger and bigger stage. How was that for you? When I interviewed you for the documentary [*Women Who Rock*], you said, "I had the exact vision of who I was as an artist." And so many people didn't have that. So many people and bands that were "evolving" with the times, like Jefferson Airplane becoming

Jefferson Starship, like, *We're gonna be here and we're gonna embody the '80s. We're not gonna embody the past*. And while you were very much a pop star at that time, you were also out of time. You were separate from time. As you said, you were your own thing, and you knew exactly what that was. How did you have that awareness? This total knowledge of who you were and what you wanted to be as an artist— where did that come from?

RLJ: The awareness: I would say it was always there. It formed pretty quickly, from the age of twenty-two, twenty-three. It started with getting to play a couple jazz songs and seeing how people reacted and going, Oh, that's—that's some of me. I'll put that right there. And then a folky kind of thing by Joni Mitchell and everybody walking by and going, *Oh, that didn't work*. When I made me, I knew that it had to be made of things that were not contemporary, because, you know, there's too many people chasing that brass ring. So you have to construct yourself out of things that aren't going to be used up and thrown away in a few years. It just has to be bigger, longer, older. And it also has to be true. So it's not gonna work for everybody. You're thinking about how to create a self that can withstand the storm that you're going to enter. Once you make yourself a public person.

I don't know how, but I just saw it. It's like a dot in the distance. I went, This is where I'm going. It's more than actually saying there were words and ideas that came. It's more like: I'm going there and I'll just keep walking till I get there. And I know what I'm made of. I'm made of my dad's jazz and I'm made of a little bit of Laura Nyro, and I'm made of something I don't know yet. There was a spot in the future. And I just knew who I was from a young age, going, I know I'm going somewhere. And, you know, even though my mom and dad… My dad's drunk and he is loading up the gun and my sister's pregnant and all these horrible things—horrible things that did not end up in the book. I know I'm going somewhere. There's some part of me, in spite of how troubled life had been, there was some part of me that was unshakable. She's still with us today. ✶

The Detour

O. Hm.

Oregon
Humanities

On *The Detour*, we talk to interesting people about important stuff.

Join us for a monthly podcast featuring writers, artists, and activists like Eula Biss, Omar El Akkad, Robin Wall Kimmerer, and Clint Smith.

Listen at **oregonhumanities.org/detour** or wherever you get your podcasts.

A REVIEW OF

THE WORLD KEEPS ENDING, AND THE WORLD GOES ON

BY FRANNY CHOI

Some of us are just now waking up to the idea that it won't go on: subways and parkways, Starbucks and Target, MMR shots and mug shots. All the things we call civilization may be swept away by rising waters, or drought, or roving RNA. What do we do with that knowledge? How do we picture our already-happening doom?

Franny Choi comes as close as any recent American poet to drawing that picture. Her collection begins by gathering scope, in poems of long lines, of collected atrocities: "brimstone eating California," "the sky, shocked with dying" over "the graves of reefs," while "Dispatches from Kenosha, // Louisville, Atlanta, arrive, arrive / like a steady kickdrum of sparrows / spatchcocked by gravity." Choi goes on, as if she could create a pile of words big enough to serve as a barricade, to protect human beings from ourselves. Many of the poems feel like epitaphs, or ineffective apologies. "I've been, undoubtedly, an American," she writes, "and done practically nothing to stop it."

These lists, these regrets, these intense, even impossible demands accumulate around the poet in distress as they might accumulate around us all. "I know I should want to be torn open," Choi writes, "by the failures of hope, but here's what I want: // a tight circle around everyone I love; / a stove that doesn't burn." Who wouldn't agree? Who can ignore—but who can concentrate full-time on—the big and burning now?

Choi's elders saw the end of another world: the middle segments of Choi's third book consider the Japanese occupation of Korea, the Korean War, and the divided nation. "If the land in me could speak / to the land I live on, what would it say?" Choi asks. "Maybe *I'm sorry*. Or, *where does it hurt?*" Her American sense of worldwide catastrophe feels like the logical sequel to the all-around catastrophes of "comfort women" (a term she uses), of refugees. Choi takes on second- and third-generation wounds, with words recurring as grief does, recycling lines from one poem as titles for others, and repeating one of those titles ("Upon Learning That Some Korean War Refugees Used Partially Detonated Napalm Canisters as Cooking Fuel") four times.

Those lists and titles point back to the present. Choi's voices are overwhelming, and overwhelmed, "counting my life mostly / as a series of small, terrible stories" within the larger terrible stories of ecological devastation, endless international conflict, police violence, exhausted soil, and oil-plagued seas. They mimic our own sense of overwhelm.

And then they don't. The best parts of Choi's new volume—making good on her poem title "Science Fiction Poetry"—come when she starts to envision how something might come after us and look back at us. The future may also see how we "clawed down walls / & ex-learned harm / & nixed cruel laws / & crowdsourced grace / & ground teeth down." Children in tropical Calgary and Fairbanks may walk through the "as-yet- / unbuilt museum / of what we had to survive." They may ask: "What was it like to live so gridded? So track-changes?" But they may exist to look back: they may be here, where "there are crises every day, and there's also bread / bubbling on the counter, pickled beans, a cat who comes home." There may be a future; there may be a home.

Choi started out as a performer: her lines now carry both the precision of print and the directness of the stage. She addresses not only blood family but also poetic allies such as "sam" (sax), "Nate" (Marshall), and "Danez" (Smith, her partner in the popular podcast *VS*). Her work isn't subtle: it is, perhaps, our "Howl." She addresses, with these poets at her side, me and you and anyone else whose "loneliness" makes us believe we've "seen / the future." And it speaks to our future: if and when we can stand the heat, we will not stand alone.

—Stephanie Burt

Publisher: *Ecco/HarperCollins* **Page count:** *144* **Price:** *$25.99* **Key quote:** *"My sister calls, and it's already too late for things to be better."* **Shelve next to:** *Octavia Butler, Cathy Park Hong, D. A. Powell, Danez Smith* **Unscientifically calculated reading time:** *Two fits of terror, one morning away from all news*

Illustration by Pete Gamlen

THE TIGER AND THE CAGE: A MEMOIR OF A BODY IN CRISIS

BY EMMA BOLDEN

It was in the eighteenth century that models of the uterus first became available to the general public in Europe. People had seized opportunities to view uteruses before, in Renaissance-era anatomy theaters, where crowds stood in concentric tiers around open female corpses. It wasn't until the 1700s, however, when enterprising male anatomists manufactured wax models of the reproductive organ to be passed around, staged, and advertised. In other words, the uterus went on sale.

These objects, splayed open and dyed, were lopped off from any contextualizing sense of body or life; there was no way of knowing that some of them had been modeled on the anatomy of real women who had died during childbirth. In such anonymous shapes of tragedy lay the promise of exciting new knowledge. Three centuries later, it is unclear how much we have learned about the uterus or the catastrophes that regularly attend it.

Emma Bolden's *The Tiger and the Cage* is a memoir about the author's experience with endometriosis, a painful condition in which a person's uterine lining grows outside the uterus. For Bolden, endometriosis has led to, among other complications, a pelvis fused with tissue, "large and hemorrhagic" cysts, and a fibroid "bulging" from the back of the uterus, bigger than the organ itself. Bolden underwent her third gynecological surgery in college, and by that time the cysts had her appendix surrounded. Because of their brown-bloodied look, her gynecologist called them "chocolate milk cysts." It was too cutesy a term, but Bolden, a poet by training, is used to language's clumsiness with bodily suffering. One of Bolden's other gynecologists told her she had dysmenorrhea, a term that simply means "painful menstruation": the symptom relabeled as diagnosis.

What do we do with pain? How do we communicate it to others without wasting ourselves on clichés, on botched metaphors, brute tautologies? Another doctor suggests to Bolden that her case is psychological: Was she perhaps molested as a child? His ineptitude inverts the premodern notion, equally cruel, that a woman's mental illness stemmed from disturbances of the womb. Today, on average, endometriosis takes six to ten years to be correctly diagnosed.

Bolden is attuned to medical misogyny, and her memoir is interspersed with reimaginings of women who suffered similar ailments, or at least similarly caustic doctors. She is fascinated by Dr. Jean-Martin Charcot, whose female "hysterical" patients at Paris's Salpêtrière Hospital were put on theatrical show in the nineteenth century: in such "pantomime scenes," Charcot would claim to hypnotize sick women, making them "lift their skirts to their knees and point their toes, or else curtsy with a smile."

Too often, the pursuit of medical knowledge makes the body an object of spectacle rather than care. Better doctors know that knowledge is a partnership, not a quest; they work to guide their patient toward greater self-discovery. William James—the nineteenth-century philosopher and brother to novelist Henry—once quipped that the ideal result would be "to eliminate the need of a physician" altogether. Yet in a time of privatized health care and *Roe v. Wade*'s dismantling, the inequality between gynecology and its patients feels larger than ever.

Henry and William had a younger sister: Alice James was, like Bolden, besieged by mysterious pain throughout her life. She was at one point diagnosed with hysteria and urged to see Dr. Charcot in France. It seems she never went, though she and her doctors continued to perplex one another, and the experience took its inevitable mental toll: "I went down to the deep sea," she wrote of one summer spent in depression; decades later, Bolden would remark that her experience felt, at times, "like drowning." The symmetry is startling. If language cannot yield precision, perhaps it grants something else: across the decades, a furtive and hard-earned fellowship.

—Zoë Hu

Publisher: *Soft Skull Press* **Page count:** *368* **Price:** *$17.95* **Key quote:** *"This flesh is not my flesh, this self not under my control."* **Shelve next to:** *Emily Ogden, Ann Patchett, Elaine Scarry, Laurel Thatcher Ulrich* **Unscientifically calculated reading time:** *Three afternoons spent indoors to escape a heat wave*

Illustration by Pete Gamlen

A MOUNTAIN TO THE NORTH, A LAKE TO THE SOUTH, PATHS TO THE WEST, A RIVER TO THE EAST

BY LÁSZLÓ KRASZNAHORKAI; TRANSLATED BY OTTILIE MULZET

László Krasznahorkai's novels are hard to put down, but not for the usual reasons. The Hungarian writer's fictions are allegorical in flavor but hostile to interpretation, dense with uneasy images and mad characters, and often indifferent to linear time. Krasznahorkai writes very long sentences: they go on for pages, they feint and double back, they abuse themselves like a trapped animal who chews through its cage and then, in a fit of madness, eats itself. In effect, they tie a reader's hands behind their back. Krasznahorkai is interested in the mind's derangements, and as his sentences map his characters' fugitive thoughts, they recruit the reader into similar patterns of thinking. When you open one of his novels, it can be a shock to see no ragged margins, just a sheer bank of language, inexorable as a funeral stela. But once you proceed down the winding path of a character's obsessive thoughts, you have no choice but to read on with a similar compulsion.

In *A Mountain to the North, a Lake to the South, Paths to the West, a River to the East*—the latest of Krasznahorkai's novels to be published in English, in a translation by Ottilie Mulzet from New Directions—his sentences turn away from the psyche to trace a character's journey through a puzzling geography. The novel begins with a man arriving at a monastery outside Kyoto. This man is known only as the grandson of Prince Genji. He has read a book called *One Hundred Beautiful Gardens*, a mysterious illustrated volume that fell into his hands by accident. The most exquisite garden in this book is the one-hundredth garden, which is perplexing in its modest beauty, impossible to find, and perhaps a joke inserted by the author. The grandson of Prince Genji suspects the garden is somewhere in this monastery, and so he roams the complex in search of it.

What follows is a meticulous consideration of the monastery and its hidden corners. Each crooked gate and hidden courtyard, each fountain, wall, and tree, each gust of air is evidence of the subtle and unrepeatable chain of events that occasioned its existence. The torii are not just gates but physical histories of the hinoki grove that supplied their timber, of the workers who felled the trees, and of the master carpenter who joined them. The monastery's library is a time line of writing technology, beginning with early bamboo sutras, and moving on to the invention of mulberry paper and the scroll, each iteration highly particular in its design, each one condensing the history of its antecedents. Everything in this ancient complex is inevitable, unable to be anything but itself, from the massive ginkgo tree with its primordial, fan-shaped leaves, like a time traveler from the Cretaceous period; to the holly bush that sprouts from its trunk; to the dog that lies down in its shade to die.

This is a book preoccupied with infinity. Krasznahorkai's project, it seems, is to thwart the passing of time through a program of looking. When a person's eye lingers, the moment swells; to describe something in excess is therefore a hedge against death. At first, Krasznahorkai's incantations seduce us. Yes, we think, time is a concertina. Everything is always. And yet, deep within the monastery, Krasznahorkai plants a counterpoint to this premise. When the grandson of Prince Genji reaches the abbot's private chamber, he finds a two-thousand-page book called *The Infinite Mistake*. The work is a refutation of infinity, written by a scholar who derides a list of famous mathematicians with "extraordinarily obscene expressions." Perhaps because I was primed by Krasznahorkai's earlier works, which are filled with apocalyptic prophecies, my mind was already inclined toward endings. A maximalist treatment of a plant or animal may attempt to halt time, but instead it only rehearses a tragic calculus. It takes millions of years of chance occurrences to make a bird in its perfect machinery and just a moment for it to be destroyed, impossible to be remade.

—*Laura Preston*

> **Publisher:** *New Directions* **Page count:** *144* **Price:** *$17.95* **Key quote:** *"…from that point onward this hidden garden never let him go, he simply could not chase it from his mind, he continually saw the garden in his mind's eye without being able to touch its existence."* **Shelve next to:** *Nicholson Baker, Jorge Luis Borges, Benjamín Labatut, W. G. Sebald, Murasaki Shikibu* **Unscientifically calculated reading time:** *One idle afternoon on a garden bench*

Illustration by Pete Gamlen

A HORSE AT NIGHT: ON WRITING

BY AMINA CAIN

Amina Cain's *A Horse at Night: On Writing* is nonfiction haunted by fiction, fragmented musings in which Cain is often possessed by her favorite literary characters, filtering her experiences through theirs. After all, reading is that rare mode by which we allow someone else to manifest our ghosts. The book, on its surface, is a diary—entries on writing give way to topics as varied as landscape painting, pets, friendship, solitude, and the authentic self. Cain leads us carefully to an understanding: personality is separate from the self—it is contextual, emerging from relationships to one's surroundings and companions. And through this understanding, we are able to glean *A Horse at Night*'s own authentic genre: not so much a diary as a tender, vulnerable self-portrait.

Cain recognizes the trap of portraiture—how it can capture the mutable self as a fixed character, something that resembles the living dead. Describing a moment in Tove Jansson's novel *The True Deceiver*, in which a woman encounters her portrait carved in ice, Cain says, "Imagine finding your likeness in that way. Are you alive or are you dead? What has been captured, there in the ice?" The brilliance of Cain's book comes in her evasion of this pitfall, conjuring herself so subtly and obliquely as to escape being frozen. It is a portrait drawn from context: descriptions of her literary fascinations, quandaries, and fears. Revelations come through analysis of other authors, as when she notes that, in Heinrich von Kleist's *The Marquise of O*, "characters are never given physical descriptions, and yet… we are able to form pictures of them… There is great value in what can be sensed."

In Cain's writerly sensibilities, we sense her self—full of insightful intelligence and curious blind spots. This is not an idealized depiction. She knows better than to elide the self-doubt of the writer: "Is it interesting to watch oneself perform? My current answer is that it is not." For a while, she says, she cut her sentiments like her sentences, until they were sparse and elegant—prose so bare as to be almost ruthless, and confident in its ruthlessness. It is a kind of rebellion against what, historically, has been labeled "feminine writing" (a rebellion perhaps best encapsulated in the ultimate cool of Fleur Jaeggy's style). Feminine writing and feminine solitude are inherent concerns of *A Horse at Night*. And yet, Cain notices that this rejection of "feminine" emotion is also a performance, a form of misogynistic self-repression. She later concludes, "In my writing, why not be fully who I am?"

It is this shifting self-awareness that keeps Cain from becoming a character—that keeps her vital. She gravitates toward painted portraits, specifically those that are aware of their frame—figures who look or point beyond the edge of the image. These works dissolve their borders, putting the viewer in the same space as the painting and vice versa—two distinct worlds superimposing upon each other. Cain, constantly gesturing beyond her pages, constructs her book similarly and creates an interior landscape into which we can project ourselves. As she puts it: "One thing laid on top of another… relaxing into each other with their outlines intact." Has there ever been a more resonant description of the magical act that is reading?

Cain questions herself unceasingly. She asks why she writes a certain way, is drawn to certain paintings, is interested in certain characters. I find myself writing back to her in the margins—the answers seem obvious. But then I recall what she says about friends: that they are capable of seeing our authentic selves in ways we cannot. It is this element that makes Cain's book the most successful kind of self-portrait: by allowing the viewer to see what the author can only question, it resists its own ghostification. It transforms the reader into a friend.

—*India Ennenga*

Publisher: *Dorothy, a publishing project* **Page count:** *136* **Price:** *$16.95* **Key quote:** *"I write to see what is inside my mind. For me, it is often far better, healthier, than recording what I know is already there."* **Shelve next to:** *César Aira, Sophie Calle, Natalia Ginzburg, Anna Kavan, Josep Pla.* **Unscientifically calculated reading time:** *Two slow summer evenings*

Illustration by Pete Gamlen

MY LIFE AS A GODARD MOVIE

BY JOANNA WALSH

In her latest book, *My Life as a Godard Movie*, Joanna Walsh uses the claustrophobia of pandemic lockdown to review what has been her lifelong obsession with the films of the late Jean-Luc Godard, or particularly the women of his films—Anna Karina, Jean Seberg, Brigitte Bardot—muses who drifted through prostitution rings, criminal underworlds, and revolutionary collectives looking effortlessly gorgeous in Dior and Givenchy until their inevitable violent demise by car crash or gunshot. Walsh's retrospective focuses on the beauty of these women—the weight of carrying such beauty, the influence of it on a viewer's desire—and the filmmaker's trade in the commodity of their beauty. In Godard films, feminine beauty is a contract for violent death.

Walsh's critique here will not be shocking to film buffs, as she finds much in common with what film theorist Laura Mulvey famously identified, in the '70s, as the problem of the male gaze in movies: "The determining male gaze projects its phantasy onto the female figure… with their appearance coded for strong visual and erotic impact so that they can be said to connote *to-be-looked-at-ness*." It is perhaps not surprising that the films of Godard offered the bulk of Mulvey's evidence; certainly, it doesn't surprise Joanna Walsh, who reminds us, "Godard plots are driven by desire. For excitement, money, utopia, sex but seldom love. Love is their by-product; beauty its currency… Beauty is not an experience for the beautiful, but the eye, the mirror, the lens."

Walsh's project blurs creative nonfiction and film critique, which seems like a nod not just to French film but to French literary modes as well, to auto-fiction and auto-ethnography—Annie Ernaux's *The Years* or Emmanuel Carrère's *My Life as a Russian Novel*, for instance—which, even when focused on objective reportage, crystallize around the author's own memoir, and the "I" overwhelms: in short, our lives will overtake anything we attempt to analyze. Or, as Walsh says of Godard, "Though

Publisher: *Transit Books* **Page count:** *112* **Price:** *$15.95* **Key quote:** *"I am trying not to make my life into a movie, but to see the movie in my life."* **Shelve next to:** *Emmanuel Carrère, Rachel Cusk, Annie Ernaux, Chris Kraus, Édouard Louis, Marie NDiaye* **Unscientifically calculated reading time:** *The time it takes to distribute* The New York Herald Tribune *to a street of Parisians, or to drink two coffees and a Pastis in a down-at-the-heel café*

many of Godard's New Wave films are *about* women, their subject is never quite a subject."

Walsh is less invested in any critical blame game, however, and keeps a relatively even hand in treating Godard's project as often outside his control—she finds that the power of the women's beauty and the women's gazes linger beyond the film, in spite of their narrative ends in Godard's hands. Walsh seems most interested in the impact that this emptying out of the female subject has on women viewers over time.

While Walsh's personal relationship to Godard's films does take center stage here, *My Life* isn't a simple indulgence of her first-person subjectivity but rather an attempt to locate or reinfuse a concept of feminine beauty that isn't voided-out by the male gaze, that moves beyond woman as a beauty commodity, without entirely losing her original love affair with the films. She writes, "I am aware that in watching Godard's film I am doing myself another obscure violence." But she also seems fully aware that an ability to deconstruct the damage wrought on our lives by culture rarely leaves us feeling less empty. Knowing that a desire is constructed or bad for us doesn't mean we don't still want the thing, or, as Walsh puts it, "How to critique femininity and still look cute?" Instead, Walsh wishes to bring readers and herself into some more hopeful terrain. "Can appearance itself be defemininised? Not *how would that look?* but *how would that feel?*… I am trying to *do* something with my body—by persistently inhabiting it unbeautified, in public—not only for myself, but for other women." For Walsh, the reading of her life through Godard is an investigation of her performance of herself-as-woman as an ongoing project, and while she attaches and detaches from Godard's tragic women, the book allows for an intimate meditation on the merger between life, art, and critique that adds softer edges and gray areas to a difficult love for the legacy of an art house auteur.

—*Joanna Howard*

Illustration by Pete Gamlen

COVER TO COVER

SURVEYING THE COVERS OF GREAT BOOKS, AS THEY CHANGE ACROSS TIME AND COUNTRY
IN THIS ISSUE: *NORWEGIAN WOOD* BY HARUKI MURAKAMI

compiled by Abigail Walker

IRAQ
*Arab Cultural
Institute, 2008*

ESTONIA
*Varrak,
2015*

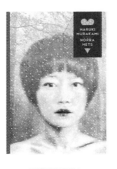

SPAIN
*Empuries
Narrativa, 2020*

TURKEY
*Doğan Kitap,
2004*

USA
*Vintage Books,
2000*

GEORGIA
*Bakur Sulakauri
Publishing, 2015*

GERMANY
*Btb Bei Goldmann,
2003*

BRITAIN
*Vintage Books,
2003*

FRANCE
*French and European
Publications, 2011*

SPAIN
*Tusquets Editores S.A.,
2007*

BRITAIN
*Vintage Classics,
2022*

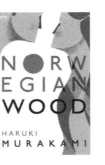

BRITAIN
*Vintage Books,
2014*

NETHERLANDS
*Atlas Contact,
2013*

BRITAIN
*Vintage Books,
2016*

IRAN
*Written Voice,
2016*

THE PUZZLE OF INCREDIBLY WIDE AND DEEP KNOWLEDGE

IF YOU COMPLETE THIS PUZZLE, YOU ARE A GENERALIST OF BROAD SKILL AND GREAT RENOWN

by Ada Nicolle, edited by Benjamin Tausig

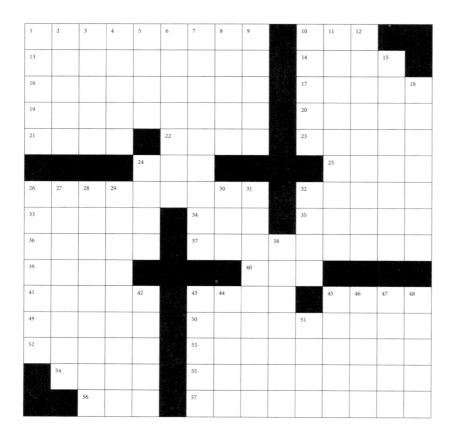

ACROSS

1. Dish with surimi, often
10. There's one opposite from six
13. First major carrier to ban smoking on all flights (1990)
14. Site of some plot brainstorming
16. Monkey bread alternative
17. Squatted in the dirt, say
19. "From what I've gathered ..."
20. Greek symbol for the isotope oxygen-18
21. Geographic word that maintains its pronunciation with an "a" appended to the front
22. Traditional offerings, e.g., for short
23. Half of rap's Black Star, along with Yasiin
24. Small problem?
25. Luxo Jr., e.g., in a Pixar short
26. Imagined anything under the sun?
32. They'll take the check
33. "Don't be ___!"
34. Rage
35. Close on set
36. Wallops
37. Ballistic Ball alternatives
39. ___ up on (study)

40. California red, briefly
41. Its subjects are often implied
43. Bulgaria's Simeon the Great, e.g.
45. Acts in succession?
49. One with a controlling partner
50. Single out on an anniversary, perhaps
52. Tricky alternative to a draw
53. Scholastic sci-fi series written under the pseudonym K. A. Applegate
54. High-quality, as weed
55. Realize with time
56. *ba-dum ___ *
57. Page attribute

DOWN

1. ___ Davis, frequent collaborator of Tyler Perry
2. Bat mitzvahs, for example
3. Noted Atlantica princess
4. Looping-in request
5. 1800s businessman (and department store founder) Andrew
6. "I'm always here for you"
7. Proof of delivery?
8. Her character was part of the first LGBTQ+ kiss in Pixar history ("Lightyear," 2022)
9. Eurovision winners of 1963, 2000, and 2013
10. Fruit that anagrams to a famous cartoon dog
11. 2013 book with the line "If one man can destroy everything, why can't one girl change it?"
12. Worker in a sewer
15. Military outfit beneath a division
18. Some vaping accessories
24. Coworkers on location, not WFH
26. Parental figures, casually?
27. Genre associated with the bands Bad Brains and Death
28. "Nothing's off limits"
29. Official war dogs of the United States Marine Corps, by breed
30. Messy fare?
31. Verse form that translates to "third rhyme"
32. PC key with an "up" counterpart
38. Beefcake calendar depictions
42. Squirts
43. Parcel of land
44. Toledo title
45. Argentina's Juan
46. Judgment-free period?
47. Remains of value, perhaps
48. Statements in passing
51. Plenty

(answers on page 144)

COPYEDITING THE CLASSICS

10 ERRORS HAVE BEEN INERTED INTO THIS PASSAGE. CAN YOU FIND THEM?

by Caitlin Van Dusen

THE WIND IN THE WILLOWS (1908)
by KENNETH GRAHAME

We others, whom have long lost the more subtle of the physical senses, have not even proper terms to express an animals' inter-communications with his surroundings, living or otherwise, and only have the word, "smell," for instance, to include the whole range of delicate thrills which murmur in the nose of the animal night and day, summoning, warning, inciting, repelling. It was one of these mysterious fairy calls from out the void that suddenly reached Mole in the darkness, making him tingle through and through with its very familiar appeal, even while yet he could not clearly remember what it was. Stopping dead in his tracks, his nose searched hither and thither in its efforts to recapture the fine filament, the telegraphic current, that has so strongly moved him. A moment, and he had caught it again; and with it this time came recollection in fullest flood.

Home! That was what they meant, those caressing appeals, those soft touches wafted through the air, those invisible little hands pulling and tugging, all one way! Why, it must be quite close by him at that moment, his old home that he had hurriedly forsaken and never sought again, that day when he first found the River! And now it was sending out its scouts and its messengers to capture him and bring him in since his escape on that bright morning he had hardly given it a thought, so absorbed had he been in his new life, in all its pleasures, surprises, its fresh and captivating experiences. Now, with a rush of old memories, how clearly it stood up before him, in the the darkness! Shabby indeed, and small and poorly furnished, and yet his, the home he had made for himself, the home he had been so happy to get back after his day's work. And the home had been happy with him, too, evidently, and was missing him, and wanted him back, and was telling him so, through his nose, sorrowfully, reproachfully, but with no bitterness or anger; only with plaintive reminder that it was there, and wanted him. *(answers on page 144)*

ChiaraWhyWon'tYouCallMeBack (NoSpacesPleaseI'mInLoveButAlso OnABudget)

Two Lines Press is accepting translations of & by contemporary Francophone Caribbean writers for a future edition of our Calico Series, now through January 28. If you're interested in submitting or in translations in general, find out more at https://www.catranslation. org/books/submit-work/

The oldest form of social media is back in style! Write a diary entry today every day. Buy a brand-new notebook to add to your collection of unused brand-new notebooks. Sincerely,
The American Notebook PAC

Hey, look Ma, I made it into a magazine print & everything —S

Normalize moisturizing your ankles! Don't worry about the whys and hows, just start doing it. Lotions available at most stores.*

Tired of that insignificant lie you once told your crush except now they're your spouse? Still trying to figure out why you get anxious at the onset of every new moon? Unsure of what the latest discourse on the world wide web is about and how you can participate? In need of advice? Send our advice columnist a letter: advice@thebeliever.net

Nightboat Books is currently reading for its 2022 poetry prize! Check out our previous winners, submission guidelines, and more at nightboat.org

I had really dry ankles. It was a really bad situation. I thought the answer was socks, but turns out the answer was lotions. Take it from me, a guy whose been there. —Arnold*

A belated happy birthday, Sarah! (And wishes in advance because I'll undoubtedly forget again next year.) —Jaron

I sprained my ankle and my doc told me I'd need a boot for 4-6 weeks. High ankle sprain, he said. Guess what? Never wore a boot, just applied lotion every day. And now I'm totally good. —Anonymous testimonial*

Hey Honeys, dig in and celebrate our second birthday with us. *Honey Literary* is now a toddler and currently open for submissions: https://www.honeyliterary.com/submit

My ankle was so stiff. Years ago, someone told me to put lotions on a sprained ankle. That it would heal the sprain. Long story short, my ankle didn't really heal well, and it was stiff all the time. But the weird thing is, someone told me, again, to put lotions on my ankle. Said it would heal the stiffness. I started doing this every day, and within two months, my ankle was better. It's never stiff anymore and also, as a nice bonus, always hydrated. Thank you, lotions. —Paul*

CLASSIFIEDS

Believer Classifieds cost $2 per word. They can be placed by emailing classifieds@thebeliever.net. All submissions subject to editorial approval. No results guaranteed.

Good luck in grad school, Sam! You got this!

Seeking mystery woman from JFK. This is a long shot but you had a copy of *The Believer* when we were sitting next to each other at terminal 8 on Wednesday, Feb. 10, 2021. We talked about the loss of Great Literature and I emailed you a draft of my unpublished novel to have a read. I haven't heard from you. Maybe you thought the novel sucked and you're ignoring me, but I've also wondered if maybe it just went to your spam? Hoping you read this and hoping it went to spam.
—Michael

Freelancing around for your design, illustration, and art direction needs. Visit lilleallen.com for more details.

Story fiends! Town criers and liars! Hand over your tale, script, copy, pod. I'll improve it and advise. Past work for *The Believer*, *The New Yorker*, Apple, and *The New York Times*. Email: editortravel at the gmail.

You say you like hot sauce, but do you? www.queenmajestyhotsauce. com. Hot sauce for cool people.

For a new magazine, we are seeking the most heroic, never-before-told stories of rescue. Firefighters, EMTs, search personnel—all are welcome. Please send inquiries or manuscripts to Rescue, 849 Valencia Street, San Francisco, 94147.

How Do Girls Do It? Find out in my newsletter about gender, dating, apocalypses, love, and despair: tinyletter.com/cuteflesh

Artist who works from 849 Valencia and often draws animals accompanied by text will send original artwork to you if you send LPs to him. The following are accepted: mid-century recordings of Chopin; early ragtime recordings; original pressings of Oscar Peterson LPs c. 1970-80; Icicle Works picture discs; and lesser known recordings by Jim Croce. Send to LPs for Artwork, 849 Valencia Street, San Francisco, 94147. This is real.

The Believer will be having a party for the release of this issue at a to-be-named bar in San Francisco. Look for more details at mcsweeneys.net. We will be selling this issue at the party so it is conceivable that you are at the party right now, reading this message. If so, welcome to the party!

In celebration of a decade of *The Margins*, Asian American Writers' Workshop presents *The Margins: Best of 2021*, now available in print with cover art by Tammy Nguyen! Featuring works by Daphne Palasi Andreades, Promiti Islam, Jaimee A. Swift, Teresa Mathew, Tamara K. Nopper, and many more! Get your copy for only $15 + shipping at aaww.org/shop

*The information, including but not limited to, text, graphics, images and other material contained in this magazine are for informational purposes only. No material in this magazine is intended to be a substitute for professional medical advice, diagnosis or treatment. Always seek the advice of your physician or other qualified health care provider with any questions you may have regarding lotions, and never disregard professional medical advice or delay in seeking it because of something you have read in this magazine about lotions.

Illustration by Tim Peacock

INTERNATIONAL BEST-SELLER LISTS

The best sellers in other countries are startlingly different than our own. See what the rest of the world is reading in this new regular feature, which will highlight a rotating cast of countries in each issue.

COMPILED BY YASMIN PATEL, ACCORDING TO 2021 ANNUAL LISTS

JAPAN

1. 推し、燃ゆ (*Idol, Burning*) by Rin Usami. *A withdrawn teenage girl learns that the celebrity she's obsessed with has been accused of assault, and she sees her own life begin spiraling alongside his.*

2. 52 ヘルツのクジラたち (*52 Hertz Whales*) by Sonoko Machida. *Kiko leaves her abusive childhood home and moves to a new town, where she meets a boy who she fears has been mistreated too.*

3. 白鳥とコウモリ (*Swan and Bat*) by Keigo Higashino. *When a prominent lawyer is found dead, one man confesses to the murder. But all is not what it seems.*

4. ブラック・ショーマンと名もなき町の殺人 (*Black Showman and the Murder in an Obscure Town*) by Keigo Higashino. *Against the backdrop of the COVID-19 pandemic, a woman's father is murdered, prompting her to return to her hometown outside of Tokyo.*

5. 元彼の遺言状 (*My Ex-boyfriend's Last Will and Testament*) by Hotate Shinkawa. *A high-powered lawyer learns that her ex-boyfriend has been murdered and left his assets to his killer.*

6. 変な家 (*Weird House*) by Rain Hole. *An outwardly normal house has a number of unexplainable features and a mysterious past.*

7. オルタネート (*Alternate*) by Shigeaki Kato. *Three high schoolers connect through a students-only dating app called Alternate.*

8. えんとつ町のプペル (*Poupelle of Chimney Town*) by Akihiro Nishino. *In a town covered in smoke, a young boy dreams of seeing the stars.*

9. 転生したらスライムだった件 (*That Time I Got Reincarnated as a Slime*) by Fuse. *An unfulfilled middle-aged man lives a dull life, until he wakes up one day as a slime monster in a new, fantastical world.*

10. 透明な螺旋 (*Transparent Spiral*) by Keigo Higashino. *In the wake of her partner's murder, a woman disappears, thereby making herself a prime suspect.*

ARGENTINA

1. *Las primas* (*Cousins*) by Aurora Venturini. *A woman named Yuna tells the story of her impoverished family in La Plata in the 1940s.*

2. *Yo recordaré por ustedes* (*I Will Remember for You*) by Juan Forn. *A collection of Forn's back-cover stories from the newspaper Página 12.*

3. *Las cosas que perdimos en el fuego* (*Things We Lost in the Fire*) by Mariana Enríquez. *This collection of short stories by Enríquez, an award-winning journalist and novelist, explores the ideas of corruption and violence in modern-day Argentina.*

4. *Los llanos* (*The Plains*) by Federico Falco. *After a devastating breakup, a man isolates himself in the countryside and reflects on his life.*

5. *Nuestra parte de noche* (*Our Share of Night*) by Mariana Enríquez. *In the wake of his mother's death, a young boy and his father travel to her childhood home and encounter the cult she grew up in.*

6. *El nervio optico* (*Optic Nerve*) by María Gainza. *A woman tells the story of her life through the history and work of her favorite artists.*

7. *Las amigas* (*Friends*) by Aurora Venturini. *In this sequel to Las primas, the same protagonist, Yuna, reflects on the few friendships that have populated her generally lonesome existence.*

8. *Sodio* (*Sodium*) by Jorge Consiglio. *The life of a chain-smoking dentist is consumed by his love for swimming and an adolescent crush.*

9. *Todas nuestras maldiciones se cumplieron* (*All Our Curses Were Fulfilled*) by Tamara Tenenbaum. *In this autobiographical novel, Tenenbaum writes about the experience of growing up in an Orthodox Jewish community in Argentina and the death of her father in the AMIA bombing of 1994.*

10. *Los peligros de fumar en la cama* (*The Dangers of Smoking in Bed*) by Mariana Enríquez. *Enríquez's first collection of short stories, published in 2009.*

SWEDEN

1. *Där kräftorna sjunger* (*Where the Crawdads Sing*) by Delia Owens. *A reclusive young girl finds herself accused of murdering a former lover.*

2. *Den saknade systern* (*The Missing Sister*) by Lucinda Riley. *Six sisters journey around the world in search of their mysterious seventh sister.*

3. *Fädernas missgärningar* (*The Sins of Our Fathers*) by Åsa Larsson. *Prosecutor Rebecka Martinsson works to solve a decades-old murder case to which she has a secret personal connection.*

4. *Box* (*Box*) by Camilla Läckberg and Henrik Fexeus. *A seasoned detective enlists the help of an offbeat mentalist to solve a peculiar murder.*

5. *Skyddsängeln* (*The Guardian Angel*) by Sofie Sarenbrant. *While investigating the recent disappearance of a close colleague, detective Emma Sköld is confronted with a murder that will soon consume her.*

6. *Där den sista lampan lyser* (*Where The Last Light Shines*) by Mari Jungstedt. *When two young boys go missing, police are determined to make a connection to a recent murder in the area.*

7. *1795* (*1795*) by Niklas Natt och Dag. *Two investigators confront the criminal underbelly of Stockholm in an attempt to find a missing girl.*

8. *Löpa varg* (*The Wolf Run*) by Kerstin Ekman. *A retired game master becomes attached to a wolf that he meets in the forest.*

9. *Solsystern: electras bok* (*The Sun Sister*) by Lucinda Riley. *A young woman mourns the death of her adoptive father and explores her biological ancestry.*

10. *Spegelmannen* (*The Mirror Man*) by Lars Kepler. *Detective Joona Linna hunts down a serial killer who targets teenage girls.*

NEW ZEALAND

1. *Auē* by Becky Manawatu. *After Taukiri leaves his violent home, he must contend with the guilt of leaving his younger brother behind.*

2. *To Italy, with Love* by Nicky Pellegrino. *Two women who are unlucky in love have a chance meeting in the Italian countryside.*

3. *Bug Week* by Airini Beautrais. *The first short story collection from the Whanganui-based poet.*

4. *Cousins* by Patricia Grace. *Three cousins grow apart and into very different lives.*

5. *Tell Me Lies* by J. P. Pomare. *When a successful psychologist witnesses the death of a patient, her seemingly perfect life begins to fall apart.*

6. *The Last Guests* by J. P. Pomare. *A young couple decides to rent out their vacation cottage, with deadly consequences.*

7. *Quiet in Her Bones* by Nalini Singh. *When a woman's body is found decades after her disappearance, her son sets out to prove that a neighbor is responsible for her death.*

8. *Remote Sympathy* by Catherine Chidgey. *A doctor at the Buchenwald concentration camp is tasked with treating the cancer of an SS officer's wife.*

9. *Inside the Black Horse* by Ray Berard. *A bungled pub robbery upends a small town.*

10. *Loop Tracks* by Sue Orr. *An intergenerational family drama that explores issues of bioethics.*

NOTES ON OUR CONTRIBUTORS

Hanif Abdurraqib is a writer from the east side of Columbus, Ohio.

Carrie Brownstein is a musician and a writer/director in film and television. She was the cocreator and costar of the Emmy and Peabody Award–winning comedy series *Portlandia*. Brownstein has directed television shows for HBO, HBO Max, NBC, Comedy Central, and Hulu. She also directed a short film for KENZO starring Mahershala Ali and Natasha Lyonne. Brownstein is a founding member of the seminal punk-rock band Sleater-Kinney and author of the *New York Times* best-selling memoir *Hunger Makes Me a Modern Girl*. She lives in Portland, Oregon.

Stephanie Burt is a professor of English at Harvard. Her new book of poems is *We Are Mermaids* (Graywolf Press, 2022).

India Ennenga is a writer, editor, and actor. She cofounded the publishing house ISOLARII and is based in New York.

Rhoda Feng is a freelance writer from New York whose work has appeared in *4Columns*, *The Baffler*, *The New Republic*, *The White Review*, and other publications.

Rachel Kaadzi Ghansah is an essayist based in New York City.

Terrance Hayes's recent publications include *American Sonnets for My Past and Future Assassin* and *To Float in the Space Between: Drawings and Essays in Conversation with Etheridge Knight*. A collection of poems, *So to Speak*, and a collection of essays, *Watch Your Language*, are forthcoming in 2023. He is a professor of English at New York University.

Jessica Hopper is an author, director, and producer based in Chicago. Her most recent book, *The First Collection of Criticism by a Living Female Rock Critic*, was published in 2022.

Joanna Howard is the author of the memoir *Rerun Era* (McSweeney's, 2019); the novel *Foreign Correspondent* (Counterpath Press, 2013); a story collection, *On the Winding Stair* (Boa Editions, 2009); and *In the Colorless Round* (Noemi Press, 2006). She cowrote *Field Glass* with Joanna Ruocco (Sidebrow Books, 2017). Her work has appeared in *Conjunctions*, *The Paris Review*, *Verse*, *Bomb*, *Flaunt*, *Chicago Review*, *The Brooklyn Rail*, and parts elsewhere. She lives in Denver and Providence, Rhode Island, and teaches at the University of Denver.

Zoë Hu has written for *The New Republic*, *The Baffler*, and *The Nation*.

Adalena Kavanagh is a writer and photographer in Brooklyn, New York. She has published stories, essays, and interviews in *Electric Literature*, *The Literary Review*, and *Air/Light*. Her photography can be found at adalenakavanagh.com.

Hartley Lin is a cartoonist based in Montreal. His graphic novel, *Young Frances*, won a Doug Wright Award for Best Book. He contributes to *The New Yorker* and other magazines.

Melissa Locker is a writer and music podcast impresario in the making. She lives on the internet and runs on coffee. You can follow her at @woolyknickers but not in real life.

Sarah Marshall hosts *You're Wrong About*, a podcast about misremembered history. She lives in Portland, Oregon, and on the open road.

Bridget Meyne is a comics maker and illustrator based in London. Frequent themes and inspirations include real-life magazines, the internet, boots, dystopian futures, and five-minute crafts.

Yasmin Patel is a college student studying English. She is originally from San Francisco.

Aubrey Plaza is an actor, comedian, and producer. She stars in season 2 of *The White Lotus*.

Laura Preston is an associate editor at *A Public Space*. Her writing has appeared in *The New Yorker*.

Annie Rauwerda is a writer, comedian, and Wikipedia enthusiast based in Michigan and New York City. Her writing has appeared in *Slate*, *Vice*, and *Input*.

Danez Smith is the author of three collections, including *Homie* and *Don't Call Us Dead*. Their work has been awarded the Forward Prize for Best Collection, the Minnesota Book Award in Poetry, the Kate Tufts Discovery Award, and has been a finalist for the NAACP Image Award in Poetry, the National Book Critics Circle Award, and the National Book Award. Former cohost of the Webby Award–nominated podcast *VS*, they live in Minneapolis near their people. Their fourth collection, *Bluff*, will be published in fall 2024.

Natalie So is a writer, researcher, and story producer who works at the intersection of true stories and TV. Her past projects include research and development for *Little America*, *The OA*, *A League of Their Own*, and the forthcoming limited series *Retreat*. She lives in San Francisco.

Oscar Villalon is the managing editor of *ZYZZYVA*, a recipient of a 2022 Whiting Literary Magazine Prize. He lives with his wife and son in San Francisco.

Ryan H. Walsh is a musician, journalist, and video/collage artist from Boston. His debut book, *Astral Weeks: A Secret History of 1968* (Penguin Press), received rave reviews in *The New Yorker*, *The Guardian*, *Rolling Stone*, and was a *New York Times* end-of-year Critics' Pick. His long-running band, Hallelujah the Hills, has toured with acts like the Silver Jews and Titus Andronicus, while releasing seven full-length albums as well as scores of singles, EPs, and experimental works. Their latest album, 2019's *I'm You*, was declared "Album of the Year" by *Glorious Noise* and "a lyrical masterpiece" by *Metro*.

Claire Vaye Watkins is the author of three books: *Battleborn*, *Gold Fame Citrus*, and *I Love You but I've Chosen Darkness*. She is a professor in the MFA Programs in Writing at the University of California, Irvine, and lives at the bottom of an ancient inland sea in Twentynine Palms, California.

Jane Wong is the author of two poetry collections: *How to Not Be Afraid of Everything* (Alice James Books, 2021) and *Overpour* (Action Books, 2016). Her debut memoir, *Meet Me Tonight in Atlantic City*, is forthcoming from Tin House Books in 2023. A Kundiman Fellow, she is the recipient of a Pushcart Prize and fellowships and residencies from Harvard's Woodberry Poetry Room, the US Fulbright Program, Artist Trust, the Fine Arts Work Center, Bread Loaf, Hedgebrook, Willapa Bay, the Jentel Foundation, and other places. She is an associate professor of creative writing at Western Washington University.

Rafia Zakaria is the author, most recently, of *Against White Feminism* (2021), which has been translated into four languages. She is a fellow at the African American Policy Forum, an intersectional think tank.

SUBMIT TO US

Jan 1 - Feb 15

Kathryn A. Morton
Prize in Poetry

Mary McCarthy Prize
in Short Fiction

Find your next
favorite book.

IN SPRING 2022, ALMOST 1,600 GENEROUS SUPPORTERS GAVE TO OUR RECORD-BREAKING KICKSTARTER CAMPAIGN.

Help poured in from near and far and came in myriad forms. This issue would not have been possible without the generosity of the following people, whom we appreciate unendingly.

A. Durbin ✶ Aaron Berkowitz ✶ Aaron Goekler ✶ Aaron Peck ✶ Aaron Weller ✶ Aaron Winters ✶ Abby Ackerman ✶ Abeer Hoque ✶ Abigail Keel ✶ Abigail Oswald ✶ abigail.lafrenz@gmail.com ✶ Ace Pumpkin ✶ Adalina Kavanagh ✶ Adam Baer ✶ Adam Blumenthal ✶ Adam Brodsley ✶ Adam Burke ✶ Adam Moody ✶ Adam Stoddart ✶ Addiekay ✶ Adena Smith ✶ Adobe ✶ Adrien Hingert ✶ Adrienne Celt ✶ Affinity Konar ✶ Aisha Sabatini Sloan ✶ Alan Jacobson ✶ Alana Post ✶ Alana Stubbs ✶ Alayne Gyetvai ✶ Aleksandra Zimonjic ✶ Alex ✶ Alex Bendig ✶ Alex Grecian ✶ Alex Kaplan ✶ Alex Reisner ✶ Alex Wirth ✶ Alexandra Marvar ✶ Alexandra Poreda ✶ Alexei ✶ Alexia Smith ✶ Alexis ✶ Alexis Gunderson ✶ Alfred Brown ✶ Alice ✶ Alice Gambrell ✶ Alicia ✶ Alicia Korenman ✶ Alisa Hartz ✶ Alison Mastny ✶ Alison Mondi ✶ Alison Naomi Holt ✶ Alix Towler ✶ Allan Weinrib ✶ Alli ✶ Allie Willemstein ✶ Allison ✶ Allison Arieff ✶ Allison Moore ✶ Ally Shwed ✶ Alondra Nelson ✶ Alyson ✶ Alyssa Schwartz ✶ Amanda ✶ Amanda Barrett ✶ Amanda Dick ✶ Amanda Niu ✶ Amanda Tennant ✶ Amanda Uhle ✶ Amanda Wallwin ✶ Amaris Ketcham ✶ Amber ✶ Amelia ✶ Amro ✶ Amy ✶ Amy Estes ✶ Amy Moran ✶ Amy Munson ✶ Amy Reardon ✶ Amy Rose Marsh ✶ Amy Silverman ✶ Amy Sumerton ✶ Amy Woodall ✶ Anant Prabhakar ✶ Andrew Wylie ✶ Andi Spark ✶ Andrea Birgers ✶ Andrea Crews ✶ Andrea Feldman ✶ Andrea Longini ✶ Andrew Altschul ✶ Andrew Baird ✶ Andrew Beckerman ✶ Andrew Benner ✶ Andrew Blauner ✶ Andrew Fay ✶ Andrew Fox ✶ Andrew Glencross ✶ Andrew Gordon ✶ Andrew Guyvijitr ✶ Andrew Hill ✶ Andrew Loquist ✶ Andrew Schuricht ✶ Andrew Vessey ✶ Andrew Wagner ✶ Andy Hunter ✶ Andy Kroll ✶ Anisse Gross ✶ Ann E Beman ✶ Ann J Kyrkostas ✶ Ann Wilson ✶ Ann-Marie White ✶ Anna Shults ✶ Anna Spysz ✶ Anne Connell ✶ Anne Fougeron ✶ Anne Hellman ✶ Anne Pessala ✶ Anne Tulloch ✶ Anne Yoder ✶ Antero Garcia ✶ Anthony Decrappeo ✶ April ✶ Ari ✶ Ariana Rosado-Fernández ✶ Arianne Hartsell-Gundy ✶ Ariel Basom ✶ Arik Gabbai ✶ Arthur Vidich ✶ Arye Dworken ✶ Ashley Jones ✶ Ashley Marcus ✶ Ashmi ✶ Austen ✶ Austin Carpentieri ✶ Austin Dryden ✶ Austin Hofeman ✶ Austin Kleon ✶ Austin Meek ✶ Austin Stahl ✶ Ayelet Waldman ✶ Backer Name ✶ Barak Krakauer ✶ Barbara Kirby ✶ Barker ✶ Barry Schwartz ✶ Basmati ✶ Becca Berge ✶ Ben Crawford ✶ Ben Gottlieb ✶ Ben I Lickerman ✶ Ben Petrosky ✶ Ben Ragle ✶ Benjamin Jahn ✶ Benjamin Liss ✶ Benjamin Russell ✶ Bernadette McVey ✶ Bernard Gastel ✶ Beth Deene ✶ Beto Segura ✶ Betsy Glenn ✶ Betsy Lam ✶ Beverley Kort ✶ Beverly Madrid ✶ Bill Clarke ✶ Bill Dawson ✶ Bill Kirchner ✶ Bill Mascioli ✶ Bill Rising ✶ Billy McDermott ✶ Birna Anna Bjornsdottir ✶ BJ Simpson ✶ Bjorn Bellenbaum ✶ Blaise Zerega ✶ Bob Proehl ✶ Bobby Baird ✶ Bon Chan ✶ Brad Adelberg ✶ Brad Laney ✶ Brad Wojak ✶ Bradley Chernin ✶ Brain Vs. Book ✶ Brainard Carey ✶ Brandon Hobson ✶ Brendan ✶ Brendan Molloy ✶ Brendan Moore ✶ Brendan Yandt ✶ Brent Colburn ✶ Brett Goldblatt ✶ Brett Slaughenhaupt ✶ Brian Cassidy ✶ Brian Contine ✶ Brian Dice ✶ Brian Pfeffer ✶ Bridget Green ✶ Brinda Gupta ✶ Brittany ✶ Brittany Fowler ✶ Brittany Lauren Wheeler ✶ Brock Allen ✶ Bruce Johnson ✶ Bruce Leibstone ✶ Bruce Lipsky ✶ Bruce Webster ✶ Bryan Gardiner ✶ Bryan Waterman ✶ Buck McWilliams ✶ C. Odal ✶ C. Van Leeuwen ✶ C.w. Hills ✶ Caitlin Archer-Helke ✶ Caitlin Burke ✶ Caitlin Van Dusen ✶ Caitlyn Dykehouse ✶ Cameo Wood ✶ Cara ✶ Cara Wood Ginder ✶ Cari Benesh ✶ Carl ✶ Carl ✶ Carl Voss ✶ Carla Jean Whitley ✶ Carla Sonheim ✶ Carli Cutchin ✶ Carmen ✶ Carmine ✶ Carol Davis ✶ Carol Lynn Rivera ✶ Carol Mammano ✶ Carol Menaker ✶ Carolyn Klein ✶ Carolyn Peterson ✶ Carolyn West ✶ Carolyn Williams-Noren ✶ Carrie ✶

Carrie & Zack Worrell ✶ Carrie Guss ✶ Carrie Niziolek ✶ Casey Denis ✶ Casey Gerald ✶ Casey Maddren ✶ Casey Quinn ✶ Cassidy ✶ Cassie Brenske ✶ Cate Fallon ✶ Caterina Fake ✶ Catherine Martin ✶ Catherine McWain ✶ Catherine Stankowski ✶ CDD ✶ Cecilia Mitchell ✶ Celia Henson ✶ Chad ✶ Chad Dupuis ✶ Chad Oldfather ✶ Chandra Steele ✶ Channing McKay ✶ Charles Allen ✶ Charles Blyzniuk ✶ Charles Fairbanks ✶ Charley ✶ Charlie Schneider ✶ Cherline Bazile ✶ Cheryl ✶ Cheryl Flack ✶ Chiara ✶ Chris ✶ Chris Baird ✶ Chris Banks ✶ Chris Borger ✶ Chris Brown ✶ Chris Friedrich ✶ Chris G ✶ Chris Gruener ✶ Chris Higgins ✶ Chris McCann ✶ Chris Naccari ✶ Chris Pikula ✶ Chris Piotrowski ✶ Chris Preston ✶ Chris Rock ✶ Chris Schmidt ✶ Chris Seidel ✶ Chris Todd ✶ Christa ✶ Christa Mrgan ✶ Christin Lee ✶ Christina Cogswell ✶ Christina Hughes ✶ Christine ✶ Christine Beeftink ✶ Christine Delea ✶ Christine Farrell-Riley ✶ Christine Harkin ✶ Christine L Whitney ✶ Christine Rener ✶ Christoph Schmitz ✶ Christopher Arnold ✶ Christopher Burton ✶ Christopher Frizzelle ✶ Christopher Lay ✶ Christopher Marks ✶ Christopher Ottolino ✶ Christopher Taylor ✶ Christy Maggio ✶ Claire Burrows ✶ Claire Rivkin ✶ Clara ✶ Clare Dunnett ✶ Clark Bosslet ✶ Claudia Cravens ✶ Cliff Mayotte ✶ Clinton Leo Gilbert Morin ✶ Colin Dickey ✶ Colin Meloy ✶ Colin Reed Moon ✶ Colin Vettier ✶ Colleen Morrison ✶ Colleen Rothman ✶ Comic Nurse ✶ Conor Moore ✶ Cordelia Derhammer-Hill ✶ Corinne ✶ Cory ✶ Courtney L. Cooper ✶ Courtney Williamson ✶ Courtney Zoffness ✶ Courtney Gillette ✶ Cristin Keely ✶ Cristina Williams ✶ Crystal Lowery ✶ Curtis Rising ✶ Cydney Stewart ✶ Cynthia ✶ D'arcy Doran ✶ Daisy Bassen ✶ Damon Copeland ✶ Dan ✶ Dan Corber ✶ Dan Kennedy ✶ Dan Manchester ✶ Daniel A Greenspun ✶ Daniel Dejan ✶ Daniel Doran ✶ Daniel Goslee ✶ Daniel Grou ✶ Daniel Russell ✶ Daniel Sanders ✶ Daniel Watkins ✶ Danielle ✶ Danielle Holke ✶ Danielle Truppi ✶ Danna ✶ Danny Wen ✶ Danny Williamson ✶ Danyelle White ✶ Darby M. Dixon Iii ✶ Daria Yocco ✶ Darren Kloomok ✶ Dave ✶ Dave Coustan ✶ Dave Hardin ✶ Dave Hyde ✶ David ✶ David A. Pratt ✶ David Conrads ✶ David Givens ✶ David Goldberg ✶ David Haggstrom ✶ David Howell ✶ David Hyde ✶ David Lackey ✶ David Lee ✶ David Moskowitz ✶ David Neal ✶ David Peattie ✶ David R Eaton Ii ✶ David Ross ✶ David Rothenberg ✶ David S. ✶ David Ulin ✶ David Zaffrann ✶ David Zielonka ✶ David Zolandz ✶ Davis Mendez ✶ Dayana Morales ✶ De Hart ✶ Deane Taylor ✶ Deborah Conrad ✶ Deborah Mills-Scofield ✶ Deefaced ✶ Delphine Sims ✶ Devin ✶ Diana Cohn ✶ Diana Elizabeth Hardy ✶ Diana Shnhn ✶ Diane Holdgate ✶ Diane Lederman ✶ Dillon Sim ✶ Dio ✶ Dirk Manning ✶ Doctor Razmataz ✶ Don Arnold ✶ Donna Bronson ✶ Donna Cousins ✶ Dora Magovern ✶ Dorothea Van Duyn ✶ Dorothy Bendel ✶ Doug Nayler ✶ Doug Rand ✶ Doug Smith ✶ Douglas Bolles ✶ Douglas Bullock ✶ Douglas Keller ✶ Douglas McGray ✶ Dov Lebowitz-Nowak ✶ Dr. Sbaitso ✶ Drew Petersen ✶ Dusty ✶ E Hyten ✶ Ealasaid A. Haas ✶ Ed Lynn ✶ Edward Aboufadel ✶ Edward Hutchinson ✶ Eileen Kirschner ✶ Eitan Kensky ✶ Elaine Froneberger ✶ Elena ✶ Elfego Baca ✶ Eli Cohen ✶ Elias ✶ Eliot Gill ✶ Elisa ✶ Elisabeth ✶ Elise Symer ✶ Elizabeth ✶ Elizabeth Engel ✶ Elizabeth Greenspan ✶ Elizabeth Kiy ✶ Elizabeth Kroner ✶ Elizabeth Kruschek ✶ Elizabeth Lane ✶ Elizabeth Lawrence ✶ Elizabeth McCracken ✶ Elizabeth Ray ✶ Elizabeth Rieke ✶ Elizabeth Salem ✶ Elizabeth Turner ✶ Ellen Gumbiner ✶ Ellen M Duffer ✶ Ellen Umansky ✶ Ellie Black ✶ Elyse Mallouk ✶ Emily ✶ Emily Bryant-Álvarez ✶ Emily Fine ✶ Emily Jackson ✶ Emily Kaplan ✶ Emily Poe-Crawford ✶ Emma Constantine ✶ Emma Conway ✶ Emma Dewald ✶ Emma Sheinbaum ✶ Eng Sengsavang ✶ Eric ✶ Eric Barron ✶ Eric Botts ✶ Eric Buell ✶ Eric Gorfain ✶ Eric Heiman ✶ Eric Johnson ✶ Eric Lubochinski ✶ Eric Pidkameny ✶ Eric Scott Ost ✶ Eric Singley ✶ Eric Tegethoff ✶ Erica ✶ Erica Christianson Davis ✶ Erica Krasovic ✶ Erik H ✶ Erik Hemming ✶ Erin Archuleta ✶ Erin Finnerty ✶ Erin Kinsella ✶ Erin Langner ✶ Erin Macnair ✶ Erin Rose Wage ✶ Erin Ruffin ✶ Erin Van Gelder ✶ Eryk Salvaggio ✶ Esme Weijun Wang ✶ Esteban Silva ✶ Ethan Nosowsky ✶ Evan Allgood ✶ Evan Gross ✶ Evan Ratliff ✶ Evan Ross ✶ Evan Suggs ✶ Eve Bowen ✶ Eve Bower ✶ F. Stewart-Taylor ✶ Farnaz Fatemi ✶ Farooq Ahmed ✶ Fern Diaz ✶ Fiona Brandon ✶ Fishmech ✶ Flávia Monteiro ✶ Frances Goldin Literary Agency ✶

Francesca Maier ✶ Francesca Richer ✶ Frank Uhle ✶ Franka Diehnelt ✶ Frankie Huang ✶ Fualana Detail ✶ Fwarg ✶ G. Cameron Robert ✶ Gab ✶ Gail Marten ✶ Gary Rudoren ✶ Gary Shank ✶ Gavin Craig ✶ Genevieve Casey ✶ Geoff Martin ✶ George Weld ✶ Georgia ✶ Georgia Rain Jackson ✶ Georgiana Nelsen ✶ Gibby Stratton ✶ Gina ✶ Gina Balibrera ✶ Gina Gionfriddo ✶ Gina Risso ✶ Gordon Cavanaugh ✶ Grace Degraaf ✶ Grace Morsberger ✶ Grace Murray ✶ Grace Prasad ✶ Graham Marshall ✶ Graham Ray ✶ Grant Heinrich ✶ Greg Hancock ✶ Greg Larson ✶ Greg Polin ✶ Greg Schnippel ✶ Greg Weight ✶ Gregory Nelson ✶ Gregory P Kavanagh ✶ Griffin Richardson ✶ Gus Szlosek ✶ H ✶ H.R. ✶ Hadil ✶ Håkan Westergren ✶ Hal Tepfer ✶ Halimah Marcus and Benjamin Samuel ✶ Handel Desa ✶ Hannah ✶ Hannah McGinty ✶ Hannah Rose ✶ Hannah Withers ✶ Hannahmaureen ✶ Hans Wuerfmannsdobler ✶ Harlean Carpenter ✶ Harley Brown ✶ Harrison Hill ✶ Harry ✶ Heather ✶ Heather Aruffo ✶ Heather Bentley ✶ Heather Bloyer ✶ Heather Hughes ✶ Heather Peterson ✶ Heidi Lackey ✶ Heidi Van Horn ✶ Helen Summers ✶ Hilary ✶ Hilary Burg ✶ Hilary Jager ✶ Hilary K ✶ Hilary Kivitz ✶ Holly Mcallister ✶ Hong-An ✶ Hua Xie ✶ Hugh Geenen ✶ Hugh Van Dusen ✶ Ian Bishop ✶ Ian Collins ✶ Ian Dannehy ✶ Ian Foe ✶ Ian Glazer ✶ Ian Krantz ✶ Ian Moe ✶ Ian Moore ✶ Ian Pearson ✶ Ian Sheddan ✶ Ieuan Jenkins ✶ Ike Chapman ✶ Ilana ✶ Iman Saleh ✶ Ingrid Burrington ✶ Ingrid H McVanner ✶ Isa Cushing ✶ Isabel Pinner ✶ J Black ✶ J Brown ✶ J Elizabeth Smith ✶ J William Semich ✶ Jack and Devin ✶ Jackie Desforges ✶ Jaclyn Adomeit ✶ Jacob Leland ✶ Jacob Thomas ✶ Jacobjacob Hauber ✶ Jade Horning ✶ Jainee McCarroll ✶ Jake Pitre ✶ James Brandes ✶ James Hanna ✶ James Klein ✶ James Kochalka ✶ James Lambropoulos ✶ James Manion ✶ James Reichmuth ✶ James Robertson ✶ James Sutton ✶ James Tynion Iv ✶ Jami Shawley ✶ Jamie Alexander ✶ Jamie Campbell ✶ Jane White ✶ Jane Whitley ✶ Jane Wilson ✶ Janeen Armstrong ✶ Janell Julian ✶ Janice Dowson ✶ Janice Goldblatt ✶ Jared Benjamin ✶ Jared Blank ✶ Jared Norman ✶ Jaron Moore ✶ Jarrod Dahl ✶ Jasmin Mittag ✶ Jason ✶ Jason Corliss ✶ Jason Gouliard ✶ Jason Hughes ✶ Jason McBride ✶ Jason McGlone ✶ Jason Sommer ✶ Jason Sugawa ✶ Jason Tobin ✶ Jason Viola ✶ Jay Moon ✶ Jay Popham ✶ Jay Price ✶ Jazz Monroe ✶ JB ✶ Je Schmitt ✶ Jeannie Mecorney ✶ Jeannie Vanasco ✶ Jed Aicher ✶ Jed Repko ✶ Jed Teres ✶ Jeff ✶ Jeff Anderson ✶ Jeff Edmunds ✶ Jeff Harper ✶ Jeff Hazlett ✶ Jeff Ross ✶ Jeff Sconyers ✶ Jeffrey Ceretto ✶ Jeffrey Hermann ✶ Jeffrey Holdaway ✶ Jeffrey Parnaby ✶ Jen Cuculich ✶ Jenefer Angell ✶ Jenna Pacitto ✶ Jenna Tang ✶ Jenne P ✶ Jennevieve Schlemmer ✶ Jennifer ✶ Jennifer Agiesta ✶ Jennifer Barth ✶ Jennifer Clarke ✶ Jennifer Day ✶ Jennifer Dowell ✶ Jennifer Fisher ✶ Jennifer Hawkins ✶ Jennifer Inglis ✶ Jennifer Isett ✶ Jennifer Kabat ✶ Jennifer Loyer-Drew ✶ Jennifer Malnick ✶ Jennifer Meyer ✶ Jennifer Morehead ✶ Jennifer Ng ✶ Jennifer Song ✶ Jennifer Wason ✶ Jeremiah Follett ✶ Jeremiah Hayden ✶ Jeremy Braddock ✶ Jeremy Cohen ✶ Jeremy Gruman ✶ Jeremy Mann ✶ Jeremy Peppas ✶ Jeremy Radcliffe ✶ Jeremy Rishel ✶ Jeremy Van Cleve ✶ Jeremy Wortsman ✶ Jerome Tolochko ✶ Jerry Englehart Jr. ✶ Jess ✶ Jess McMorrow ✶ Jesse Nathan ✶ Jessica ✶ Jessica Clare ✶ Jessica Farquhar ✶ Jessica Gilkison ✶ Jessica Lawrence-Hurt ✶ Jessica Manack ✶ Jessica Martinez ✶ Jessica Petelle ✶ Jessica Silverstein ✶ Jessica Taylor ✶ Jessica Young ✶ Jill Guthrie ✶ Jillian Lubow ✶ Jim Fassold ✶ Jim Kosmicki ✶ Jim McElroy ✶ Jim Welte ✶ Jim Withington ✶ Joanna E. Rapf ✶ Joannet ✶ Jodie ✶ Jodie A. Shull ✶ Joe Distefano ✶ Joe Dizney ✶ Joe Germuska ✶ Joe Sutton ✶ Johanna Maron ✶ Johanna Schwartz ✶ John E. Sullivan ✶ John Glassie ✶ John Hardy ✶ John Hawkins ✶ John Hill ✶ John Kern and Heather McDonald ✶ John Lavine ✶ John Mastin ✶ John Muller ✶ John Nusse ✶ John Pearce ✶ John Petersen ✶ John Pribble Iii ✶ John Skelton ✶ John Tollefsen ✶ John Weiner ✶ John Wirkner ✶ Jon Callas ✶ Jon Cappadona ✶ Jon Leland ✶ Jon Lickerman ✶ Jon Robin Baitz ✶ Jon Sailer ✶ Jonathan ✶ Jonathan Ellingson ✶ Jonathan Fretheim ✶ Jonathan Huang ✶ Jonathan Kiefer ✶ Jonathan Lethem ✶ Jordan J. ✶ Jori Lom ✶ Josee Pronovost ✶ Joseph Didomizio ✶ Joseph Edmundson ✶ Joseph M. Gerace ✶ Josh Cook ✶ Josh Fischel ✶ Josh Halpern-Givens ✶ Josh Riedel ✶ Josh Rutner ✶ Josh Sucher ✶ Joshua Dickerson ✶ Joshua Gooden ✶ Joshua Leto ✶ Joshua Lewis ✶ Joyce Hennessee ✶ JSB ✶ Juan Cuellar ✶ Judith Mitchell ✶

Judson ✶ Julia ✶ Julia Forbess ✶ Julia Kinsman ✶ Julia S ✶ Julia Strohm ✶ Julia Tranchina ✶ Julianna Fomenko ✶ Julie ✶ Julie Phillips ✶ Julie Schmidt ✶ Julie Shapiro ✶ Julie Wroblewski ✶ Juniper Sage ✶ Just B.e. Productions ✶ Justin McIntosh ✶ K ✶ Kaitlin Matesich ✶ Kameelah Rasheed ✶ Kara Bowers ✶ Kara Loquist ✶ Karen Broyles ✶ Karen Gansky ✶ Karen Stilber ✶ Karina A. ✶ Kasee Kozel ✶ Kat King ✶ Kat Manalac ✶ Kate ✶ Kate Fritz ✶ Kate Haney ✶ Kate Rutledge Jaffe ✶ Katherine May ✶ Katherine May Williams ✶ Katherine Ross ✶ Katherine Vloet ✶ Katherine Williams ✶ Kathleen Barksdale ✶ Kathleen Schaefer ✶ Kathryn ✶ Kathryn Larson ✶ Katie ✶ Katie Bovenzi ✶ Katie Swalm ✶ Katrina Dodson ✶ Katy Parker ✶ Katy Wight ✶ Kayla Pastor ✶ Kayla Sansevere ✶ Kayleigh Zaloga ✶ Keith Grauman ✶ Keith O'neill ✶ Kellen Ray ✶ Kelley ✶ Kelly ✶ Kelly Caldwell ✶ Kelly Conroe ✶ Kelly Danver ✶ Kelly Miller-Schreiner ✶ Kelly Pollard ✶ Kelsey Young ✶ Ken Krehbiel ✶ Kenneth Epstein ✶ Kenneth T. White Iii ✶ Keri Bertino ✶ Kerry Sonia ✶ Kevin Adams ✶ Kevin Cracraft ✶ Kevin Dean ✶ Kevin Dumont ✶ Kevin Freeman ✶ Kevin Purring ✶ Kevin Simowitz ✶ Khart ✶ Kie ✶ Kiele Raymond ✶ Kim Beil ✶ Kim Dale ✶ Kim Roche ✶ Kim Wishart ✶ Kimberly Hensle Lowrance ✶ Kimberly Herbert ✶ Kirtan Nautiyal ✶ Kitania Folk ✶ Klaas Berkeley ✶ Klovasz ✶ Kris Fernandez-Everett ✶ Kris Majury ✶ Kristen ✶ Kristen Grayewski ✶ Kristen Iskandrian ✶ Kristen Kieta ✶ Kristen Radtke ✶ Kristen Reed ✶ Kristin Bye ✶

Kristin Gorecki-Martin ✶ Kristin Nielsen ✶ Kristopher Wood ✶ Kristy Duncan ✶ Kyla Morgan ✶ Kyla Sweet ✶ Kyle Connors ✶ Kyle P. Edmonds ✶ Kyle Paoletta ✶ Kylie Russell ✶ Lacy Simons ✶ Lagorio ✶ Lana ✶ Larry Agnello ✶ Larry Doyle ✶ Lars ✶ Lars Laing-Peterson ✶ Laura ✶ Laura George ✶ Laura Gibbs ✶ Laura Green ✶ Laura Greene ✶ Laura Matter ✶ Laura Perkins ✶ Laura Zinn Fromm ✶ Laurel Leckert ✶ Lauren ✶ Lauren Joost Stachowiak ✶ Lauren Markham ✶ Lauren Waterhouse ✶ Leah Newsom ✶ Leeanne Gm ✶ Lena ✶ Lesley ✶ Lesley Siegel ✶ Leslie Walker Burlock ✶ Leslie Woodhouse ✶ Leslie Ylinen ✶ Lester Nelson-Gacal ✶ Letterform Archive ✶ Liishi ✶ Lila Byock ✶ Lilavati ✶ Lily Frenette ✶ Linda Hinrichs ✶ Linda McLarnan ✶ Linda Nace ✶ Linda Sue Larose ✶ Lindsay Ferguson ✶ Lindsey Darrah ✶ Linnea Hegarty ✶ Lisa Alfelt ✶ Lisa Keller ✶ Lisa Korytowski ✶ Lisa Lucas ✶ Lisa M. Geller ✶ Lisa McNeilley Phd ✶ Lisa Olstein ✶ Lisa Snyder ✶ Lisa Yoder ✶ Lish ✶ Liz ✶ Liz Bowen ✶ Liz Cohen ✶ Liz Findley ✶ Lloyd Goldfine ✶ Lms ✶ Long Vo ✶ Loredana Spadola ✶ Loren Lieberthal ✶ Loren Marple ✶ Lorien ✶ Lorin O ✶ Lucy Corin ✶ Lukas Fauset ✶ Lyz Lenz ✶ M Margaret Terry ✶ Madeline Dye ✶ Maggie ✶ Maggie Breslin ✶ Maggie Sattler ✶ Maggie Smith ✶ Mandeep Ubhi ✶ Mandy Jenkins ✶ Mandy Sampson ✶ Marc Allen ✶ Marc Kevin Hall ✶ Marcy Dix ✶ Margaret Fishkind ✶ Margo ✶ Margot Atwell ✶ Marguerite Fenwood ✶ Mariana Fisher ✶ Mariel Ashlinn ✶ Maris Kreizman ✶ Marisa Aveling ✶

Marisa Brown ✶ Marissa Flaxbart ✶ Mark ✶ Mark Dober ✶ Mark Dwight ✶ Mark Kaufman ✶ Mark Kingsley ✶ Mark McKnight ✶ Mark Oldach ✶ Mark Roelke ✶ Mark Springberg ✶ Marley Richmond ✶ Marnie Galloway ✶ Martha Neth ✶ Martin Scherer ✶ Mary Bedia Bushkar ✶ Mary Daniels ✶ Mary Herr ✶ Mary Humphreys ✶ Mary Kate ✶ Mary Kay Fleming ✶ Mary Larson ✶ Marya Kuklick ✶ Mason Cassady ✶ Mat ✶ Matt Beatty ✶ Matt Conner ✶ Matt Connolly ✶ Matt Davies ✶ Matt Elvin ✶ Matt Haber ✶ Matt Henriksen ✶ Matt King ✶ Matt Mantsch ✶ Matt Roren ✶ Matt Spada ✶ Matthew ✶ Matthew Aron ✶ Matthew Batt ✶ Matthew Herscovitch ✶ Matthew Poirier ✶ Matthew Storer ✶ Maura Schneider ✶ Maureen ✶ Max Paladino ✶ McSwanwick ✶ Meg McGuire ✶ Megan ✶ Megan Lasswell ✶ Megan McDonald ✶ Megan Molteni ✶ Meghan Cason ✶ Meghan Gilmore ✶ Melanie Appelbaum ✶ Melanie Ford ✶ Melanie Kahl ✶ Melinda Kennedy ✶ Melissa ✶ Melissa Demarest ✶ Melissa East ✶ Melissa Faliveno ✶ Meredith Ennis ✶ Meredith McCracken ✶ Merlyn Schultz ✶ Merritt Poling ✶ Mi Ann Bennett ✶ Micah McLain ✶ Michael Albo ✶ Michael Boyce ✶ Michael Brace ✶ Michael Chartrand ✶ Michael Eckblad ✶ Michael Epstein ✶ Michael Ferris ✶ Michael Frank ✶ Michael Ge ✶ Michael Goldberg ✶ Michael Hsu ✶ Michael Kelly ✶ Michael McKinley ✶ Michael Moore ✶ Michael Munley ✶ Michael Patrick Cutillo ✶ Michael Rebok ✶ Michael S. Brown ✶

Michael Schneiderman ✶ Michael Todd Cohen ✶ Michael Wilson ✶ Michele Moses ✶ Michele Stafford ✶ Michelle Bowles ✶ Michelle Brower ✶ Michelle Cotugno ✶ Michelle Covington ✶ Michelle Repko ✶ Michelle Robertson ✶ Michelle Yee ✶ Mickey Hadick ✶ Mike ✶ Mike Hutchinson ✶ Mike McVicar ✶ Mike Morrow ✶ Mike Plante ✶ Mike Rogge ✶ Mike Taylor ✶ Miko McGinty ✶ Mimi ✶ Mimi Kramer ✶ Mindy Aronoff ✶ Minerva Projects ✶ Miquel Ramirez ✶ Miranda ✶ Miranda Zickler ✶ Miriam Feuerle ✶ Miriam Lawrence ✶ Mj Engel ✶ Molly Dickinson ✶ Molly Mary McLaughlin ✶ Molly Pearson ✶ Molly Taylor ✶ Mona Wolfe ✶ Monica De La Torre ✶ Monica Snellings ✶ Monica Sofia Guzman Lenis ✶ Moses ✶ Muckdart ✶ Murray Browne ✶ Nacho Nova ✶ Nancy Koerbel ✶ Nancy Levinson ✶ Nancy Smith ✶ Naomi Hawkins-Rowe ✶ Natalie Green ✶ Natalie Slack ✶ Natasha Boas ✶ Natasha Friedt ✶ Nate Brown ✶ Nathan Griffith ✶ Nathan Rostron ✶ Neil Blanck ✶ Neil Jacobson ✶ Neil Shapiro ✶ Nelda Carlisle-Gray ✶ Nguyên Khôi Nguyễn ✶ Nicadoodle ✶ Nicholas ✶ Nick Hammer ✶ Nick James ✶ Nick Kangas ✶ Nick Pham ✶ Nick Yulman ✶ Nicki Ittner ✶ Nicole ✶ Nicole Avril ✶ Nicole Wilkins ✶ Nidhi R ✶ Nikky Southerland ✶ Nikolas McConnie-Saad ✶ Nissa Cannon ✶ Nitish Pahwa ✶ Noah Kardos-Fein ✶ Noah Rosen ✶ Noah Swartz ✶ Nora Feely ✶ Nora Flanagan ✶ Nora Fussner ✶ Nora Sharp ✶ Norah Vawter ✶ Ns ✶ Ola Jacunski / Aleksandra Hill ✶ Olia Natasha Ougrik ✶ Olivia Hammerman ✶ Oriana Leckert ✶ Oscar Herrera ✶ P Smith ✶ Padmasini ✶ Parashar Bhise ✶ Parker Gregory Shpak ✶ Parker Higgins ✶ Pat Fox ✶ Patrick ✶ Patrick A. Sutton ✶ Patrick Carrick ✶ Patrick Cottrell ✶ Patrick Freebern ✶ Patrick McCaw ✶ Patrick Schilling ✶ Patrick Taffe ✶ Patty Nolan ✶ Paul Bendix ✶ Paul Collins ✶ Paul Flippen ✶ Paul Haahr ✶ Paul Krauss ✶ Paul M Herkes ✶ Paul Rogers ✶ Paul Rosenberg ✶ Paul Van Zwieten ✶ PD Rearick ✶ Pegana ✶ Penfist ✶ Perry Ladel ✶ Pete ✶ Peter ✶ Peter Ginna ✶ Peter Koshland ✶ Peter Laughlin ✶ Peter Paul ✶ Peter Ramkissoon ✶ Peter Rednour ✶ Phat B ✶ Phil Wait ✶ Philip Aromando ✶ Philip Fracassi ✶ Post-Soviet Depression Press ✶ Potter Earle ✶ Pucci Dellanno ✶ R Kenyon Corbett Iii ✶ Rachael Small ✶ Rachel Applebach ✶ Rachel Cantor ✶ Rachel Fouché ✶ Rachel McKenny ✶ Rachel Monroe ✶ Rachel Moore ✶ Rachel Victor ✶ Rachel Vilsack ✶ Rachel Wilson ✶ Radovan Grezo ✶ Ramona Naddaff ✶ Ramses Madou ✶ Rante Cimafranca ✶ Rascher M Alcasid ✶ Raymond Kutch ✶ Raysha Gallinetti ✶ Rebecca ✶ Rebecca Ackermann ✶ Rebecca Amann ✶ Rebecca Arzoian ✶ Rebecca Makkai ✶ Rebecca Taylor ✶ Rebecca Thomas ✶ Rebecca Worby ✶ Rebeccastevenson ✶ Rebekah Falkner ✶ Rekha Murthy ✶ Richard Chlopan ✶ Richard Conlin ✶ Richard McGuire ✶ Richard Naples ✶ Richard Newman ✶ Richard Osler ✶ Richard Polt ✶ Richard Robert Hansen ✶ Richard Weinman ✶ Richard West ✶ Rick Ayre ✶ Rick Puhl ✶ Rick Webb ✶ Rim Linge ✶ Rob ✶ Rob Haley ✶ Rob Richard ✶ Robert Arvid Nelsen ✶ Robert Cantwell ✶ Robert Goldman ✶ Robert Hay ✶ Robert Klevay ✶ Robert Stover ✶ Roberto Quesada ✶ Robin ✶ Robin Becht ✶ Robin Zebrowski ✶ Robyn Todd ✶ Rochelle Schmidt ✶ Rodney Franks ✶ Roger Klorese ✶ Ron Charles ✶ Ron Nurwisah ✶ Roni Devlin ✶ Rosa Tampinco ✶ Rosanne Gangi-Gaertner ✶ Rose Kim ✶ Ross Bullen ✶ Ross Drummond ✶ Ross Murray ✶ Roughan Sheedy ✶ Rubi ✶ Ruth Franklin ✶ Ryan Bradley ✶ Ryan Closs ✶ Ryan Flores ✶ Ryan Godfrey ✶ Ryan Grant ✶ Ryan Leggett ✶ Ryan McCabe ✶ Ryan Pitts ✶ S. Lopez ✶ Saad Arif ✶ Safwat Saleem ✶ Sam ✶ Sam Fitzpatrick ✶ Sam Glannon ✶ Sam Gold ✶ Sam Maclaughlin ✶ Sam Schuman ✶ Sam Stander ✶ Sam Van Wetter ✶ Samantha Grillo ✶ Samantha Hunt ✶ Sami Emory ✶ Samuel Bass ✶ Sandro Olivieri ✶ Sapuska ✶ Sara ✶ Sara Clemens ✶ Sara Duff ✶ Sara Gurwitch ✶ Sara Harvey ✶ Sara Ortiz ✶ Sara Yenke ✶ Sarah ✶ Sarah Burnes ✶ Sarah Chihaya ✶ Sarah Dalton-Erickson ✶ Sarah Hanson ✶ Sarah Herbert ✶ Sarah Howard ✶ Sarah Jl ✶ Sarah Kellner ✶ Sarah Min ✶ Sarah Rosenthal ✶ Sarah Selzer ✶ Sarah Sharp ✶ Sarah Tricky Perry ✶ Sarah Weinman ✶ Sarah Wyatt Swanson ✶ Sari Botton ✶ Sasha Graybosch ✶ Sasha Statman-Weil ✶ Satkirat Thethy ✶ Schleska ✶ Scott ✶ Scott A Vignola ✶ Scott Eden ✶ Scott Faingold ✶ Scott Feschuk ✶ Scott Goeke ✶ Scott Rinicker ✶ Scott Zagrodny ✶ Sean ✶ Sean Langmuir ✶ Sean Leow ✶ Sean McCoy ✶ Sean McGurr ✶ Sean Murphy ✶ Sel ✶ Serena Burman ✶ Seth Geiser ✶ Sha ✶ Shane Pedersen

✳ Shannon ✳ Shannon Geis ✳ Shannon Kerr ✳ Shannyn Rew ✳ Shari Basom ✳ Shari D Rochen ✳ Sharlyn Lauby ✳ Sharon H. ✳ Shauta Marsh ✳ Shawn Calvert ✳ Shawn Clark ✳ Sheila Donley ✳ Sheila McCormick ✳ Shelby Shaw ✳ Shelley Estelle ✳ Shelley Vinyard ✳ Sheon ✳ Sheri Evans ✳ Sheri Malman ✳ Shirley Chan ✳ Siena Oristaglio ✳ Simon ✳ Simon Ogden ✳ Sk ✳ Skynet ✳ Sofia Anastassiou ✳ Sofia Gates ✳ Sofia Manfredi ✳ Sonia Mistry ✳ Sonia Turek ✳ Sonya Unrein ✳ Stacey W. ✳ Steig ✳ Steph Bozzo ✳ Steph Hammell ✳ Stephan Hardeman ✳ Stephanie ✳ Stephanie Mankins ✳ Stephanie Rizzo ✳ Stephen Bronstein ✳ Stephen Fuller ✳ Stephen Hahn ✳ Stephen Smith ✳ Stephen Wake ✳ Steve Bozich ✳ Steve Gideon ✳ Steve Kalkwarf ✳ Steven Brower ✳ Steven Fisch ✳ Steven Friedman ✳ Stuart McCall ✳ Stuart Watson ✳ Summer Brennan ✳ Susan Black ✳ Susan Chun ✳ Susan Crutchfield ✳ Susan Ito ✳ Susan King ✳ Susan Maffei ✳ Susan Menick ✳ Susana Ponce ✳ Susannah Brodnitz ✳ Susanne Reece ✳ Suzan Whitlach ✳ Suzanne Campbell ✳ Suzanne Dell'orto ✳ Suzi Albertson ✳ Sydney Scardino ✳ Sylvia Lindman ✳ Sylvia Raymond ✳ Syncione Bresgal ✳ Taidgh ✳ Tanya Sepulveda Estes ✳ Tara ✳ Taylor Houston ✳ Taylor Michael ✳ Taylor Smith ✳ Taylor Willson ✳ Ted Gioia ✳ Ted Hromadka ✳ Tedder ✳ Tee I. ✳ Temim Fruchter ✳ Teresa ✳ Teresa Berry ✳ Teresa Ibarra ✳ Terri Ann Lyons-Hedtke ✳ Terry Kates ✳ Terry Keshner ✳ The Creative Fund By Backerkit ✳ The Yellow Dress ✳ Thepru ✳ Thi Bui ✳ Thomas Andrew ✳ Thomas Devlin ✳ Thomas Knight ✳ Thomas M Dale ✳ Thomas Paluck ✳ Thomas Shrack ✳ Threemoons ✳ Thu Ha ✳ Tia Shearer ✳ Tiffany Larsen ✳ Tiffany Troy ✳ Tim Kenny ✳ Timonty Legion ✳ Timothy Faust ✳ Timothy Hudson ✳ Timothy Mills ✳ Timothy Schuler ✳ Tina Burns ✳ Tina Crandell ✳ Tobias Carroll ✳ Toby Drake ✳ Todd Guill ✳ Todd Kaplan ✳ Tom Benton ✳ Tom Dufner ✳ Tom Fitzgerald ✳ Tom Goren ✳ Tom Healy ✳ Tom Kaczmarek ✳ Tom Keekley ✳ Tom McDermott ✳ Tom Mueller ✳ Tom Overby ✳ Tonia Allen ✳ Tony Burrett ✳ Tove Danovich ✳ Traci ✳ Tracy ✳ Tracy Bromwich ✳ Tracy Honn ✳ Travis Lafleur ✳ Trevor Sieben ✳ Trey Moody ✳ Trifin J Roule ✳ Trinity Ray ✳ Trisha Low ✳ Tristan ✳ Tristan Wagner ✳ Tyler ✳ Tyler Cushing ✳ Valerie Hickman ✳ Valerie Woolard ✳ Valorie Clark ✳ Van Jensen ✳ Vesna Jocic ✳ Vic Brand ✳ Vicki ✳ Vince Leo ✳ Viola McGowan ✳ Vitor ✳ Vivian Lee ✳ Vlad ✳ VS ✳ W Wolf ✳ Walt Opie ✳ Wendy Cloudberry ✳ Wendy Wimmer Schuchart ✳ Wesley and Lourey Savick ✳ Whitney Gaines ✳ Whitney Morrill Brown ✳ Will Sloan ✳ William Casper Spaulding ✳ William Donahoe ✳ William K ✳ William Lockwood ✳ William Morris ✳ William Riot ✳ William Tucker ✳ William Willett ✳ William Yale ✳ Wolf ✳ Wyatt Walker ✳ Wythe Marschall ✳ Yacov Bar-Haim ✳ Yancey Strickler ✳ Yen Ha ✳ Yohanca Delgado ✳ Yukiko Takeuchi ✳ Yvonne Conza ✳ Zac Hill ✳ Zach Donovan ✳ Zach Shepherd ✳ Zachary Lane ✳ Zadie ✳ Zena Barakat ✳ Zoe Harris ✳ Zoethegoat

WE WOULD ALSO LIKE TO RECOGNIZE SEVERAL PEOPLE WHO WENT TO EXTRAORDINARY LENGTHS TO REVIVE AND SUSTAIN THIS MAGAZINE.

✳✳✳

OUR BOUNDLESS THANKS TO:

Kellen Braddock
Carli Cutchin
Carol Davis
Brian Dice
Caterina Fake
David Friedman
Jeremy Radcliffe
Jed Repko
Nikky Southerland

✳✳✳

The Believer is published by McSweeney's, a nonprofit literary arts organization that is sustained by a unique community of readers. Be part of our work by subscribing to our publications, or consider donating directly to McSweeney's Literary Arts Fund to support thousands of readers and writers around the world.

✳✳✳

For more information, visit: mcsweeneys.net/donate

IN THE NEXT ISSUE

Not all contents are guaranteed; replacements will be satisfying

---

CROSSWORD SOLUTIONS
(PAGE 132)

C	R	A	B	S	A	L	A	D		P	I	P	
A	I	R	C	A	N	A	D	A		L	A	I	R
S	T	I	C	K	Y	B	U	N		U	M	P	E	D
S	E	E	M	S	T	O	B	E		O	M	E	G	A
I	S	L	E		I	R	A	S		T	A	L	I	B
		I	M	P					L	A	M	P	
D	A	Y	D	R	E	A	M	T		P	A	Y	E	E
A	F	O	O	L		I	R	E		G	L	E	N	N
D	R	U	B	S		N	E	R	F	D	A	R	T	S
B	O	N	E			Z	I	N					
O	P	A	R	T		T	S	A	R		P	L	A	Y
D	U	M	M	Y		R	E	R	E	L	E	A	S	E
S	N	E	A	K		A	N	I	M	O	R	P	H	S
	K	I	N	E		C	O	M	E	T	O	S	E	E
	T	S	S			T	R	A	N	S	N	E	S	S

COPYEDITING THE CLASSICS SOLUTIONS
(PAGE 133)

We others, whom (1) have long lost the more subtle of the physical senses, have not even proper terms to express an animal's (2) inter-communications with his surroundings, living or otherwise, and only have (3) the word, (4) "smell," for instance, to include the whole range of delicate thrills which murmur in the nose of the animal night and day, summoning, warning, inciting, repelling. It was one of these mysterious fairy calls from out the void that suddenly reached Mole in the darkness, making him tingle through and through with its very familiar appeal, even while yet he could not clearly remember what it was. Stopping dead in his tracks, his nose searched (5) hither and thither in its efforts to recapture the fine filament, the telegraphic current, that has (6) so strongly moved him. A moment, and he had caught it again; and with it this time came recollection in fullest flood.

Home! That was what they meant, those caressing appeals, those soft touches wafted through the air, those invisible little hands pulling and tugging, all one way! Why, it must be quite close by him at that moment, his old home that he had hurriedly forsaken and never sought again, that day when he first found the River! And now it was sending out its scouts and its messengers to capture him and bring him in (7) since his escape on that bright morning he had hardly given it a thought, so absorbed had he been in his new life, in all its pleasures, (8) surprises, its fresh and captivating experiences. Now, with a rush of old memories, how clearly it stood up before him, in the the (9) darkness! Shabby indeed, and small and poorly furnished, and yet his, the home he had made for himself, the home he had been so happy to get back (10) after his day's work. And the home had been happy with him, too, evidently, and was missing him, and wanted him back, and was telling him so, through his nose, sorrowfully, reproachfully, but with no bitterness or anger; only with plaintive reminder that it was there, and wanted him.

(1) who (nominative pronoun: subject of the verb *have long lost*); (2) *animal's* (misplaced possessive apostrophe: *animal* is singular, not plural); (3) have only (*only* should directly precede the word or phrase it modifies); (4) delete comma (comma suggests that *smell* is the only "word"); (5) He stopped dead in his tracks, his nose searching (fix the dangler: he, not his nose, stopped dead in his tracks); (6) had (change present perfect to past perfect); (7) insert period and capitalize *Since* (to fix run-on sentence); (8) its surprises (add *its* for parallel structure); (9) delete *the* (repeated word); (10) insert *to* (missing word)